ROAD TO DAMNATION

ROAD TO DAMNATION

The Wrongful Conviction of Robert Farquharson

Chris Brook

Clear Decks Media

All rights reserved by the author. No part of this book may be reproduced or used in any manner without written permission of the copyright owner except for the use of quotations in a book review. For more information: chris@sci-cri.com.

ISBN 978-0-6489417-1-2 (paperback)

ISBN 978-0-6489417-0-5 (ebook)

Cover design by Eva Guerra

Clear Decks Media

CONTENTS

1.	Damned	1
2.	Obsessed	5
3.	The Dad Test	11
4.	Sinking Fast	15
5.	Making a Mark	23
6.	Let's call it Forensic Science, but do we really need those pesky sciency bits that we all hated at school?	35
7.	The Ways We Fool Ourselves	43
8.	Under Pressure	49
9.	You Get What You Ask For	59
10.	Taking Extreme Measures	67
11.	Condemned to Repeat It	77
12.	Bearing False Witness	89
13.	Memories of a King	99
14.	The Gist of It	109
15.	A False Dawn	119
16.	Strange Behaviour	129
17.	Pants on Fire	143
18.	The Gorilla in the Room	155
19.	Angry, Angry, Angry	165
20.	Innocent or Genius	177
21.	Into the Tunnel	187
22.	Tricks of the Trade	197
23.	Unindicted Co-Ejaculator Theory	203
24.	The Age of Innocents	209

25. The Supermarket Carpark	223
Appendix A: The Reconstruction	227
Appendix B: Other 'Changing Stories'	255
Appendix C: Professor Naughton's Report	259
Appendix D: Dawn Waite testimonies	263
About the Author	271

CHAPTER 1

DAMNED

It is pitch black. Jai is shaking him. 'Daddy, daddy.' He is dazed, at the wheel. He starts to feel around. We are off the road, he thinks, must be in a ditch. But then Jai starts to open the passenger door and water starts rushing in. He reaches over Jai, shuts the door quickly. The car lurches left. The kids are yelling now. 'Just settle,' he says, 'I'm gonna try to get youse all out of here'. He starts to follow the routine for taking the kids out of the car. Get out, go around the car and grab Bailey out of his baby seat, then Tyler will jump over the baby seat, Jai gets out the front door. Routine. He turns off the engine and the headlights before he gets out of the car. Routine. He sinks. He cannot touch the ground. He is swimming. Goes under. Comes up. He can't touch the bottom. Why is it so deep? The car is sinking. Fast. He reaches out, tries to hold on to it. But it's gone. Fuck. Fuck.

He dives down. Nothing. Where is the bottom? It is night and the water is dark and cold. He takes another breath. Dives as deep as he can, feeling around. Nothing. Why is it so deep? He dives again. Shit. What the fuck just happened? How could that have happened? The kids! Holy shit! Fuck fuck fuck. He goes down again. Nothing. Comes to the surface and screams. 'Help! Somebody! Help!' It is pitch black and he kicks his feet to stay afloat.

This is the innocent version of the night Robert Farquharson killed his children. In a way, he'd already lost them. His wife Cindy had asked for a divorce 10 months prior, taking custody, the house, the good car. Cindy explained that she had loved him, but had never been 'in love' with him. She had started a new relationship with the man who had laid the concrete for what was supposed to be Rob and Cindy's new home. Rob had moved in with his dad who lived nearby, staying close to his children, now the focus of his life[1]. He hated living with his dad. He still loved Cindy. He hated her new man. 'Dickhead'.

He is still in the water when he sees the headlights of a truck. He swims toward them but it feels like he is swimming forever, that the water won't end. When finally his feet touch mud he crawls out, onto the bank. He looks back at the dam, and sees nothing. He looks toward the road and sees nothing. The truck is long gone. Propelled forwards, he crosses the paddock and clambers over a fence and up the bank to the road. Now there are more headlights. He waves frantically but the car drives past. 'I'm late,' he is thinking, 'Cindy is waiting for us. Oh fuck. What am I going to tell Cindy? Oh fuck. Fuck. They're dead. I've fucking killed the kids.'

The next car he sees he steps out and stands in front of. He is covered in mud and soaked. It swerves around him, keeps going. Then another follows it and another. But then there is another, it stops. Two locals, Shane Atkinson, 22 and Tony McClelland, 23, get out. 'What the fuck are you doing standing on the side of the road?' yells Shane. 'Are you trying to kill yourself mate?'

'Fuck! No! No! No! I've just killed me kids. No! No! No! Fuck Fuck Fuck! What have I done?' His mind is racing. What happened? This is what will be asked. And it is. The men are staring at him. Think. What happened? Here is the road, there is the water. 'I must have done a wheel bearing, put the car in the dam,' he says. 'I've killed the kids. I have to tell their mother.' But still thinking, what the fuck happened? He can remember coughing. One of the guys tells him to calm down. And again asks, what happened?

And this here is where it begins, the trial of Robert Farquharson. The trial that repeated itself, that saw volumes of

---

1. This is not in dispute. Plenty of evidence was forwarded during both trials that Farquharson's life at that time revolved around his relationship with his kids, e.g. Trial at p1236-1238 & p2835.

titillating memoirs and naïve observations, of vitriol, a trial by police, by media and in the justice system, applauded novel-length reportage by one of Australia's most celebrated non-fiction writers, and in the seven years all this took, one person's narrative remained unchanged.

'I blacked out'. Robert, on the side of the highway with two confused young men, remembered. He was coughing. He had been for days. He was coughing and then they were in the dam. 'I was havin' a coughing fit, next thing I remember we were in the dam. I must'a blacked out'. 'I tried to get the kids out. I need to tell their mother. I tried. I couldn't get 'em out.' he says to the men. 'Cindy is waiting for us. I need to tell her.'

'Mate, what the fuck are you talking about??'

Oh fuck. I need a cigarette. Oh fuck. 'Can ya gimme a smoke mate? You gotta drive me to Cindy. I gotta tell their mother. Fuck. I gotta tell her. Fuck. What am I going to tell her? Fuck. They are dead. Cindy. Fuck. She is going to fuckin' kill me. Fuck.'

Farquharson is not making any sense, he is not coherent, he is just babbling. The two guys do not move, just stare at him. 'Mate, calm down, take a breath and tell us where the kids are?'

'I blacked out and put the car in the dam. The kids, they are in the car. I tried to get them out. I couldn't get them out. The kids, they are in there.'

Shane and Tony looked at the dam. The dam was still. Is this guy insane?

'Should we go down and try to get them out?' asks Shane.

Still no cigarette.

'Mate, do you want to call the police?' asks Tony.

Farquharson just keeps babbling.

'Get me to their mother. It is too late. I fucking killed 'em. Fuck! Gimme a smoke, can ya? I gotta tell Cindy. Drive me to Winch.'

The crazy fucker is pointing to Geelong. Is he insane? He is clearly not the full dollar. Has he got Downs Syndrome? wonders Shane.

'Winch is that way mate' says Shane, pointing in the right direction.

'Ok, drive me there, I got to tell Cindy. I fucking killed the kids. I gotta tell her.'

'You sure we shouldn't call the cops, mate?'

'It's too late. I gotta tell Cindy. Fuck. She's their mother. I gotta tell her. She's waiting. I gotta tell Cindy. Drive me to Winch.'

CHAPTER 2

OBSESSED

It was Father's day, September 4th 2005, and Robert Farquharson had been driving his three young sons home to their mother's house in Winchelsea after taking them to dinner at KFC in Geelong, 30 minutes up the Princes Highway. Just a few minutes before reaching Winchelsea, the car went off the road and into a dam. The three children, Jai aged 10, Tyler 7 and Bailey 2 years old, all drowned. Robert Farquharson escaped the sinking car.

Tyler and Bailey were found lifeless in the back seat when the 1989 Commodore Berlina, the 'shit car', was winched from the dam later that night. Jai was found protruding from the front door by police diver Rebecca Caskey, who pushed him back inside before the car was winched out. Was it worse that he nearly made it?

The community of Winchelsea was shocked. The boys' school flew their flag at half-mast and provided counselling to Jai and Tyler's class mates, who planned a memorial garden. Bouquets of flowers were laid at the side of the dam. Media interest was intense at the funeral of the three boys at the Church of John the Baptist in Winchelsea. Farquharson and ex-wife Cindy Gambino cried, wailed, embraced. This was raw grief and the scenes, captured by tv and print media, are distressing.

Or was Farquharson putting it on? Were these crocodile tears?[1] Initially, the police reported the deaths as 'a tragic accident' and

Robert Farquharson and Cindy Gambino console
one another at the funeral of their three boys. ©
Newspix/Kelly Barnes

there was enormous sympathy for Robert Farquharson. Within days, however, the police started casting suspicion. Surely this was not murder? Unthinkable. 'How could anyone be that evil?' thought Sergeant Jeffry Smith who was in charge of police operations on the night of the children's deaths.

Within months, Robert Farquharson would be charged with murdering his three sons. He was found guilty at trial in 2007. Farquharson appealed and won the right to a new trial, and was found guilty of murder for a second time in 2010. He appealed again, first to the Supreme Court of Victoria and then to the High Court of Australia, and lost. Farquharson is currently in prison, serving a 33 year sentence.

Who is Robert Farquharson, and how could he be that evil?

A lot has been written about Robert Farquharson, with two full length books on the case, and a chapter in a third book written by a psychologist purporting to explain 'why he did it'. None of the authors actually spoke to Farquharson, however one

---

1. see e.g. Megan Norris *On Fathers Day* Bonnier Publishing Australia 2013 5526 (kindle).

author, Megan Norris, did speak extensively to Cindy Gambino, his partner for 12 years. A portrait emerged of a very ordinary Aussie bloke.

In the 1990's, John Howard's rise to prime minister of Australia was attributed by many to his appeal to 'aussie battlers', ordinary working class individuals. Howard described a battler as 'somebody who finds in life that they have to work hard for everything they get… normally you then look at it in terms of somebody who's not earning a huge income but somebody who is trying to better themselves, and I've always been attracted to people who try to better themselves.' Prior to being thrust into the public domain as the embodiment of evil and of male violence, Farquharson had embodied the term 'little aussie battler'. He was literally little, around 5 foot 2 inches in the old scale. He worked long hours as a cleaner in a hotel, having worked previously for the city council and then as a lawn mower. He was an 'old school' husband and father who left the housework and child raising to the Mrs, and whose interactions with the boys revolved around sports. He was 'a good provider'[2] who was very close to his boys[3].

Helen Garner, renowned author of a critically acclaimed narrative nonfiction book on the case, embraced Farquharson's ordinariness as a touchstone for exploring the human psyche and, as is her want, her own psyche 'I'm interested in apparently ordinary people who, under life's unbearable pressure, burst through the very fine membrane that separates our daylight selves from the secret darkness that lives in every one of us.'[4]

Does it though? Are we all capable of murdering our own children?

I have spoken to Robert Farquharson on multiple occasions, but I don't purport to have great insights into his psyche. I visited him in the protective custody section of prison, where he has spent more than a decade. No-one likes a child killer, making him unsuitable for mixing into the general population of

---

2. Norris, M. *On Fathers Day* 3914 (kindle)
3. Norris, M. *On Fathers Day* 281 (kindle)
4. Garner, H, *On Darkness*, in *Everywhere I Look* Text Publishing

prisoners. An outcast from society's outcasts, the lowest of the low. Sitting across from me, wearing a green jump suit, in an ordinary room with ordinary chairs and ordinary tables, he comes across as an ordinary aussie bloke. But consider that at the next ordinary table sits another ordinary looking bloke, also clad in a green jump suit, chatting amiably with his mother. That ordinary looking bloke is doing a life sentence for a string of brutal rapes that culminated in a horrific rape and murder. The ordinary table across from us was occupied by another ordinary looking bloke wearing a green jump suit, and his family; father, mother, sister. They seemed pretty ordinary too. This bloke, who savagely killed two elderly neighbours, casually had his arm around his sister as the family chatted.

When Farquharson told me the story of what happened the night his children died, I could not look into his eyes and tell whether he was lying. I don't have that ability. I cannot read minds. I can tell you that he stuck by his story of blacking out after coughing. Of coming to in the dam. Of trying to dive down. Of not reaching the car. Of going for help. That by the time he reached the road he had gone into shock. That the only thing that came into his mind was the need to tell Cindy, the boys' mother. I can also tell you that I believed him. Not because he sounded earnest, and not because he looked me in the eyes, as though that matters. I believed him because I had spent the past two years looking closely at the evidence used to convict him, and had concluded that the evidence indicates that he is innocent.

But he was found guilty! Twice! Not by one jury, but by two juries! The cries of protestation from those familiar with the case ring loud in my ears. I encounter them whenever I mention that I am researching the case. Why bring this case back up again? Hasn't Cindy suffered enough?

Nothing can console Cindy Gambino for losing her three sons, but if I am right, then an innocent man has now been locked up for more than a decade and will remain so for a long time to come. A man who lost *his* three sons.

Like most people from the state of Victoria, I have known about the Farquharson case from the beginning. Like many, I wanted to better understand how a seemingly normal bloke could be driven to kill his three sons. I read the two books that have been written on the case, *On Father's Day* by Megan Norris and *This House of Grief* by Helen Garner. Both authors followed the trials closely, but both accounts left me with a nagging doubt. Did he really do it? Something did not add up. Sure, there are horror stories of men seeking revenge on their partners by killing their children, but Farquharson did not seem to fit the script of a violent man.

But what did I know about Farquharson, and for that matter what did I know about who was capable of such things? What drew me into looking at the evidence in this case was not pop-psychology, trying to assess who is capable of murder. It was something far more mundane: the accident reconstruction evidence that was central to the prosecution case. I am a physicist, and the descriptions I had read of this evidence seemed hopelessly wrong. Was something getting lost in translation? Or was the evidence really as poor as it seemed?

Compelled to find out more I scoured the internet, finding snippets of detail here and there. I read the appeals decisions that contain summary information of the case and, although there were not enough details to understand it fully, the accident reconstruction evidence continued to look shaky. I wanted to find the full details of this reconstruction evidence but soon discovered that evidence and reports from criminal cases are not publicly available. Not even court transcripts, where I could at least read the expert witness testimony, are publicly available. I still wonder why not. Isn't this *our* justice system? Why shouldn't justice be fully transparent?

I decided to contact Farquharson's barrister, Peter Morrissey, to ask if he could provide me a copy of the transcripts. I wondered how many crazy people contact him about high profile cases like this. Psychics and the like. So when contacting him, I emphasized my credentials as an academic and scientist, and even signed using 'Dr. Brook', a title I only draw upon when contacting real estate agents when I am looking to rent a flat. I really don't know if any of that mattered, but Morrissey replied and after a bit of back and forth, said he would forward my details to a woman named Anne Irwin, who was a friend of Robert Farquharson.

Anne got in contact and sent me the court transcripts of both trials. I would later learn that any sliver of hope was welcome by Farquharson's small band of dedicated supporters. I would also come to learn of the profound scepticism coming from Farquharson's family, particularly his sisters Carmen and Kerri, about anyone seeking information. Carmen and Kerri have developed a deep mistrust of the media. My coming from an academic background counted in my favour with Anne and besides, she did not need to tell the sisters just yet.

I have now come to know Anne Irwin as a remarkable woman who is Farquharson's lifeline, and Farquharson's family as steadfast in their support, but concern for Farquharson's welfare was not on my mind at the time. Surely the evidence of guilt will be clear in the transcripts, considering that two different juries had no reasonable doubt about his guilt. Considering that he was sentenced to 33 years in prison. Considering that he had exhausted all avenues of appeal, his appeals dismissed and rejected by all courts including the High Court of Australia.

Upon reading the transcripts, instead of being somewhat comforted by the thought that at least he got his just desserts, I was struck by the hopelessly poor standards of analysis of the evidence, and the huge gap between the calibre of enquiry and analysis that I encounter in my career in science, and those in our justice system. As a scientist, I shook my head in disbelief at the manner in which the evidence was analysed and presented. Is this the system by which our society seeks justice for three drowned children, and their grieving family? Is this the system by which our society condemns a man to spend 33 years in jail? The further I read and understood the evidence, the more uneasy I felt. The more uneasy I felt, the more I was driven to find out more. I became obsessed.

Chapter 3

THE DAD TEST

'What about your children, why didn't you get them out?' demanded Stephen Moules to Rob Farquharson on that fateful evening. Moules was Cindy's new partner at the time, and the two are now married. When Farquharson arrived at Cindy's house, Cindy had called Moules, who leapt into action. He rushed to the dam and plunged into the water, searching for the car, searching for the children. Again and again, Moules dived into the freezing, blackened water. The contrast between Moules as a 'furious hero'[1] who 'kicked off his lace up boots, and flung his red jacket to the ground'[2] as he bounded down to the dam, and Farquharson as a cowardly wimp who left his kids to drown, then 'stood by and did nothing'[3] as others joined the search, is etched into the mythology of this tragedy.

At sentencing, Justice Cummins made special mention of Moules, 'a brave and good man'[4]. 'He nearly died just doing what he did. He spent 45 minutes in and out of that icy cold water'[5] said Cindy. 'Very brave, what you did, very brave' said 60 minutes reporter Peter Overton during an interview in 2007, in which Moules laments that 'I know if it was me in that situation, I believe that if my children weren't here today, I wouldn't be

---

1. Helen Garner *This House of Grief* 2463 (kindle)
2. Megan Norris *On Fathers Day* 563 (kindle)
3. Megan Norris *On Fathers Day* 5314 (kindle)
4. DPP v Farquharson [2007] VSC 469 (16 November 2007), 10
5. *60 Minutes*, Nine Network, 25 Oct 2007

here today 'cause if I couldn't save 'em, I'd huddle around them and say, 'Well, we're going together kids', and that's all there is to it. You know, your kids are helpless, they don't understand. I mean, poor Bailey was two years old. Pitch black, cold water — he would not have had a clue. Let alone what Tyler and Jai would have been feeling'.

These sentiments were shared by many in the public, as can be garnered from comments on news articles on the case, 'Real loving parents die trying to save their kids. Not swim and leave…'[6], reads one 'I am a mother of four boys, I would not have left my boys in that car I would have rather died trying to save them'[7] reads another, and another 'Do you know of any parent that wouldn't have to be forcefully restrained to keep them from diving into the water to save their babies? From diving until they don't have the strength or breath to swim any more?'[8], and 'there is no way I would ever leave the water without getting my kids out. If my kids were in a car submerged in water, I wouldn't leave that area – dead or alive I would get them out. I myself would die trying to get them all out. GUILTY!'[9]

In the eyes of the public, Farquharson had 'failed the "Dad Test". If his kids had to die, why hadn't Farquharson shown a willingness to die in their rescue?'[10] The notion that Farquharson should have been able to get his children out of the car put him immediately under suspicion, casting a long shadow over the case from the beginning.

These sentiments played a very real part in Farquharson's trials. Both juries were shown a video of a submergence test performed by the police, using the same type of car as Farquharson's. The police lowered the car into a dam, to demonstrate how it would sink. Author Helen Garner, who sat through both Farquharson's trials, described the video where

---

6. username mvvandieman, https://www.youtube.com/watch?v=IZtjz38szRc
7. username jig678, https://www.youtube.com/watch?v=IZtjz38szRc
8. http://hellbeasts.com/?p=1234
9. Christine on Robin Riley's Blog 07 Oct 2007
10. Carlyon, P., Devic A. & Buttler, M. Robert Farquharson: The dad who killed his three sons Sunday Herald Sun August 30

'gradually, gradually, nose down, on an angle, heavy and slow, in endless silence, the commodore sinks into the dam'[11], whilst the view from inside the car showed the water coming up 'leisurely and secretive, commandeering the space with unstoppable authority, its surface twinkling and wriggling. It rises and rises until it covers the two seat-backs, and engulfs the camera itself.'[12] Garner described the video as 'terrible… unbearable… visually so horribly vivid… just unthinkable, I can hardly even talk about it now, and I think that everyone in the court room was just speechless with horror.'[13] The judge in the second trial, Lex Lasry, described the submergence videos as 'the worst part'[14] of the trial, exclaiming that he 'never wanted to revisit them'[15].

The car in the police reconstruction video had taken more than eight minutes to sink. 'To me that was very compelling, that you had time where you could collect your thoughts, collect the boys, work out a plan, and say "this is how we are going to get out"'[16] observed the lead investigator in the case, Detective Sergeant Gerard Clanchy of the homicide squad. Prosecuting barrister Andrew Tinney impressed upon the jury that 'the behaviour claimed by the accused in the course of the event where his car became submerged in the dam and his children died, completely defies belief'[17] and that 'no loving father would dream of departing from the car without securing the safety of his children first or going at least close to dying in the process.'[18]

Indeed, this is compelling. It is not possible to know the reasons for the jury's verdict, but at least one court reporter concluded that 'the fact that Robert Farquharson wasn't willing to die saving them [the children] convinced a jury of his guilt.'[19]

---

11. Helen Garner *This House of grief* 1379 (kindle)
12. ibid.
13. Helen Garner on *Conversations with Richard Fidler*, ABC radio Sept 4 2014
14. Brennan, Bernadette *A writing Life Helen Garner and her work* 2017, 3431 (kindle)
15. ibid.
16. *Crimes that Shook Australia* Series 2 episode 1
17. Trial 2 p4865
18. Trial 2 p4864
19. Elissa Hunt *He had no interest in saving his kids* Herald Sun July 23 2010

Chapter 4

SINKING FAST

Between 30 seconds and two minutes. That is how long it takes for a car to sink once it is driven into water, according to the research of Dr. Gordon Giesbrecht, a professor at the University of Manitoba. Dr. Giesbrecht and his colleague Gerren McDonald conducted more than 100 car and truck submersions with people in them. 'When your vehicle hits the water, you have about a one-minute window of opportunity to get out,'[1] concluded Giesbrecht. 'Before you know it, you're under water, you're panicking and your odds of survival are very, very low'[2].

Based on these experiments, Dr. Giesbrecht wrote an academic paper[3] as well as instructional brochures on how to escape a sinking car. In summary[4]: exit through the window. Fast.

The difficulty of escaping a sinking car has resulted in a significant number of deaths. Vehicle submersions cause about 400 fatalities in North America annually, and account for up to 10% of all drownings in the U.S., New Zealand and Canada. In Australia, The Royal Life Saving Society puts the number of such deaths at 10 to 15 per year[5], a slightly lower per capita rate than

---

1. Kelly, C. How to get out of a sinking car The Star, Nov 4 2009
2. ibid
3. Giesbrecht G, McDonald G. *My car is sinking: automobile submersion, lessons in vehicle escape.* Aviat Space Environ Med 2010; 81:779–84.
4. The acronym SWOC describes what to do: SEATBELTS off, WINDOWS open; OUT immediately; CHILDREN first.

North America, presumably due to the dryer conditions of the Australian continent. These are not cases of people being fatally injured during the crash; people get trapped in the car as it sinks, and they drown.

It is not hard to find real life horror stories that underline the importance of Giesbrecht's research and message. Shanell Anderson, 31, lost control of her car and drove into a pond in Cherokee County. She called 911. The respondent spent crucial time trying to confirm the address of the accident, which was not showing up on the system. By the time emergency services arrived 20 minutes later, Shanell had drowned.

Giesbrecht advises against using a mobile phone to call emergency services if you drive into a body of water, as time is of the essence; the best chance of escaping through a window comes during the floating phase. Tragically for Shanell, the emergency respondents were unaware of Giesbrecht's research, and did not tell her to hang up the phone and get out the window.

In 2007, five Australian SAS soldiers, all in their early twenties, were driving back to their army barracks on Swan Island, returning from having a couple of drinks at a bar in Queenscliff. These were elite servicemen having a few beers, it was not a bender.[6] Three were in the front car, two followed in another car just 30 seconds behind. The front car missed a bend and ran off the Swan Island bridge and into Port Phillip bay. The depth of the water was not greater than the length of the car, such that that the rear was poking out of the water when the front of the car had settled in the sand at the bottom. Yet the soldiers could not open the doors. They also failed in their attempts to break the windows. The two soldiers in the following car tried to help, grabbing rocks to try to break the window. In spite of the efforts of those inside and outside the car, all three of the SAS soldiers in the front car drowned.[7]

---

5. Royal Life Saving National Drowning Report 2014, 2015
6. Blood alcohol levels of two soldiers were above legal driving limits were recorded but it was not clear who was driving.
7. Report of the commission of inquiry concerning the deaths of Sgt Craig Martyn Linacre, Cpl Michael Anthony McAvoy Cpl David Graham O'Neill, 3 Sept 2008

It is not easy to get out of a sinking car. In water, cars are death traps.

The Nissan pathfinder of Phil Budding and Dr. Kerry Arrow.

In November of 2016, Dr. Kerry Arrow and her husband Phil Budding were leaving their Healesville home to visit their newborn baby in Mercy Hospital. Their Nissan Pathfinder veered off the steep driveway and into their dam. Phil managed to escape the submerging car but by the time he dragged his wife out it was too late. Kerry Arrow was taken to hospital but never recovered, dying two weeks later. A photo of the Pathfinder protruding from the still water of the dam reminds me of a crocodile poking its eyes above the surface, belying the terror of what has taken place in these tranquil waters.

Other tragic cases show that it is not easy to get children out of a sinking car. In March 2016 Ruth Daniels, 57, her daughter Jodie Lee Daniels, 14, Sean McGrotty, 49, and his sons Mark, aged 12, and Evan 8, all drowned when their car slipped off a pier in Donegal, Ireland. A number of people were present and witnessed the tragedy. One man swam out to the car and was able to grab a 4 month old baby, who was handed out the window before the car sank. Emergency response teams rushed to the scene, but were too late to save the remainder of the family. 'I knew the services were all on their way, and I was hoping against hope that the car would stay up until the people came,' said eyewitness Francis Crawford. 'I was watching the car and then it started to dip, and then all of a sudden the whole car just went down'.[8]

In Monroe, North Carolina, three young children and a 26 year old man all drowned when a car rolled into Lake Lee. Two other men, including the children's uncle who was fishing from the bank, tried to save the children, without success.[9]

In another case, three children drowned[10] when a car slid into Arlesey lake in Bedfordshire, England. Their parents and another passenger had scrambled out of the vehicle as it slid down a gravel bank into the water. Rescue crews rushed to the scene. A paramedic dived into the water, but could not reach the car, as the water was almost seven metres deep. Another waded in with a length of rope and a snorkel, managing to reach the car, but he could not pull the children free.

I asked Dr. Giesbrecht about Farquharson's story, that he had blacked out and ended up in the dam, and was unable to get his kids out as the car sank very fast once he got out the door. 'Bottom line if you open a door, water rushes in, the car sinks quickly slamming the door. You stand a good chance of being trapped when the door slams shut on you, but if you do get out the rest of the people in the car will be trapped and go down quickly with the car.'

I then directly asked Giesbrecht's opinion on the plausibility of Farquharson's claimed scenario. 'No question that a quickly acting adult could get out if he opened the door early before it sunk too deeply. Then the water would rush in, car would sink quickly and the door would close.... After this it would be virtually impossible to open doors or windows from inside or outside. The car would land on the bottom quickly and it would

---

8. Jess Staufenberg, *Buncrana Pier accident* The Independent 16 March 2016
9. The Tuscaloosa News - Apr 10, 1974
10. Demetriou, D. *Three children die as family car plunges into lake* The Telegraph 29 Jul 2001

be very difficult to swim down to it in 7.8-meter deep water. I have actually demonstrated what happens when you open the door with two US Special Forces Para Jumpers (PJs) who could not get out after opening the door and having it slam shut on them. They had to wait until the crane brought the car back up to the surface. Therefore, the result in this case is not surprising. The only thing that is questionable is if he drove in the water accidentally (then he's innocent) or on purpose (then...).'

The result was not surprising. The only thing that is questionable is if he drove in the water accidentally or on purpose. Once the car was in the dam, whether deliberately or by accident, then the situation was beyond Farquharson's control, and it was not surprising that the children drowned.

There is a stark contrast between these conclusions that were based on Giesbrecht's scientific research, and the manner in which the events were presented in Farquharson's trial. In the police reconstruction video watched by the jury, the car had taken more than eight minutes to sink. The reason it took so long was that the dam used in the police 'reconstruction' was only 2.8 metres deep, while the car was 4.8 metres long. 'If a 4.8-meter long car is placed in 2.4-meter deep water, the front end will hit the bottom when the car is still more horizontal and it will take much longer for it to fill up with water.' says Giesbrecht.

The dam where Farquharson's car sank was 7.4 metres deep. The water was freezing, there was a new moon and it was pitch black. According to his story, Farquharson woke from being unconscious and was not aware of where he was. The car was floating, and he did not know that the dam was so deep. When he got out the door, he went under, and had to swim to the top. The car sank fast. To the bottom. When compared with Giesbrecht's experiments, this is a plausible story. When compared with Phil Budding's horrific experience of losing his wife Kerry Arrow, this is a plausible story. Yet compared to what the jury was shown and told by the prosecutors, the story appeared very hard to accept.

What about Farquharson's claims that he dived down but could not reach the car? Stephen Moules was not the only person to enter the freezing water that night, in search of the car. James Cromer was just 17 years old and a member of the urban fire brigade that rushed to the scene. Along with another local Phil Lindsay, Cromer volunteered to enter the water and search. Other members of the brigade attached ropes to Cromer and Lindsay, to ensure their safety, and set up lighting to help direct their search. They found where the car entered, due to the debris at the edge of the lake, and searched in patterns to ensure they did not keep going back over the same areas. They could not locate the car. 'I had assumed that ... to find a car in a normal dam would take a matter of seconds, not knowing... how deep the dam in fact was.'[11] explained Cromer.

Other would-be rescuers also heroically entered the dam. One was Kiri Fausett[12], a Winchelsea local and state emergency service (SES) volunteer. Fausett testified that he tried 'doing pin drops as deep and as far as I could go',[13] but he was not able to reach the bottom of the dam and that 'the water just got colder and colder and I was starting to feel for my own wellbeing'.[14] Making matters worse, the dam was full of 'black water', with zero visibility due to suspended sediment.

People entered from both sides of the dam. None could reach the car.

Stephen Moules had trained as a surf lifesaver, and was no slouch in water. Cromer, Lindsay and Fausett has similar expertise. So, whilst Stephen Moules really was heroic that night, as were the others who entered the freezing water, their fruitless efforts highlight how difficult it was to dive down to the car. This evidence supports Farquharson's claims that he dived down but could not reach the car, before deciding his best hope was to swim to shore and flag down a passing car for help.

The Search and Rescue squad arrived at the dam 9.47pm, and police diver Senior Constable Rebecca Caskey was tasked with finding the sunken car. Attached to a rope, wearing a wetsuit

---

11. Trial 2 p1736
12. Trial 2 p1866
13. Trial 2 p1866
14. Trial 2 p1868

and using a scuba tank, Caskey felt around in the mud at the bottom of the dam while a colleague gradually slackened the tether, allowing her to sweep in concentric arcs. It took several arcs and 23 minutes to locate the car.

Looking purely at the evidence, Farquharson's story surrounding the events in the dam is credible. The evidence shows that Farquharson had little chance of saving the children, especially after he made the error of opening the door. This conclusion is based on detailed experiments done by independent researchers who had no knowledge of the Farquharson case. According to these experiments, there is less than two minutes between Farquharson crashing into the water, regaining consciousness, awakening dazed and confused, and the sinking of the car to the bottom of the dam. We also know that Farquharson's attempts to dive down and find the car would have been futile, because many others, far better swimmers than Farquharson, had not been able to reach the car.

CHAPTER 5

MAKING A MARK

Is it possible that Robert Farquharson, as a loving parent, could escape from a sinking car, whilst his three children drowned? Two ways of answering this question have been explored; one was presented by prosecutors in a court of law, the other by researchers in a scientific journal, using scientific methods. Two very different perspectives. One appeals to our emotion and nourishes the natural parental instinct that no innocent man would leave his children to drown; the other to our intellect, and challenges our initial emotional reaction. Two different answers, one which infers the guilt of Robert Farquharson; the other is consistent with innocence.

It is the latter that I rely upon in my attempts to unravel the truth in the case, as I resolved to apply scientific methods of enquiry and analysis, developed during my career working as a scientist, to the evidence in the Robert Farquharson case.

What are scientific methods of enquiry and analysis? Indeed, what is science? In the words of the astrophysicist Neil De Grass Tyson, science 'is made possible by generations of searchers strictly adhering to a simple set of rules. Test ideas by experiment and observation. Build on those ideas that pass the test. Reject the ones that fail. Follow the evidence wherever it leads, and question everything.' Nobel Prize winning physicist Richard Feynman says that science is a method for separating ideas, 'try one to see if it worked, and if it didn't work, to eliminate it.'

Simply stating a theory, or giving an opinion, is not good

enough for science. Science is a system designed to understand whether a given theory or opinion is correct, testing it by analysing evidence. Scientific analysis allows us to question our intuitions, our emotional responses, formally and systematically putting them to the test to determine if they are correct.

Knowledge based on scientific methods of testing and experiment helped me understand what would happen once Farquharson's car entered the dam. The plausibility of his story does not prove his innocence, but it does allow the remainder of the evidence to be explored with an open mind, with the presumption of innocence maintained.

What about the accident reconstruction evidence that got me interested in this case? After finally gaining access to exhibits and reports, stored at Victoria Legal Aid, I was in a position to properly analyse this evidence.

As presented in the committal hearing, two voir dires (pre-trial hearings), and two trials, the reconstruction evidence is a sprawling mess of examination and cross examination, claim and counter-claim, accusations and denials of mistakes and incompetence, inconsistent testimonies, unsubstantiated assertions and opinions, unending forays into irrelevant minutiae, and jumps back and forth from one aspect to another without any coherence. And so much of it was just so tedious. Helen Garner decried that 'the air of the court became a jelly of confusion and boredom'.

The combination of confusion and boredom in the reconstruction evidence was possibly fomented by the defence barrister Peter Morrissey, in a bid to overwhelm and confuse the jury and leave them with an underlying 'reasonable doubt'. This is a standard tactic in any defence barrister's kitbag. But this tactic may have played into the hands of the prosecution, because amongst all the confusion and boredom, the prosecution expert stuck to a simple theme and simple conclusions, which did not change: three steering inputs were required for the car to follow its path from the road to the dam. This assertion was clearly conveyed to the jury, who could be forgiven for having very little idea of the foundations upon which the conclusions were based.

This message that Farquharson must have been steering the car was central to his conviction.

After sifting through the mess and organizing all the information and testimony, I made a detailed analysis of the prosecution's reconstruction evidence that you can find in Appendix A. I will look at one part of the evidence below, as an example, but I do encourage you to read the appendix for yourself if you want to understand why I am so confident that the reconstruction evidence presented by the prosecution was fatally flawed. In summary, my analysis indicates that an un-steered car that followed the slope of the terrain could have left all the physical evidence that was found.

In my analysis, I explored the limits of what could be interpreted from the physical evidence at the scene, and found that a range of paths were consistent with that evidence. Some of those paths were possible for a car that was not being controlled by a conscious driver. Others were not. The limits on the available evidence mean that it is not possible to distinguish between those paths, and therefore one could not determine whether or not the car was being steered.

By contrast, when the prosecution reconstruction expert, Sergeant Glen Urquhart, reached the limits of what could be interpreted from the evidence, he proffered opinions.

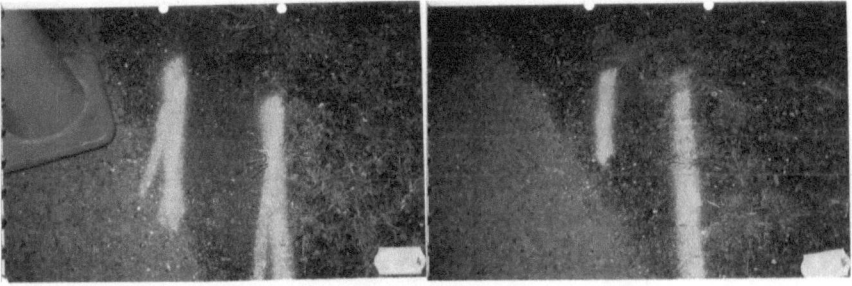

The left and right marks on the edge of the road, purported to be where the car left the road, as photographed by Senior Constable Courtis. Yellow paint added by Sergeant Exton.

To illustrate what I mean, consider the evidence pertaining to a mark that Urquhart used in his reconstruction as indicating where the car left the road. Originally, two marks were identified by police officers on the scene that night, officers Exton and Kok. They believed that the marks showed where the left and right wheels of Farquharson's car had left the road, and marked them with yellow paint. Sergeant Urquhart arrived at the scene just after midnight, around five hours after the car went in the dam. Urquhart inspected the marks and initially 'concurred... that was the position where the car had left the road'. It was only after he put them on a scale plan that Urquhart realized that they could not both be correct. The marks were too close together to match the distance between the wheels of Farquharson's car. Although there was a lot of confusion and inconsistencies between witnesses on this point, Urquhart chose the right hand mark as being left by a car. 'There was something that I observed within the yellow paint marks that led me to believe that a tyre had travelled over that...'

The question remained as to whether the mark was made by Robert Farquharson's car, as multiple other cars had also crossed over the edge of the road that evening. The task was to establish a link between the mark and the tyres of Robert Farquharson's car. Such a task falls under the broad umbrella of pattern evidence, which constitutes a large fraction of forensics, and includes blood splatter analysis, hair comparisons, bite marks, handwriting comparisons, shoe impressions, ballistics, CCTV image matching, and fingerprinting.

The traditional methods employed in these disciplines were developed by police officers in the field for the purpose of examining evidence, without testing the validity of the methods scientifically. Crime labs created to handle this type of forensic evidence were operational rather than research facilities. They built upon methods in a case by case manner as was required, without conducting the requisite scientific studies to determine how reliable such methods were. It was convenient for labs to have deep ties with the police force, allowing close and timely communication, facilitating the transfer of evidence, and streamlining record-keeping. And also introducing bias. The overall result is that the reliability of pattern evidence varies enormously, with little standardization within or between the disciplines.

Most, if not all of the disciplines of pattern evidence have been at the centre of miscarriages of justice. Take George Perrot, who was just seventeen years old when he was arrested for raping a 78 year old woman in 1992. No blood or semen was present, ruling out DNA testing. The victim testified that Perrot did not look like the attacker. However, a single hair found at the scene was said to be a match to Perrot's. The expert witness, an FBI hair and fibre specialist, testified that cranial and pubic hair were distinctive and could be used to identify individuals. It was not until 2013 that the FBI admitted that the whole foundation of 'hair comparison evidence' was deeply flawed. When scientific studies finally tested the validity of the methods employed, it became apparent that microscopic analysis of hairs is not able to identify individuals. George Perrot was finally freed in 2016, having spent 30 years in jail for a crime that he did not commit.

Then there is Ray Krone, who became known as the 'snaggle tooth killer' when an impression of his jagged teeth was matched to bite marks on the body of a murdered Phoenix bartender. A bite mark expert was the key witness for the prosecution, with no other evidence tying Krone to the crime. Krone was released in 2002 when DNA from saliva and blood from the crime scene was matched to a convicted rapist. He had spent 21 years in prison. Thankfully, his death sentence had been commuted to life imprisonment. A review of the science underlying bite mark analysis made in 2016 found that methods developed by odontologists (forensic dentists) to match bite marks to suspects were 'clearly scientifically unreliable' and that 'available scientific evidence strongly suggests that examiners cannot consistently agree on whether an injury is a human bite-mark and cannot identify the source of bite-mark with reasonable accuracy.'

Yes, you read that correctly. When tested in a scientific environment, bite mark experts could not even determine whether the mark was made by a human.

Bite mark evidence can be traced back as far as the Salem

witch trials in 1620, and has been employed in modern policing since the 1950s, highlighting that presenting forensic techniques as being 'well established' and 'standard procedure', as is often asserted in trials, does not mean that the methods have any scientific validity. Assertions of how well established procedures are, or how experienced an analyst is at performing these techniques, are no substitute for rigorous scientific testing.

On 14 September 1964, Alexander McLeod-Lindsay returned from work to his suburban Sydney home to find his wife and son had been brutally beaten. Both their skulls had been fractured, with Pamela McLeod-Lindsay also suffering abdominal injuries, a broken collar-bone, broken nose, and severe lacerations. Her skull fracture was so severe that brain tissue was exposed. Miraculously, both Pamela and their son lived. The police suspected Alexander McLeod-Lindsay and eventually charged him with attempted murder. Pamela insisted that her husband was not the person who attacked her and their son, but the prosecution asserted that she was lying to cover up for her husband.

The prosecution case against McLeod-Lindsay centred on 'expert' evidence that blood stains found on his jacket was 'impact splatter' from the attack. Detective Sergeant Norman Merchant from the Scientific Section of the Criminal Investigation Bureau was adamant that the stains could only be impact spatter from blows delivered vertically to the head by a right handed man, standing with his right leg forward. Such is the sway of 'scientific' forensic evidence that McLeod-Lindsay was found guilty of attempted murder, in spite of his wife steadfastly maintaining that it was someone else who had attacked her. He spent 9 years in prison for a crime that he did not commit, before being released on parole. In 1990, McLeod-Lindsay was exonerated after a review of the evidence found that the blood on his jacket was clotted, indicating that it was not impact splatter, but was instead consistent with McLeod-Lindsay's repeated claims that his wife had coughed the blood onto his jacket as he cradled her in his arms.

A 2009 review of blood splatter evidence found that the

methods developed by police were 'more subjective than scientific' and that 'the uncertainties associated with bloodstain pattern analysis are enormous'.

So, what does all this mean for the marks where Farquharson's car allegedly left the road? The scientific working group for Shoeprint and Tire Tread Evidence (SWGTREAD) was initiated in 2004 by the FBI to standardize and advance the forensic analysis of shoeprint and tyre tread evidence, to make it more scientific. Protocols for matching tyre prints to particular car wheels were proscribed, and include procedures for making castings of the prints and for taking detailed photographs. Guidelines were set out for how the results should be presented in court, depending on the level of certainty for a match. Despite such advances, a 2016 review found that significant scientific validation work was still lacking in this field, and the ability of experts to make positive identifications remains unclear, as do their rates of error.

How was the evidence of the mark on the side of the road presented in the trial of Robert Farquharson? Sergeant Exton, who first identified the marks, testified that 'I can clearly say where the yellow paint touches the bitumen surface is exactly where the driver's side front tyre of the VN Commodore left that bitumen surface.'

Based on what?

What about Sergeant Urquhart, the expert witness who did the reconstruction? Referencing the right hand mark and a set of rolling prints through long grass off the road, the latter of which clearly *were* made by Farquharson's car, defence barrister Peter Morrissey asked Urquhart, 'What you say is they could be produced by the same car?'

'I say they are produced by the same car.'

Based on what?

No castings were made. No photographs depicted tyre tread markings. No analysis was made to match the right mark to Farquharson's tread. Yet a definitive match between that right mark and Farquharson's car was asserted by two prosecution witnesses, leaving no room for doubt, with no indication of any uncertainty relayed to the jury.

Let us accept that the right hand mark is indeed a rolling print made by a vehicle, rather than a scuff mark that could be made in any number of other ways, although the evidence for this is, at best, ambiguous (see appendix A). With this caveat, we can ask how Sergeant Urquhart established that it was Farquharson's car that made the mark, rather than some other vehicle. A significant number of vehicles had crossed over the road's edge that evening, but no one was monitoring exactly how many or where they crossed. Yet only two marks were found at the edge of the road, meaning most vehicles crossed the edge without leaving a mark. Why couldn't the right mark have been made by the car of Shane Atkinson and Tony McClelland when they were stopped by a hysterical Farquharson waving them down? What about the ambulance, firetruck, SES trucks, or the various cars of people who had rushed to the scene prior to the arrival of the police from the Major Collisions Unit?

Given that no photos depicted any tyre tread in the marks, no moulds were taken, what evidence was presented to link that right mark to Farquharson's car in particular? Urquhart asserted that the differentiating feature was speed. 'At a higher speed you're more likely to get a disturbance of gravel even for a car travelling straight than you are at lower speeds. That's not to say that at lower speeds it can't happen. My view is that it's just simply more likely at a higher speed.'

Firstly note that he says 'more likely': so why did he testify so definitively that the mark was made by Farquharson's car? Why did he not state that it was 'more likely' made by Farquharson's car than other vehicles?

Secondly, is speed really the most important factor in determining whether a car will leave such a mark? No studies were cited, and no experiments were done. The assertion was not scientific in nature, and it may not even be true. Why would a car that is moving fast be more likely to leave a mark on the side of that particular road than a slower moving car? What about weight? Wouldn't a fire-tuck, or SES vehicle, be more likely to leave a mark than a car? What about braking? Tony McClelland and Shane Atkinson braked heavily in that region when they were flagged down by a frantic Farquharson. What about turning the wheel at that point? What if someone who rushed to the scene had turned their wheels to navigate down the embankment? Would that have been more likely to leave a mark than a car travelling straight? What about the differences in the soil in different areas, where some soil may be looser than other soil? If speed is shown to be a factor, it will not be the only factor.

Finally, even if it was shown that a car travelling fast is more likely to leave a mark, we need to know how much more likely. Is it twice as likely? Three times as likely? Any increase in likelihood needs to be assessed against the number of cars that crossed the road that night: if a fast moving car is three times more likely to leave a mark, but six cars crossed the road that night, then overall it is still twice as likely that another car left the mark than Farquharson's.

All this makes any link between the mark and Farquharson's car uncertain. Highly uncertain. Meaning that the reconstruction expert should have explained this uncertainty to the jury, and should have explored alternative plausible paths. Instead, he presented a reconstruction based on that mark being where Farquharson's car had left the road.

Urquhart then went further. Not only did he assert that the right mark was made by Farquharson's car: he asserted that it was made by the right wheels of Farquharson's car. So, even if we accept that this non-descript mark was made by a car tyre, and then accept the speculative argument, based on speed, that the mark was made by Farquharson's car rather than another vehicle, what evidence was presented that it was made by the right wheels rather than the left wheels? No rationale was ever proffered for this assertion, despite the question being raised multiple times over the various hearings and trials. Urquhart simply stated 'that's my opinion that I believe the vehicle was travelling over that mark', and 'it's always been my position that the driver's side tyres have crossed that right side mark'. When again pressed for the reasoning, he says 'That's always been my position' and when asked 'is there more to it?' Urquhart responded 'No, no, and I think we went through it in quite a lot of detail in the last trial, and my position hasn't changed.'

Indeed, Urquhart's position did not change: he made the same unsubstantiated assertion in both trials. An assertion that was not supported by any physical evidence at the scene, and is totally unscientific in nature. An assertion that helped form the basis for Urquhart's reconstruction, the most important piece of evidence used against Robert Farquharson.

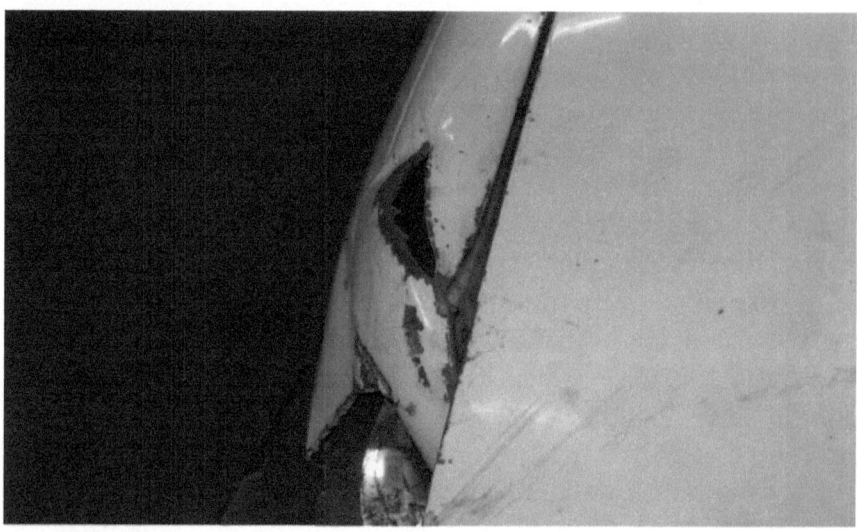

Farquharson's car went through a wire fence, between the road and the dam. The fence ripped through the metal of the car on the front right hand side. The prosecution asserted, without any testing, that this collision could not have caused the car to pull rightward.

This was not the only unsubstantiated opinion that was proffered by Sergeant Urquhart. As outlined in Appendix A, Urquhart gave his opinion that the car was travelling at 60km/h; that the road camber sloped left, and when that opinion was shown to be wrong, that the right sloping camber could not explain the car's path off the road; that there was a straight section through the long grass; and that hitting a fence with the front right side of the car would not cause the car to pull rightwards (see picture). Meanwhile, another prosecution expert witness, Robert Leguier, expressed an opinion that having a left tyre that is 10 mm higher than the right tyre could not cause the car to veer rightward and Sergeant Exton gave his opinion that striking and running over the top of fence posts could not have caused a deviation of the car.

Each one of these opinions went against Farquharson. Without these opinions, none of the asserted three steering inputs, so crucial to the prosecution's case, are necessary. Without these opinions, the forensic reconstruction evidence no longer points to guilt. None of these opinions were supported by the evidence at the scene, none were supported by experiments done by the police, none were supported by experiments that they could cite from other researchers in the reconstruction field. In other words, none of these opinions had any scientific basis. But isn't forensic evidence supposed to be scientific? Don't we call it forensic science?

CHAPTER 6

LET'S CALL IT FORENSIC SCIENCE, BUT DO WE REALLY NEED THOSE PESKY SCIENCY BITS THAT WE ALL HATED AT SCHOOL?

The admission of unverified, unscientific opinions by expert witnesses is at the heart of an ongoing crisis in forensic science, not just in Australia but throughout the world. Much of forensic science is just not science at all. This is not my opinion, but the findings of several important reports[1,2,3,4,5] into forensic science over the past decade in the U.S., Canada, and the U.K[6]. The most significant and comprehensive of these reports is

---

1. National Research Council. *Strengthening Forensic Science in the United States: A Path Forward.* The National Academies Press. Washington DC 2009 p178, 179
2. Law Commission of England and Wales, *Expert Evidence in Criminal Proceedings in England and Wales,* 34 Law Com Report No 325, Hon Stephen Goudge
3. Hon Stephen Goudge, *Inquiry into Pediatric Forensic Pathology* (Toronto: Queen's Printer of Ontario, 2008) [Goudge Inquiry]
4. Lord Campbell, *The Fingerprint Inquiry Report* (Edinburgh: APS Group Scotland, 2011).
5. PCAST (op cit 50)
6. These reports explored the scientific underpinnings of various forensic sciences. This is not confined by national boundaries. So the lack of scientific underpinnings found in the report applies to Australia, and all countries. Further, international societies exist to share forensic analysis methods. Many procedures and methods used in Australian forensic sciences are therefore the same as those used in the countries where the reports were written. Also, many Australian forensic scientists are trained and certified in the UK and the US. For example, the certification to practice accident reconstruction in Australia is granted by the U.K based Institute of Traffic Accident

Strengthening Forensic Science in the United States: A Path Forward[7], undertaken by the National Academy of Sciences as commissioned by the U.S. National Research Council (NRC). The multidisciplinary committee that wrote the report was composed of forensic scientists, statisticians, law professors, biologists, a chemist, an engineer, computer scientists, a medical examiner, and was chaired by Judge Harry T Edwards. At the end of an exhaustive two-year process, Edwards concluded that 'I simply assumed, as I suspect many of my judicial colleagues do, that forensic science disciplines typically are well-grounded in scientific methodology and that crime laboratories and forensic science practitioners follow proven practices that ensure the validity and reliability of forensic evidence offered in court. I was surprisingly mistaken...'[8] The Report observed that 'some forensic science disciplines are supported by little rigorous systematic research to validate the discipline's basic premises and techniques.'[9]

At the root of the problem is the fact that our legal system does not *require* that forensic evidence be scientific. Our courts introduce 'science' into trials in a manner that pays scant regard to the scientific method, ignoring the essential aspects that define what science is.

Forensic evidence is introduced into the court as an exception to rules that prevent witnesses from proffering 'opinions'.[10] Most witnesses in a trial are restricted to describing facts, such as what they saw or heard, and are prevented from expressing their

---

Investigators, while officially recognised training has been provided by external institutions such as Northwestern University in Illinois, and courses of the London City and Guilds. See also Edmond , G. & Matire K., Antipodean forensics: a comment on ANZFSS's response to PCAST Australian Journal of Forensic Sciences, 50:2, 140-151

7. *Strengthening Forensic Science in the United States: A Path Forward* National Research Council 2009
8. H. T. Edwards, *Solving the Problems That Plague the Forensic Science Community* 2009
9. *Strengthening Forensic Science in the United States: A Path Forward* National Research Council 2009
10. In Victoria, the rules surrounding the introduction of such evidence are codified in the Uniform Evidence Law 1995, which also applies in New South Wales, Tasmania, the ACT and the Northern Territory

interpretation of these facts, or giving their opinion as to what can be inferred from the facts. It is up to the jury to interpret the evidence, not the witnesses. However, it is recognized that the analysis and interpretation of some types of evidence requires a degree of expertise, or 'specialized knowledge'.[11] Therefore, courts allow experts to analyse that evidence and provide their opinion as to how it can be interpreted.

Experts are provided great leeway in what opinions they can express. A study comparing[12] the admission of forensic evidence in the U.S., the U.K., Canada and Australia found that 'there is almost no expert testimony so threadbare that it will not be admitted if it comes to a criminal proceeding under the banner of forensic science.'[13] In Victoria,[14] where Farquharson was tried, experts are required to have 'specialized knowledge', and their opinions must be 'wholly or substantially based on that knowledge'. However, the legal system applies their own standards as to what constitutes the basis of knowledge and how this can be applied to interpret evidence. Generally, the requirement of a nexus between the basis of knowledge, the evidence and the interpretation given in courts is set at a level that facilitates a liberal allowance of opinion, once the expertise of a witness has been established.

Consider evidence given by Sergeant Urquhart in the first trial. Urquhart asserted that the path of Farquharson's car required a 220° turn of the steering wheel, which would imply that Farquharson had not blacked out. The assertion of a 220° turn was objected to by the defence but permitted by the judge. The allowance of this evidence formed part of the appeal of the case in 2009. The Court of Appeal found that the opinion was

---

11. Uniform Evidence Law 1995
12. Details of the laws and rules surrounding the introduction of expert opinion evidence do differ between countries and states For example, in the U.S. there is a requirement that evidence is 'reliable', see Daubert v. Merrell Dow Pharm., Inc., 509 U.S. 579 (1993). In Australia, this requirement of *reliability* was explicitly rejected in *R v Tang* (2006) 65 NSWLR 681.
13. G. Edmond, S. Cole, E. Cunliffe, and A. Roberts *Admissibility Compared: The reception of incriminating expert evidence (i.e. forensic science) in four adversarial jurisdictions*, 2013
14. s79 of the Evidence Act

admissible, 'based on the articulated assumption that the car was travelling in its correct lane. There was admissible evidence upon which this assumption could be made.'[15] However, the fact that the car started in the left lane only provides the basis for a right turn of *any magnitude*. It provides no basis for a turn of 220°. Such a flawed interpretation of the nexus between evidence and opinion is an example of the liberal admittance of incorrect expert evidence in criminal trials, evidence that does not withstand the scrutiny that is inherent in science.

The emphasis of the legal system is not on the scientific quality of the evidence presented.[16] Instead, great emphasis is placed on the credentials[17] of the person presenting the evidence. Has the person done a course in the relevant field? How much experience do they have? How many court cases have they presented evidence in? The roots of this approach are understandable. If an expert has qualifications and experience in a field of *specialized knowledge,* then how is the court, which presumably does not have such expertise, supposed to second guess the opinion of the expert?

However, this emphasis on the credentials of the experts, without requirements of scientific validity and reliability, created a system that is at odds with the principles of science. Let me turn again to Richard Feynman[18], as he explains the process of looking for a new theory. 'First we guess it', he says. The use of the word *guess* has significance: he is not affording initial opinions any status, at this stage it is nothing more than a guess. It may be an educated guess, but it is still just a guess. 'Then', he continues, 'we compute the consequences of the guess' and 'we compare the computation results to nature... to experiment or experience... to see if it works. If it disagrees with experiment, it's wrong. That simple statement is the key to science.' What Feynman says next

---

15. R v Farquharson [2009] VSCA 307 (17 December 2009) p32 at 130
16. see e.g. G. Edmond *Forensic Science Evidence and Rational (Jury) Evaluation* 2015 p99
17. e,g, G. Edmond, S. Cole, E. Cunliffe, and A. Roberts *Admissibility Compared: The reception of incriminating expert evidence (i.e. forensic science) in four adversarial jurisdictions,* 2013
18. Feynman, R. *The Character of Physical Law* (1965), The MIT Press, Chapter 7 p156

is this 'It doesn't make a difference how beautiful your guess is, it doesn't make a difference how smart you are, or what your name is. If it disagrees with experiment, it is wrong'. Science is absolutely not interested in who you are, it has no regard for qualifications or experience.

Even Einstein made mistakes, and those mistakes were uncovered by the scientific method of testing by experiment. For example, Einstein added a constant term to his equations of relativity so that the equations would describe a Universe that is static, as he believed it to be. However, it was subsequently discovered by the experiments of Edwin Hubble that the Universe is expanding and not static. Hubble measured the velocities of galaxies, finding that they are, in general, moving away from us in all directions, and that the more distant the galaxy, the faster it is receding. This implies expansion in all directions. More recently, Nobel Prize winning research led by Brian Schmidt of the Australian National University, Adam Reiss of John Hopkins University and Saul Perlmutter of the University of California in Berkley, has shown that the rate of this recession of galaxies is accelerating, meaning that a constant term has actually been re-instated to the relativistic equations that describe the Universe. This does not mitigate the fact that Einstein was wrong in making an assumption of a static Universe.

The validation of an opinion by reference to a person's credentials is a well-known fallacious argument called an 'appeal to authority', and it has no place in science. Yet appeals to authority have formed the foundations of much forensic 'science', and the consequences of this approach are far reaching and profound. Not only are un-validated and unsubstantiated expert opinions admitted in criminal trials, whole fields of 'specialized knowledge', such as bite mark analysis and blood splatter analysis, developed and evolved to meet the standards required for admittance in court, rather than the standards required to withstand the scrutiny that is inherent in science.

An illustrative case of how credentials can be attained in these fields can be seen in Tom Bevel, who developed an interest in blood spatter during his 20 plus years working in the Oklahoma City Police Department. Bevel had no scientific background, so he took a few professional courses in relevant topics but never trained or worked as a scientist. Having gained experience in cases working for the police force, he contracted out his services as a blood-spatter expert, primarily testifying for the prosecution. He taught courses on blood splatter analysis, and published a textbook[19]. His un-scientific testimony sent Warren Horinek to prison for 30 years for shooting his wife, despite the medical examiner having ruled the death a suicide, and despite the lead detective also believing that it was a suicide. Horinek has spent 15 years in prison and is still fighting for his freedom.

The history of the analysis of patterns left by fires[20], and implications regarding whether arson was involved, has a similarly alarming history. Ditto for ballistics evidence[21] and as stated earlier, hair comparisons[22], bite marks and blood splatter[23]. You get the picture. All these fields of 'specialized knowledge' developed over decades under the standards of analysis and enquiry set by the legal system, rather than within a scientific environment. A long list of wrongful convictions is the result[24].

In the Australian context, unscientific forensic evidence helped result in the wrongful convictions of, amongst others, Lindy Chamberlain, Edward Splatt, and the aforementioned Alexander McLeod-Lindsay.

The fact that courts have not required forensic analysis to be scientific in nature allowed non-scientific analysis to become pervasive, organized, and institutionalized. Many forensic fields have made efforts to introduce more science into their methods,

19. *Bloodstain Pattern Analysis* with an Introduction to Crime Scene Reconstruction.
20. e.g. G Gorbett, B Meacham, C Wood & N Dembsey *Use of damage in fire investigation: a review of fire patterns analysis, research and future direction* 2015 Fire Science Reviews
21. e.g. K Servick *Reversing the legacy of junk science in the courtroom* in *Science* Mar. 7, 2016
22. PCAST (op cit 50) at p118
23. See research by the Innocence Project. A review of bite mark analysis is being undertaken by the Forensic Science Commission. Preliminary findings caused them to put a moratorium on all bite mark evidence
24. see e.g. the wrongful conviction blog edited by M. Godsey

however this has not been driven by any significant change in the way our legal system admits expert evidence, meaning that unsubstantiated opinions that have no basis in science continue to have great influence on the outcomes of criminal trials. Indeed, new fields such as 'forensic gait analysis' continue to be created and evolve within this system, without having a scientific basis[25]. The emphasis of courts on the credentials of expert witnesses, rather than on the quality of the science, has proven to be misguided, to put it mildly.

In the case of Robert Farquharson, it was opinions and assertions, rather than science, that formed the basis of the prosecution claims that three steering inputs were required for the car to get from the road to the dam.

---

25. Edmond, G. & Cunliffe E., *Cinderella Story? The Social Production of a Forensic "Science"*, 106 J. Crim. L. & Criminology (2016).

Chapter 7

THE WAYS WE FOOL OURSELVES

In 1909, Robert Millikan used falling oil drops to measure the charge on an electron, balancing the electric force with the gravitational force by adjusting the voltage until the drops were suspended in the air. Millikan obtained a value for the electric charge that we now know was almost correct, but not quite. His error came from using an incorrect value for the viscosity of air. The interesting part of this story comes next, when other scientists performed experiments to refine the value: each subsequent measurement became a little larger, and a little larger, slowly moving from Millikan's value toward the higher, correct value. Why didn't those experiments discover the actual value straight away? Why did they creep towards it? According to Richard Feynman 'It's a thing that scientists are ashamed of, this history, because it's apparent that people did things like this: When they got a number that was too high above Millikan's, they thought something must be wrong and they would look for and find a reason why something might be wrong. When they got a number closer to Millikan's value they didn't look so hard.'[1]

The scientists had been biased by the experiments that had come before.

Beyond the central notion of testing ideas by experiment, perhaps the most important ingredient of the scientific method has been the development of systems to prevent us from being

---

1. ibid

led to the wrong answer by biases and emotional responses. Richard Feynman put it like this 'We have learned a lot, from experience, about how to handle some of the ways we fool ourselves.'[2] Scientists are invested in doing their experiments in a manner that is free of biases, because 'the truth will come out.'[3] Other scientists will repeat the experiments, and nature will either agree or disagree with the proposed theory. If experiments are wrong due to researchers being biased, they will not get correct results and will not gain a good reputation as a scientist.

Training of scientists occurs through a system of organised mentorship, as students undertake their first experiments with the aid of supervisors. Supervisors are tasked with questioning each aspect of their student's experiments, probing methodological flaws, trying to poke holes in the logic, suggesting new ways to test theories. Scientific research is often done with other experienced collaborators, who perform similar dissections. When a study is deemed ready and is submitted for publication, the journal assigns one or more referees to study the analysis and the reasoning, again trying to determine if there are any flaws in the study. If everything passes these processes, the study will be published.

However, the scrutiny of the research is certainly not over once a study is published. Other scientists in the field are sceptical, and do not just accept published papers as being true. They question them, they try to find flaws and to think of new ways to test the underlying theory. Therefore, science is under constant review, and no theory is above scrutiny. Studies that take short cuts or have their results affected by natural human biases, get found out and shown to be wrong.

These scientific methods are not restricted to physics, biology, chemistry and the like, but can be applied to a range of questions, including those regarding human nature. Researchers of human behaviour employ scientific methods in their execution, taking care to include a statistically relevant number of participants,

---

2. Feynman, R. *Surely You're Joking, Mr. Feynman!: Adventures of a Curious Character*, 1985 WW Norton
3. Ibid, although the quote may derive from 'the truth will come to light' and 'the truth will out' in *the Merchant of Venice*, quotes based on proverbs that have been traced as far back as the 11th Century, at least.

comparing to a control sample, and trying to exclude factors beyond those being tested. At least, that is what the good practitioners attempt to do.

Again, biases can be quite subtle. In 2008, a statistician at Columbia University, Andrew Gelman, published a study that concluded that Democratic candidates in the U.S. could get more votes if they moved slightly rightward on economic policy. Five years later, a student named Yang Yang Gu tried to replicate these results and discovered that Gelman had used a minus sign for one of the variables in his code, which should have been a plus sign. A simple coding error had led to incorrect results. Gelman explains that the 'results seemed perfectly reasonable. Lots of times with these kinds of coding errors you get results that are ridiculous. So you know something's wrong and you go back and search until you find the problem. If nothing seems wrong, it's easier to miss.'[4] Gelman would have looked harder, and found the bug in his code, if the results were not within the realms of his expectations. Gelman published a correction to the study.

Sometimes mistakes are not so innocent. The background to the next story is that a large number of studies[5] have shown that people do not readily change their minds, regardless of how much contradictory evidence they are confronted with. Many ideas on how to change people's minds have been explored, but none worked. This may not be surprising to anyone who has tried to reason with an anti-vaxxer. In fact, the difficulty in changing the mind of an anti-vaxxer is not just anecdotal. A 2014 study[6] tried to determine the best way to change the minds of parents who did not want their children to have the measles-mumps-rubella shots. The experimenters tried four different ways to change their minds; one explaining the lack of evidence that vaccinations cause autism; one explaining the dangers of the disease; one presenting images of children afflicted with the

---

4. Regina Nuzzo *Fooling Ourselves* **Nature** Vol 526 Oct 2015
5. e.g. Brehm, J. W. (1956). Postdecision changes in the desirability of alternatives. *The Journal of Abnormal and Social Psychology, 52*(3), 384-389.
6. Nyhan, B et al. *Effective Messages in Vaccine Promotion: A Randomized Trial* 2014 PEDIATRICS 133, 4

diseases; and one telling the story of a child who almost died of measles. None of the methods worked.

Just to clarify, studies[7] show that when people do not care deeply about an issue, they *will* change their minds when presented with evidence. It is strongly held beliefs that are the hardest to change. 'If information doesn't square with someone's prior beliefs, he discards the beliefs if they're weak and discards the information if the beliefs are strong.'[8] Processing information in a biased manner that fits our current world view is not only common, it appears to be the dominant manner in which we process information[9]. Misconceptions are readily accepted, and correct information rejected, if they confirm people's prior beliefs and expectations[10].

This tendency is now referred to as *confirmation bias*[11], but is a characteristic of human nature that has been known for a long time. A quick perusal of Wikipedia throws up quotes from Thucydides in ancient Greek times (around 400BC), St. Thomas Aquinas in *The Devine Comedy* (1320), and by Sir Francis Bacon (1620). In *The Life and Opinions of Tristram Shandy, Gentleman,* Laurence Sterne (1759) put it this way, '*It is the nature of a hypothesis, when once a man has conceived it, that it assimilates everything to itself, as proper nourishment; and, from the first moment of your begetting it, it generally grows the stronger by everything you see, hear, read, or understand.*'

Nor was it a recent discovery that beliefs which are closely held are the hardest to change. In 1897, Tolstoy observed that 'most men—not only those considered clever, but even those

---

7. R. Kelly Garrett and Brian E. Weeks. 2013. *The promise and peril of real-time corrections to political misperceptions.* In Proceedings of the 2013 conference on Computer supported cooperative work (CSCW '13). ACM, New York, NY, USA, 1047-1058; Sol Hart, P., & Nisbet, E. C. (2012). Boomerang Effects in Science Communication: How Motivated Reasoning and Identity Cues Amplify Opinion Polarization About Climate Mitigation Policies. *Communication Research, 39*(6), 701–723.
8. Konnikova, M, *I don't want to be right*, The New Yorker, May 16, 2014
9. e.g. Lord, Ross, and Lepper 1979; Kunda 1990; Redlawsk 2002; Taber and Lodge 2006; Nylan & Reifer 2016 *The roles of information deficits and identity threat in the prevalence of misperceptions*
10. Steele, C. 1988. "The Psychology of Self-affirmation: Sustaining the Integrity of the Self." In Advances in Experimental Social Psychology, edited by Leonard Berkowitz, Vol. 21, 261–302. New York: Academic Press.
11. Wason, Peter C. (1960), *On the failure to eliminate hypotheses in a conceptual task,* Quarterly Journal of Experimental Psychology (Psychology Press) **12** (3): 129–140

who are very clever, and capable of understanding most difficult scientific, mathematical, or philosophic problems—can very seldom discern even the simplest and most obvious truth if it be such as to oblige them to admit the falsity of conclusions they have formed, perhaps with much difficulty—conclusions of which they are proud, which they have taught to others, and on which they have built their lives.'[12]

These are some of the biases that scientists must mitigate when they 'follow the evidence, wherever it leads'.

In this context, a stunning result[13] by UCLA PhD candidate Michael La Cour and University of Columbia professor Donald Green, of ways to change the minds of people who are against same-sex marriage. By engaging people in extended conversations, gay canvassers were able to persuade 15% percent of participants to have a lasting change in their opinion. These conversations were not preaching and they were not presenting facts. The canvassers simply engaged the participants, relating personal experiences and allowing the respondents to speak their own mind freely. The study found that these conversations worked. The size of the result, with 15% of participants changing their opinions over a long term, was huge compared to any other study previously published. The study was accepted for publication in the prestigious journal *Science* and stunned researchers in the field.

Too bad that La Cour had faked the data. This was uncovered when other researchers tried, and failed, to reproduce the study by following the same methodology. David Broockman from UC Berkley and Joshua Kalla from Stanford wanted to test whether they could obtain the same results for transgender issues. The initial stage of the methodology was an online survey to engage participants, but the researchers got only around one quarter of the response rates of the La Cour and Green study. Such a large discrepancy raised alarm bells, so the researchers looked closer and found other anomalies in the original study. When confronted with these issues, LaCour could not produce the raw

---

12. Tolstoy, Leo "What Is Art?" 1897
13. La Cour & Green 2014 *When contact changes minds* **Science**, vol 346, 6215, pp. 1366-1369

data from which he made his analysis. His co-author, Dan Green, withdrew the publication, having misplaced his faith in the honesty of his collaborator. LaCour had his offer of a prestigious position at Princeton University rescinded.

The truth will come out.

Total fakery is relatively rare in science, although this case is certainly not isolated[14]. A broader issue is the pressure on scientists to get results in order to attain employment, to attract funding, and indeed to gain fame and notoriety, at least within their own scientific community. Do we look as closely at results that are exciting and new, in order to make sure there are no errors? Are we biased toward evidence that proves current theories wrong, when we know that such studies gain more attention than those supporting the status quo? Will this result please my supervisor or the head of my department because it supports her theory? These are some of the questions that scientists need to continually ask themselves. Being human, scientists have all the foibles you would expect, including stubbornness, ambition, and ego, and also the cognitive biases that are inherent in the way that humans process information. If scientists fall prey to their own vices and biases and end up fooling themselves, they can easily be led to the wrong answer, but the truth will come out.

These are ongoing issues in science: in the words of astrophysicist and Nobel laureate Saul Perlmutter, 'science is an ongoing race between our inventing ways to fool ourselves, and our inventing ways to avoid fooling ourselves.' Scientists continue to devise better ways of de-biasing data analysis, in order to arrive at results that will stand up to scrutiny because, in the long-run, the worth of a scientist is judged by the amount of scrutiny that their results can withstand. Incorrect results attained due to human biases will be scrutinized and eliminated.

Not so in the criminal justice system.

---

14. Marcus, A. & Oransky, I. *Retraction Watch* tracks, amongst other things, fraudulent scientific results

Chapter 8

UNDER PRESSURE

Sergeant Geoffrey Exton took the call at the Major Collisions Investigation Unit (MCIU) of the Victoria police: a car had run into a dam near Winchelsea and three children were believed to have died. Exton called his boss, Senior Sergeant Jeffry Smith who was head of the MCIU. Smith sent Exton to the scene, to secure it and to start collecting evidence.

Exton and his team inspected the site but could find no evidence to support Farquharson's account of an out of control vehicle.[1] 'Where motor cars run off the road, the driver panics and he oversteers the car, they lose control and we see those marks regularly on our roads… We set up lighting and didn't find any marks, and that concerned me greatly…'[2]

Exton spoke with Cindy Gambino's new partner, Steven Moules. Moules told Exton what he knew, and that `I smell a rat. Something is not right here'.[3] By this early stage, Exton suspected murder.[4,5]

Meanwhile, Senior Sergeant Smith went with Senior Constable Courtis to Geelong hospital to interview Farquharson, prior to heading to the scene. The officers became suspicious of Farquharson's demeanour during the interview. Smith's gut

1. Megan Norris *On Fathers Day* 15% location
2. Channel 7, Crimes that Shook Australia Season 2 Episode 2
3. Megan Norris *On Fathers Day* 15% location
4. Anthony Dowsley, Herald Sun July 23, 2010
5. Megan Norris *On Fathers Day* 84% location

told him there was something dubious about the story that Farquharson told,[6] that his responses to questions did not 'feel right'.[7] From the hospital, Smith rang his crew who were at the scene. Before he could say anything about his own suspicions, he was told by Exton 'This is bullshit. He's driven into the water.'[8]

After arriving at the scene and making his own examination, Senior Sergeant Smith concurred with Exton that there was no evidence to support Farquharson's account, enhancing his suspicions.[9] By the following morning, Smith had brought the homicide squad into the investigation. He compiled a list of more than 10 reasons that made him believe it was a deliberate act of murder, and only a single reason that supported an accident. 'That one reason was that no one could be that evil'. Smith said that 'We always thought the hardest thing about convicting him would be getting people to believe anyone could be that evil.' [10]

36 hours after the death of the three Farquharson boys, the case had become a homicide investigation, led by Sergeant Gerard Clanchy of the homicide squad. Along with Senior Constable Andrew Stamper, Clanchy immediately brought Farquharson to police headquarters for an interview. At the end of the interview, in which Farquharson maintained that it was a horrible accident, that he had blacked out after a coughing fit, Clanchy and Stamper both determined that he was lying. For Clanchy, Rob's comment that he only had 'two arms and two legs. I cant save three' confirmed his gut feeling that Farquharson was 'lying through his teeth.'[11]

The problem is that studies have comprehensively shown that people are not good at detecting lies.[12,13] Studies also show that police are no better at spotting liars than anyone else.[14] In fact,

---

6. Megan Norris *On Fathers Day* 12% location
7. Megan Norris *On Fathers Day* 12% location
8. Andrew Rule, Herald Sun, July 25, 2013
9. Megan Norris *On Fathers Day* 15% location
10. Aleks Devic, Mark Buttler And Patrick Carlyon, *How Could A Dad Kill His Sons?*, Sunday Herald Sun August 30, 2015
11. Megan Norris *On Fathers Day* 17% location
12. Bond, C. F., & DePaulo, B. M. (2006). Accuracy of deception judgments. Personality and Social Psychology Review, 10, 214– 234,

police have a bias toward thinking that people are lying,[15] and are guilty,[16] compared to other citizens who generally have a bias toward thinking that people are telling the truth.[17] Compared to other people, however, police are *more confident* in their abilities to spot liars.[18]

So Exton became suspicious due to a lack of evidence of a driver having panicked and over-corrected, even though Farquharson was claiming to have blacked out, whilst Smith and then Clanchy became equally suspicious when they thought they were able to spot a liar. From a very early stage in the investigation, there was a strong feeling amongst members of the investigation team, both within the homicide squad and the MCIU, that Farquharson was guilty.

This feeling amongst police officers that Farquharson was guilty created a serious issue with respect to the reconstruction evidence. Sergeant Glen Urquhart, the reconstruction expert, worked within the MCIU. Senior Sergeant Smith was his boss. In this particular investigation, Urquhart was working under the umbrella of the homicide squad and Gerard Clanchy. So Urquhart's boss within the MCIU, the overall boss of the investigation, and other colleagues at the MCIU such as Geoffrey Exton, all believed that Farquharson was most likely guilty from an early stage in the investigation. The accident reconstruction work in the Robert Farquharson case was done within this environment that was inherently compromised, an incubator of bias.

13. Sporer, S. L., & Schwandt, B. (2006). Paraverbal indicators of deception: A meta-analytic synthesis. *Applied Cognitive Psychology*, 20, 421–446.
14. Meissner, C. A., & Kassin, S. M. (2002). "He's guilty!": Investigator bias in judgments of truth and deception. *Law and Human Behavior*, 26, 469–480. See also De Paulo & Pfeifer 1986; Eckman & O'Sullivan 1991; Garrido & Masip 2001; Kassin, Meissner & Norwick 2005
15. Meissner, C. A., & Kassin, S. M. (2002). "He's guilty!": Investigator bias in judgments of truth and deception. *Law and Human Behavior*, 26, 469–480.
16. S M. Kassin, C. A. Meissner, and R. J. Norwick 2005 "I'd Know a False Confession if I Saw One": A Comparative Study of College Students and Police Investigators
17. although University students dominate the participation in the literature studies
18. S M. Kassin, C. A. Meissner, and R. J. Norwick 2005 "I'd Know a False Confession if I Saw One": A Comparative Study of College Students and Police Investigators

'I spent 34 years as a Police Officer and from Day One as a junior Constable I had it drummed into me that the gathering of evidence had to be thorough and completely unbiased. If ever there was a case where this did not happen it is Farquharson's'. This is David Axup, the defence reconstruction expert in the case. After I had analysed the reconstruction evidence, I emailed Axup to get his opinion on the evidence, how it played out in court, and what he thought in hindsight. Axup had testified that Farquharson's car followed the slope of the terrain in a gentle arc that lead from the road to the dam. He found no evidence that the car needed to be steered to follow that path. He stood by that testimony.

But Axup is also biased, right? Toward the defence? Aren't defence experts just hired guns? Axup had added in his reply that 'I do not know whether Farquharson is guilty of deliberately driving into the dam. If he is he deserves to rot in jail.' So Axup was not sounding particularly biased toward Farquharson, and he is a former cop himself. However, bias is not always conscious. I wanted to be sure that I was not just accepting Axup's word because it agreed with my own analysis.

Around the time I had contacted David Axup, Anne Irwin informed me that the Innocence project at Edith Cowan University in Perth had spent some time looking into the Farquharson case. I made contact and they informed me that a reconstruction expert over there, Bob Davey, had also looked into the evidence. I email Davey, who told me he had 'looked at the case out of professional interest' (i.e. he was not paid by anyone) and that 'while the crash reconstruction evidence from the prosecution expert was flawed, it was only part of their case. His actions after the crash didn't help'. So again, a reconstruction expert was telling me, without equivocation, that the prosecution reconstruction evidence was flawed, whilst at the same time emphasizing that this does not mean that Farquharson is innocent. In fact, it seemed like he thought that Farquharson is guilty.

Several months later Anne Irwin emailed to inform me that someone else was showing interest in Robert Farquharson's case.

Freelance journalist and recent law graduate Luke McMahon had been in touch with her, and was interested in looking at the evidence. The Farquharson case had formed part of his criminal law exam, and Luke had sensed that something was wrong. 'This is bullshit' is how he put it to me, after Anne Irwin had put us in contact. I showed Luke the research I had done, which by then had been extended to the analysis of most of the evidence in the case, and he was in. We have been working on the case together ever since. Luke has a strong sense of justice but at this point of the story, the thing to note is that he is particularly good at hunting people down and is happy to approach them. Not so easy for me, as I was living in Spain at the time.

In the files relating to Farquharson's appeal, Luke found a report by another reconstruction expert, Dr. Shane Richardson. Richardson is a forensic engineer, who has conducted over 1000 vehicle collision investigations and has provided expert evidence in the Supreme, County, Magistrate and Coronial Courts related to collisions and incidents. He has been engaged by both the defence and the prosecution. Richardson had looked at the evidence for the defence, but had not testified in the case. Luke met with Richardson, and taped the conversation. Richardson was blunt in his assessment of the flawed evidence that helped convict Farquharson 'How could he say this shit in court?'. Richardson explained that the prosecution 'asserted... that the only way that that track can occur in that direction is by someone deliberately steering the vehicle' but that 'they haven't actually proven that. They have asserted it. They didn't provide enough evidence, in my opinion, that the only way that the car could have travelled that route is by steering inputs.'

Richardson's assessment of the evidence mirrored mine. And Axup's. And Davey's. There was just not enough evidence at the scene to conclude that someone had been steering the car. Richardson said that 'if you run a vehicle across a slope, and you have a change in slope, the vehicle direction will change as it runs across the slope. And that could have been the reason why you get changes in directions in the Farquharson case.'

Richardson spoke extensively of the problems of the Major

Collisions Investigation Unit and their relationship with investigating police, 'They have obligations to their colleagues, they have interactions with the families of the victims', and because they are so 'entwined' in the investigation 'it becomes personal and... I don't think they can separate themselves'.

Such problems of bias in forensic analysis have been well known by the legal community for a very long time. In an English case back in 1873 the judge, Sir George Jessel, stated that 'Undoubtedly there is a natural bias to do something serviceable for those who employ you and adequately remunerate you.'[19]

I am sorry CSI fans, but the analysis done by the investigators in the tv series is performed in an environment that is hopelessly biased, meaning that the whole premise of the show is the antithesis of how forensic science should be performed. Avoiding such compromised environments for conducting forensic work is precisely why the U.S. National Research Council[20] recommends that forensic work is done outside the police force, and within independent research institutions. 'The institutional regime of police forensics influences the preferences of forensic workers and may bias their reasoning. The institutional context creates a kind of "motivated reasoning" among forensic workers.'[21]

Looking back, this bias was often overt, as summed up by this quote from an FBI forensic lab worker 'People say we're tainted for the prosecution. Hell, that's what we do! We get our evidence and present it for the prosecution.'[22]

In Australia's most infamous miscarriage of justice, when Lindy Chamberlain was found guilty of murdering her infant daughter Azaria, who had been killed by a dingo, the bias of forensic biologist Joy Kuhl was of a different nature, but was equally as overt. In the evening after giving (false) forensic evidence at the trial, Kuhl told reporters, whist having a drink

---

19. Abinger v. Ashton, 17 L.R.Eq. 358, 374 Ch. 1873
20. *Strengthening Forensic Science in the United States: A Path Forward* National Research Council 2009
21. Koppl, R. *How to Improve Forensic Science*, Eur J Law Econ (2005)
22. ibid

at a local bar, that Chamberlain '...is, you know, a witch. I could feel her eyes burning holes through my back.'[23] This bias can be linked to a media frenzy that surrounded the case.

The bias of forensic analysts is no longer so overt. Our legal system, having recognized that bias is a problem in expert testimony, has created rules that are intended to suppress bias.[24] In Australia, expert witnesses are technically officers of the court, to which they pledge a duty to provide unbiased testimony.[25] Similar provisions exist in other countries[26] including the U.S. and U.K. The details of the provisions differ, but the idea is to compel the experts to be unbiased.

Yet experts continue to be engaged by the prosecution and defence, not by the courts. In a 2013 study[27] a number of expert witnesses were asked for reports on a defendant. Each expert was given the exact same evidence, but some were told that the report was for the prosecution and others that it was for the defence. The study found that the reports were slanted toward supporting the case of those who employed them. This was a real world experiment, and concerned no trivial matter: the experts who believed they were working for prosecutors tended to conclude that sexually violent offenders were at greater risk of re-offending than did experts who thought they were working for the defence.

The implication is not that the experts are dishonest. They simply looked more critically at evidence going against the interests of those who engaged them, while more readily accepting the evidence that supports their interests.

---

23. Bryson, J *Evil Angels* 1985 Summit Books p432
24. Supreme Court (Chapter I expert witness code amendment) Rules 2016 (sr no 52 of 2016)
25. Uniform Civil Procedure Rules 2005 (NSW) r 31.23; Court Procedures Rules 2006 (ACT) Schedule 1; Federal Court Rules 2011 (Cth) Practice Direction CM 7; Supreme Court Civil Supplementary Rules 2014 (SA) r156; Uniform Civil Procedure Rules 1999 (Qld) r 249
26. E.g. U.K., Practice Direction 25b – The Duties Of An Expert, The Expert's Report And Arrangements For An Expert To Attend Court
27. Murrie D. et al., *Are Forensic Experts Biased by the Side That Retained Them?*, 24 PSYCHOL. SCI. 1889 (2013).

In the Farquharson case, Sergeant Urquhart's colleagues at the MCIU were involved in other aspects of the investigation, such as conducting interviews of Farquharson. And further, Urquhart was now part of the homicide investigation. Was Urquhart privy to other information pertaining to the case when he did the reconstruction work? Information that was not relevant to his own work, but was considered by his colleagues to be evidence of Farquharson's guilt? No protocols were in place within the MCIU to isolate Urquhart from the work that his colleagues were doing on the case.

Another problem is that information can leak the other way, from the forensic experts to other witnesses. Forensic analysts who work in a biased environment can express their interpretations and opinions to other witnesses, whose own independence is then compromised. This back and forth has been referred to the 'biasing snowball effect.'[28] Cross-contaminated evidence can be (mis)-represented at trial as being separate lines of evidence that independently corroborate one another.

Consider that prior to the trial, Urquhart met with the prosecution team including the prosecutor Mr. Rapke, lead investigator Detective Sergeant Clanchy, and members of the MCIU who had collected evidence at the scene, including Sergeant Exton[29]. Urquhart explained his theory regarding the path of the car, and how he had interpreted the evidence from the scene. At the trial that followed soon afterwards, Exton was asked to describe the evidence he found at the scene, including the marks in the region where the car left the road. Exton knew that Urquhart was using those marks as part of his reconstruction. Were Exton's confident assertions that the marks showed where Farquharson's car left the road influenced by the fact that he knew that Urquhart relied on those marks? Clearly,

---

28. Edmond, G. et al. *Contextual bias and cross-contamination in the forensic sciences: the corrosive implications for investigations, plea bargains, trials and appeals*, Law, Probability and Risk, 14, 1, 2015, pp 1–25
29. Trial 1 p716, 717, 726, 730 , 1936

this would totally subvert the nexus between the evidence and conclusions in the reconstruction.

There are just so many problems that are caused when forensic work is not done in an independent way. The good news is that this is being recognised by the people that count: in 2017, after an extensive review, the forensic reconstruction section of the MCIU was relocated to the Forensic Services Division of Victoria Police, a body set up at arm's length from the investigating police. Unlike the producers of CSI, the Victorian police have understood the imperative of bias mitigation in forensic analysis. Too late for Robert Farquharson.

Dr. Richardson was also critical of the level of training provided to police reconstruction 'experts'. Speaking of the pre-2017 arrangements, he emphasized that the MCIU did a 'very good job' of scene attendance and the documentation and collection of data, but was of the firm opinion that they do not do reconstruction work well. 'I think that they are unsupported with respect to training and qualifications. They are self-teaching what they do'. Although they have studied science or engineering, they 'haven't actually worked in the area... they have worked as police officers... they are under-supported, overworked for what they do and they are being asked to do something beyond their skills.' This assessment gains support from the Victoria police report into the police accident reconstruction, that recommends 'That Victoria Police investigates the feasibility of seconding suitably experienced reconstructionists from other jurisdictions' and makes a range of recommendation regarding the qualifications and training that reconstruction experts should attain.

More certain than ever that the reconstruction evidence presented against Farquharson was horribly wrong, Luke and I decided it was time to approach Glen Urquhart, the prosecution expert witness. Luke wanted to confront him with my research, to get his reaction. Luke spoke with Urquhart on the phone and they agreed to meet. We really wanted to know whether he stood by his evidence.

It did not turn out to be that simple.

When they met over coffee, Urquhart told Luke that he had not slept the night before, such were the ongoing effects of the stress he had suffered from the Farquharson case. Just the thought of talking about the case had kept him up all night. He claimed that he had the symptoms of Post Traumatic Stress Disorder (PTSD), which he traced directly to the case. This was the case that caused him to leave the police force.

Luke suggested that Urquhart read some sections of my analysis, giving him the chance to respond. Urquhart said he could not look at the evidence of this case, that it was not good for his mental health. Giving a clue as to the type of pressure he had been under during the case, Urquhart revealed that, as he entered the court to give evidence in the first trial against Farquharson, a police officer involved in the case had told him 'the case rests on you'. His worst nightmare was that Farquharson would be granted a retrial and that he would have to give evidence again.

Despite not being willing to defend any of the questionable details of his evidence, or to discuss any specific aspects of it, Urquhart stood by the evidence he had given against Farquharson, pointing out that it had all been challenged in court. Luke, in turn, pointed out that many wrongful convictions had resulted from faulty forensic evidence and that such evidence had also been challenged in court. Urquhart agreed, 'don't get me wrong. I've asked myself many times if I've helped convict an innocent man'.

CHAPTER 9

YOU GET WHAT YOU ASK FOR

'I think I just went over the overpass', said Robert Farquharson in the interview recorded that night, 'and I started coughing and um, I don't remember anything, and then all of a sudden I was in the water'.

Like his story of not being able to get the kids out of the sinking car, Farquharson's story of blacking out after coughing 'provoked credulity and scorn'.[1] When Luke McMahon told a prominent barrister that he was looking into the Farquharson case, the barrister responded that 'the guy had no hope going to trial with that bullshit story about passing out after coughing'.

To cough and then pass out… is that even a thing?

It turns out that there is a condition known as *cough syncope* in which loss of consciousness follows a violent cough or prolonged bouts of violent coughing. Could Farquharson have had the condition? The trial delved into this question and once again, the court required the help of expert witnesses. If medical evidence could show that Farquharson did not have cough syncope then his whole story falls apart, regardless of how poor was the reconstruction evidence. Perhaps this medical evidence would alleviate my growing concern that an innocent man may be 'rotting in jail'? Not to mention the ongoing nightmares of Glen Urquhart.

The prosecution medical witness was Professor Matthew

---

1. Garner, H. *This House of Grief* Kindle location 110.

Naughton, whose credentials took 28 minutes to elucidate. Naughton was an extremely well credentialed witness indeed: the head of General Respiratory and Sleep Medicine at the Alfred Hospital, a Fellow of the Royal Australian College of Physicians, and an adjunct Professor of Medicine at Monash University. Naughton's duties included teaching and research on top of treating patients in the hospital. Naughton has published more than 100 research studies in international medical journals, written chapters for numerous text books, and at the time of the trial was sitting on the editorial board of the *American Journal of Respiratory and Critical Care Medicine*, the world's premier journal for his field of medicine.

Being a member of the editorial board makes Naughton a gatekeeper for scientific standards of that journal. One would hope that he would apply these scientific standards to the evidence in the case. I am sure that is what the police and the courts hope when they elicit the evidence of such well credentialed experts.

Despite his expertise in respiratory and sleep medicine, cough syncope was not within Naughtons field of specialty. Naughton had never had a patient with cough syncope, nor published any papers on the subject. Naughton himself stated[2] that neurologists and cardiologists would be better equipped to answer questions on cough syncope. Compare this to scientific journals. When a study is submitted for publication, an editor assigns a referee who has published a paper on that topic. The reasons for this are clear: it is far easier to assess a study after you have actually researched the field in detail. Should not the court, and the accused, be granted the same standards as our best scientific journals?

Naughton's expertise was challenged by the defence, but the court found him to be qualified to give expert opinion on cough syncope. This decision was upheld by the Court of Appeal who found[3] that cough syncope could reasonably be assumed to come

---

2. Trial 1 p 95

3. As laid out in the 2001 case *Makita (Australia) Pty Ltd v Sprowles*

'within the ordinary knowledge of a specialist thoracic physician'.[4]

Regardless, let us move on and accept Naughton's right to give an opinion on these matters. Naughton is clearly a clever person with related knowledge; he could read the literature on cough syncope, analyse the relevant symptoms displayed by Farquharson and convey an opinion to the court.

For Naughton, this process did not involve checking the patient, for at no stage did he examine Farquharson in any manner[5]. Rather than access to the patient, Naughton was given a summarized version of the Farquharson case file by the head of the investigation, Detective Sergeant Clanchy. This file contained all the incriminating evidence that the police had gathered, including the (flawed and misleading) reconstruction evidence, and witness evidence by Greg King that I will explore later in the book.

Of what use is reconstruction evidence in determining whether Farquharson suffered from cough syncope? This is a classic example of domain irrelevant information. i.e. information about a case that is not directly relevant to an expert's analysis. A 2006 study[6] showed that even fingerprint analysis can be swayed by contextual information about a crime. Various analysts were given the same sets of prints, but some were told that the suspect had confessed to the crime, whilst others were told that the suspect was in police custody at the time the crime was committed. In 17% of the cases, the analysts changed their result in the direction suggested by the extraneous, domain irrelevant information. It is for this reason that the National Research Council report on the state of forensic science recommends that forensic scientists should not be exposed to 'domain irrelevant information': information sharing between police investigators and forensic scientists creates the strong possibility of unconscious bias[7].

When Naughton made his report in 2005, perhaps these issues

---

4. R v Farquharson 2009 VSCA 307 p21 point 80
5. e.g. Trial 1 from p77, Trial 2 p.3012
6. Dror, I. E. & Charlton, D. J. *Forensic Identification* **56**, 600–616 (2006).

were not as well known by the law enforcement officers and the court, although one could argue that they should have been. However, Naughton himself was an editor of a scientific journal. Didn't he understand the dangers that are posed by bias? Why did he accept this extraneous material? Why did he read it? Richard Feynman offers a possible explanation. 'The long history of learning how not to fool ourselves—of having utter scientific integrity–is, I'm sorry to say, something that we haven't specifically included in any particular course that I know of. We just hope you've caught on by osmosis.'[8]

Having been compromised by the incriminating report, Naughton commenced his research into the condition of cough syncope. He read the following sentence from a textbook,[9] 'Like sleep apnoea cough syncope is a cause of impairment because of the potential for loss of consciousness'. He also read from an American Thoracic Society article that `somewhat analogous to sleep disorders, cough syncope is a cause of impairment because of the potential loss of consciousness. Thus jobs that require vigilance should be proscribed [prohibited]'.[10] That was the extent of Naughton's research.[11] From this, and the material he had been given by the police, Naughton provided the police with a report stating that it was 'extremely unlikely that Robert Farquharson suffered from cough syncope'.

Again, compare this to scientific practice. Articles published in journals such as the *American Journal of Respiratory and Critical Care Medicine* include an introduction section summarizing the current state of the field, demonstrating that the author is up to date with the relevant literature. If an editor were to receive a research paper with such a shallow review of previous literature as Naughton's report, that paper would be rejected. It is not even close to scientific standards. The literature review was not even

---

7. e.g. Dror, et al. (2006) 'Contextual Information Renders Experts Vulnerable to Making Erroneous Identifications', Forensic Science International, 156, pp 74–78.
8. Feynman, R. "*Surely you are joking Mr Feynman*" p342
9. The Textbook of Respiratory Medicine eds John F. Murray & J.A. Nadel
10. American Thoracic Society, article
11. Trial 2 p3014-3015, see also *R v Farquharson* 2009 at 81, p21

up to University undergraduate standards. Imagine Professor Naughton setting an assignment at Monash University for his students to review the literature on cough syncope, and they read a couple of sentences? Fail! So why would he offer an opinion on a condition about which he has never undertaken a study, nor had a patient, after such scant research? Again, this lack of research was challenged by the defence but the Court of Appeal found it 'goes to the weight of Dr Naughton's evidence, not its admissibility.'[12]

After being questioned by the defence barrister in the pre-trial hearing (voir dire), where this lack of research was exposed, a chastened Professor Naughton did read more literature prior to the trial. However, the fact that Naughton did subsequent research does not alleviate the impact of his initial report on the process of investigating and prosecuting this case. It helped to confirm the suspicions of the police regarding guilt and this can lead to tunnel vision. The extra research also did not alter the opinion that Naughton had already formed. Yet we know that people generally, including researchers, find it difficult to change their opinions once they are formed. When doing research, the idea is to gather all available information *before* forming an opinion.

With this deeper research, Naughton discovered that cough syncope is 'poorly described in the modern medical literature',[13] that the cause of the loss of consciousness is 'not absolutely clear',[14] and that the literature is mainly composed of a series of 'case reports'[15] which he describes as 'the lowest'[16] form of scientific evidence. Essentially, a lot of uncertainty remained

---

12. 2009 *R v Farquharson*, p21
13. Trial 1 p1599
14. Trial 2 p2963
15. Trial 1 1641
16. Trial 1 p1642

(and remains[17]) concerning the condition, as it has not been well studied within clinical trials.

These are important points that Naughton identified. When something is scientific, it does not mean that results are certain. Quite the opposite. That man again, Richard Feynman, explains that 'what we call scientific knowledge today is a body of statements of varying degrees of certainty. Some of them are most unsure, some of them are nearly sure, but none is absolutely certain.'[18] So what is the point of science then, if nothing is certain? Doesn't science have answers? Or do we not really know anything? Bertrand Russell said that 'When one admits that nothing is certain one must, I think, also add that some things are more nearly certain than others.'[19]

Remember, scientific ideas (or theories) are tested by experiment or by experience. The more experiments that are done, the more certain the idea becomes. Results of a particular experiment may favour an idea, but sometimes the evidence attained from that study is relatively weak. It can take a multitude of experiments, over a number of years, for an idea to gain a reasonable level of certainty. As an idea survives more and more tests, when it is shown time and again that nature accords with the consequences of the idea, then that piece of scientific knowledge increases in certainty. The certainty of scientific knowledge is a measure of how much scrutiny it has withstood.

With cough syncope, very little experimental testing has been done. There are several different ideas concerning the causes[20]

17. e.g. Chih-Ping Chung, et al. 2013 op cit P. Dicpinigaitis L. Lim & C. Farmakidis *Cough syncope* 2014 Respiratory Medicine 108, 244, stated that ``cough syncope appears to be the final common pathway of several pathophysiologic processes", that it is not yet known whether ``different pathophysiological processes prevail in individual patients, or, whether cough syncope is the result of simultaneous contributory events.", and nor is it known ``whether all individuals are vulnerable to cough syncope under certain threshold conditions".
18. Feynman R. "The Value of Science," public address at the National Academy of Sciences (Autumn 1955); published in *What Do You Care What Other People Think* (1988);
19. Bertrand Russell, *Am I An Atheist Or An Agnostic?, 1947*
20. e.g. Chih-Ping Chung, et al. 2013 op cit; P. Dicpinigaitis L. Lim & C. Farmakidis *Cough syncope* 2014 Respiratory Medicine 108

of the condition, and each idea carries significant uncertainty because they have not been subject to sufficient testing. This sense of uncertainty was not expressed by Naughton, who wrote that it was 'extremely unlikely that Robert Farquharson suffered from cough syncope'.[21] In his testimony, Naughton repeatedly used the words 'extreme' and 'extremely'[22] to express his level of confidence in his diagnosis.

So, there are clear differences in the manner in which uncertainties are portrayed in the courts and in science, and the portrayal of uncertainties is a central tenet of science. Essentially courts, and police, do not require that expert reports be scientific in nature. What they request is the opinion of a scientist or other expert. What they get is the opinion of a scientist or some other expert. That is often different to requesting, and therefore getting, a scientific analysis.

---

21. Naughton's report is reproduced in Appendix C
22. E.g. Trial 2 p3005 at p3008 and at p3011

Chapter 10

TAKING EXTREME MEASURES

The fact that cough syncope was not Naughton's specialized field of knowledge, that he did scant research before forming an opinion, and that he read biased, irrelevant information about the case, does not necessarily make Naughton's opinion wrong. I was concerned by the process leading to Naughton's report and testimony, but I wanted to know if the conclusions were nevertheless correct.

The first aspect of the medical evidence that got a lot of attention in both trials was the rarity of cough syncope. How common is it for people to black out after coughing? Do certain traits make people more susceptible to the condition? Does Farquharson have those traits?

As well as Professor Naughton, the court heard testimony from Professor John King, a neurologist at the Royal Melbourne Hospital, and Dr. Chris Steinfort, who was head of thoracic medicine at Geelong Hospital. All three medical experts agreed[1] that it was *possible* that Farquharson had suffered from cough syncope.

What distinguished Professor Naughton's testimony was his repeated use of the adjective *extremely*. Naughton emphasised that cough syncope is 'an extremely rare condition',[2] 'extremely uncommon',[3] an 'extremely rare condition'.[4] The prosecuting

---

1. e.g. Trial 2 p3025 (Naughton), Trial 2 p2869 (King), Trial 2 p4497 (Steinfort)
2. Trial 2 p3003
3. Trial 2 p2969

barrister, Andrew Tinney, re-enforced this language in his closing address to the jury: 'the distinct rarity of the condition',[5] 'an extremely rare condition',[6] an 'extremely uncommon'[7] form of syncope, 'an extremely rare condition based on sensible evidence',[8] an 'extremely rare medical condition'.[9]

Prof. King agreed that cough syncope was 'rare',[10] and 'an uncommon cause' of syncope,[11] but did not say 'extremely'. Dr. Steinfort agreed that it is 'a rare condition. I wouldn't say it's extremely rare.'[12]

It seems that the word *extremely* was used by the prosecution to counter the accepted fact that it was possible that Farquharson had cough syncope. The idea was to make that possibility seem so remote that it did not provide the jury with *reasonable doubt*. By contrast, the defence barrister Peter Morrissey tried to emphasise that 'the medical evidence… says it's possible'.[13] So the differences in terminology used by the experts seems to have been influenced by our adversarial system. I wanted to look past the language of advocacy, which has no relevance to the analysis. What evidence was presented for the rareness of cough syncope?

To demonstrate the rareness of the condition, Prof. Naughton pointed out that he had never personally had a patient who had cough syncope.[14] He asked colleagues at the Alfred Hospital if they ever had any cases, including two lung transplant specialists, a cystic fibrosis specialist, and some physiotherapists who work with HIV patients. From these inquiries only one case was reported, involving a patient with cystic fibrosis.[15]

4. Trial 2 p3003
5. Trial 2 p4981
6. Trial 2 p5002
7. Trial 2 p5003
8. Trial 2 p5003
9. Trial 2 p5005
10. Trial 2 p2886, 2901 Trial 1 p1575
11. Trial 2 p2863
12. Trial 2 p4549
13. Trial 2 p5362
14. Trial 2 p2976
15. Trial 2 p2978

The problem is that specialist doctors working in a large hospital are assigned cases depending on their speciality, and the needs of the patients. Cough syncope patients would not be assigned to any of these specialists. In fact, cough syncope is not likely to be referred to a specialist doctor at all. So this information did not help in understanding how rare the condition is.

Naughton then referred[16] to several text books, noting that references to cough syncope are sparse, asserting that this provided further evidence of the rareness of the condition. He also noted that cough syncope is not specifically mentioned in Australian driving guidelines,[17] again alluding to its rareness.

Prof. King estimated[18] that he had diagnosed about six patients with cough syncope over his 40 year career. However, King spent much of that time as a specialist in a major hospital, so it is again not surprising that cough syncope patients were not being referred to him.

Dr. Steinfort testified that he had approximately 20 cases of cough syncope over 15 years. However, a number of people who had suffered cough syncope, and who had heard about the Farquharson case, contacted Victoria legal aid, who referred these patients to Dr. Steinfort. This filtering of cases *toward* Steinfort needs to be considered when interpreting how these 20 cases in 15 years pertains to the overall rarity of cough syncope. Prior to these referrals from Victoria legal aid, Steinfort had 10 cases of cough syncope over a 12 year period. After the referrals started, he had 10 cases in 3 years.

The other evidence regarding the rareness of cough syncope pertained to the fraction of *syncope* cases which were *cough* syncope. Of the patients who were treated for syncope (fainting), how many of those cases were precipitated by heavy coughing? Prof. Naughton testified that `I'm approximating here but I would say it would be well and truly less than 1 percent'[19]

---

16. Trial 2 p3002
17. Trial 2 p3035 'Assessing Fitness to Drive'
18. Trial 2 p2868
19. Trial 2 p2970

although he admits this is an 'opinion' and an 'estimate', and provides no evidence to back it up. Prof. King quotes a research paper as showing that 'about 2 percent of all cases of syncope'[20] are cough syncope.

After reading all this evidence and testimony I still had no idea how rare cough syncope is. Why didn't any of the expert witnesses explore medical data bases? Hospitals keep detailed records which are compiled and analysed by the Department of Health, amongst others. To find out how rare a condition is, why ask a physiotherapist for anecdotes when you could ask an hospital administrator to explore the data? Why was the court even asking doctors about the rarity of the condition? Why not ask a Health Department statistician?

I decided to search for some data.

Australian Emergency departments collect data on the more general 'syncope', without breaking this down to sub-components such as cough syncope. There were 80,000 syncope cases recorded[21] in Australian Emergency departments in a single year spanning 2014/2015. Syncope is surprisingly common.

I looked up the research[22] quoted by Prof. King, regarding the fraction of syncope cases that are caused by coughing. The paper says that 2.5% (rather than 2% as quoted by King) of syncope cases over a 3 year period at a particular clinic were cough syncope. I then found a more recent 2014 review paper[23] on cough syncope that looked at 3244 cases of syncope within 5 studies, and found 2.6% of them were *cough* syncope.

If around 2.5% of the 80,000 syncope cases at Australian Emergency departments are *cough* syncope, as the research papers suggest, that would mean 2000 people were treated for

20. Trial 2 p2863
21. Australian hospital statistics: Emergency Department care 2014/2015, AWAHI, http://www.aihw.gov.au/publication-detail/?id=60129553619
22. H. William Bonekat, Robert M. Miles, and Bruce A. Staats, *Smoking and Cough Syncope: Follow-up in 45 Cases*, International Journal of the AddictionsVol. 22, Iss. 5, 1987
23. P. V. Dicpinigaitis, L. Lim, C. Farmakidis *Cough syncope* Respiratory Medicine 2014 108, 244e251

cough syncope in Emergency departments each year. That is around 40 per week.

Ok, that is a little more informative, although there remains significant uncertainty. In particular it may under-estimate the number of cases because unconsciousness during cough syncope lasts a matter of seconds, and recovery is relatively rapid[24] so many cases would go to their doctor rather than the emergency department. In fact many may not seek treatment at all. It is well established[25] that males with health issues often do not seek medical care, and cough syncope patients are almost exclusively male. However, at least we have some guidance, an 'order of magnitude' telling us that the number is likely to be 'in the thousands'; it is not likely to be in the hundreds, nor in the tens of thousands.

A second source of data I found comes from Scotland.[26] In the United Kingdom, drivers are prohibited[27] from driving for 6 months following a single episode of cough syncope, and for 12 months if they suffer multiple episodes over a 5 year period. In Scotland in the year spanning 2014/2015, 216 such prohibitions were recorded.[28] A separate study[29] shows that only 30% of NHS doctors are aware of the guidelines pertaining to cough syncope, meaning that the true number of cough syncope cases presenting to doctors is likely to be three times higher, making around 600 cases in that year. If we account for the population difference

---

24. study here... which was it??
25. e.g. Jamie Doward 4 Nov. 2012 *Men risk health by failing to seek NHS help, survey finds* The Guardian UK; Tom Geoghegan 17 July 2009 *Why are men reluctant to seek medical help?* BBC Magazine
26. I note that it has not been studied as to whether some ethnic groups are more prone to cough syncope than others: in this regard Scotland is probably a safe place to source data in this particular case as Farquharson is a Scottish name, and Rob Farquharson retains Scottish physical attributes
27. *Advice for medical professionals for drivers with neurological disorders* DVLA: Assessing fitness to drive: guide for medical professionals
28. Helen McArdle 19 Oct 2015 *Revealed: 46% of "blackout" drivers in Scotland get their licence back within months* **Herald Scotland**
29. Ng K. et al. 2015 *Knowledge of Driving Vehicle Licensing Agency guidelines among NHS doctors: a multicentre observational study* Journal of the Royal Society of Medicine Vol. 6 1-8

between Scotland and Australia, the 600 cases per year would translate to around 3000 cases in Australia, a similar enough number to the estimate I made above using different data, i.e. 'in the thousands'.

The final data I found came from the U.K. Driver and Vehicle Licensing Agency (DVLA), which attributes approximately 25 road fatalities per year to cough syncope.[30] The U.K. has about 50% more road fatalities[31] than Australia per year, so this would translate to around 17 such fatalities in Australia per year. Although this figure has its own uncertainties,[32] there are multiple recorded road accidents attributed to cough syncope, from a significant number of sources and studies.[33] There is ample evidence from which to conclude that road accidents caused by cough syncope do happen.

By this stage, I felt like I had a bit more of an understanding of how common cough syncope is, beyond the anecdotes of a few doctors and vague references to 'rare' or 'extremely uncommon'.

30. Chris Sherrard 15 May 2014 *Driver who ploughed in to hero lollipop lady had severe coughing fit behind the wheel* Mirror U.K. I was able to verify these numbers with Prof. Alyn Morice from the International Society for the Study of the Cough who attained the information from the DVLA, but I was not able to get a response from the DVLA directly.
31. World Health Organisation data
32. Uncertainties arise as the proportion of various causes of fatalities are likely to be different in the two countries. In particular, falling asleep is a more common cause of road accidents in Australia where distances are large. Further, distinguishing any form of syncope from falling asleep can be difficult if an accident is fatal.
33. e.g. DVLA data, (op cit 35); Whitty C. *On the so called "laryngeal epilepsy"*. Brain 1943, 66:43e54; Symonds C. *Cough syncope, frequent fainting, and epilepsy*. Proc Roy Soc Med 1962, 55:179e80; Bonekat H, Miles R, Staats B. *Smoking and cough syncope: follow-up in 45 cases*. Int J Addict 1987, 22:413e9; Hanawa T, Ikeda S, Funatsu T, et al. *Development of a new surgical procedure for repairing tracheobronchomalacia*. J Thorac Cardiovasc Surg 1990,100; Jayarajan A, Prakash O. *Cough syncope induced by enalapril*. Chest 1993, 103 327e8; Fitzsimons M. *Case report: cough syncope in a U.S. Army aviator*. Aviat Space Environ Med 1998, 69:515e6; McCorry D, Chadwick D, Barber P, Cooper P, Wroe S. *Cough syncope in heavy goods vehicle drivers*. QJM 2004, 97:631e2; Marinella M. *A car crash complicating influenza*. Mayo Clin Proc 2004, 79:1087e8; Spring P, Kok C, Nicholson G, et al. *Autosomal dominant hereditary sensory neuropathy with chronic cough and gastro-oesophageal reflux: clinical features in two families linked to chromosome* Brain 2005, 128:2797e810.

What about the characteristics of cough syncope sufferers? If it only affects elderly women, then clearly Farquharson is in trouble. According to Prof. Naughton, the literature[34] tells us that 'the typical cough syncope patient is someone who is often a middle aged male, who is often either slightly or moderately overweight. They have often been a heavy smoker. And usually there is a history of alcohol, moderate to large alcohol consumption, that's in the background.'[35] Farquharson conforms to all these characteristics. He was 36 years old, overweight, a smoker and a drinker.

Most cough syncope sufferers also have chronic obstructive airways disease[36]. Although there are no systematic studies to identify the fraction of such cases, the available case studies[37] put the number at around 80%. Dr. Steinfort reported that 16 of his 20 cough syncope patients had chronic airways disease, again 80%. For the remaining 20%, a large range of other conditions have been associated with cough syncope. The 2014 review paper[38] on cough syncope lists no fewer than 30 disorders ranging from influenza A, to whooping cough[39], to pulmonary hypertension and cerebral tumours.

If the number of cough syncope cases per year in Australia is indeed a couple of thousand, as I estimated from the available data, then the number of cases in patients who do not have chronic obstructive airways disease is several hundred. Farquharson did not have chronic obstructive airways disease.

---

34. e.g. P. V. Dicpinigaitis, L. Lim, C. Farmakidis *Cough syncope* Respiratory Medicine (2014) 108, 244e251
35. Trial 2 p2970
36. e.g. Dicpinigaitis, P. V. 2014 op cit.
37. Kerr Jr A, Derbes VJ. *The syndrome of cough syncope.* Ann Intern Med 1953;39:1240e53;Bonekat HW, Miles RM, Staats BA. Smoking and cough syncope: follow-up in 45 cases. Int J Addict 1987, 22:413e9; Chung et al. *Jugular venous reflux and plasma endothelin-1 are associated with cough syncope: a case control pilot study* BMC Neurology 2013, 13:9
38. P. V. Dicpinigaitis, L. Lim, C. Farmakidis *Cough syncope* Respiratory Medicine (2014) 108, 244e251
39. See also Kogan, Y., Elias, N., Slobodin, G., Odeh, M. *Recurrent Cough Syncope Due to Pertussis in Adults: Report of Three Cases and Review of the Literature.* Journal of Medical Cases, North America, 7, jun. 2016

On the other hand, it is well documented that in the two weeks leading up to Fathers day 2005, he had a respiratory tract infection and a terrible cough.

So, I finally had some ball-park idea of how rare is cough syncope in people with similar attributes as Robert Farquharson. Each year a few hundred middle aged, overweight Australian males who smoke and drink alcohol but do not have chronic obstructive airways disease will have an episode of cough syncope.

How does this information help determine whether or not Farquharson is guilty?

It is important not to confuse the rarity of cough syncope with the likelihood that Farquharson actually had the condition on that night in 2005. Doing so is a statistical fallacy that is so commonly employed by prosecutors that it is termed 'the prosecutors fallacy'. The rarity of cough syncope does not directly translate to the likelihood of Farquharson having had cough syncope that night. Determining the likelihood that Farquharson had cough syncope on the night requires consideration of all relevant information and evidence pertaining to the case.

What do I mean by this?

Consider how rare it is for fathers to kill their children. Between 20 and 25 children[40,41,42] are killed by a parent each year in Australia, on average. Fathers are responsible for around one half of the cases[43], around 12 per year. Of these cases, revenge or retaliatory filicide is an *uncommon* motivation,[44] with most cases involving mental illness[45] and an 'altruistic' belief by the

---

40. Mouzos, J. and Rushforth, C. *Family Homicide in Australia* Australian Institute of Criminology, Trends & Issues in Crime and Criminal Justice, June 2003, No. 255
41. Cussen, T., & Bryant, W. (2015). *Domestic/family homicide in Australia* Research inPractice no. 38. Canberra: Australian Institute of Criminology
42. Brown, T., Tyson, D., & Fernandez Arias, P. (2014). Filicide and parental separation anddivorce. *Child Abuse Review,* 23 (2), 79–88.
43. Op cit. Cussen, T., & Bryant, W. (2015)
44. Resnick PJ. Child murder by parents: A psychiatric review of filicide. Am Psychiatry. 1970; Resnick PJ. *Filicide in the United States* Indian J Psychiatry. 2016 Dec; 58(Suppl 2)

perpetrator that they are somehow saving the child from the horrors of this world.[46] In Australia between 2001 and 2012 there were twelve cases of filicide classified as having a motive of revenge,[47] around one per year, and those figures include the Farquharson case. Should we conclude that it is 'extremely unlikely' that Farquharson killed his sons based on the extreme rareness of filicide and even more extreme rareness of retaliatory filicide? Following this logic, should we find all men accused of filicide not guilty because it is such a rare phenomenon? Of course not, just as we cannot conclude that Farquharson didn't have cough syncope just because it is rare.

There are two options; either Farquharson had cough syncope or Farquharson committed filicide. Both are rare, but one of them must be correct.

---

45. Flynn SM, Shaw JJ, Abel KM (2013) *Filicide: Mental Illness in Those Who Kill Their Children*. PLoS ONE 8(4)
46. Resnick PJ. Child murder by parents: A psychiatric review of filicide. Am Psychiatry. 1970
47. Tominson et al. 2016, *Filicide in Australia: A national study*, presented at the 21st ISPCAN International Congress for the Prevention of Child Abuse and Neglect, 28-31 August 2016, Calgary, Canada. Data comes from National Homicide Monitoring Program

CHAPTER 11

CONDEMNED TO REPEAT IT

To this day there is no consensus on the mechanisms that cause cough syncope.[1] The causes are 'probably multifactorial',[2] and different mechanisms may be involved in different sufferers. The expert witnesses, Naughton, King, and Steinfort, all agreed that the causes remain unclear[3] and that there is no test, such as a blood test or an electroencephalogram (EEG), that can determine whether a person suffers from cough syncope.[4]

So how do we determine whether someone has cough syncope? How are we supposed to know if Farquharson had it?

The experts all agreed that the diagnosis of cough syncope is based *entirely* on history.[5] Beyond simply taking the word of the patient as to what occurred, Professor King pointed out that it is 'very helpful to have an eye-witness account, because the patients themselves are not always clear on what happened.'[6] Naughton concurred, saying that 'Ideally, we like to see a collateral history, in other words, someone having witnessed what went on... If someone, more than one person perhaps,

---

1. P. V. Dicpinigaitis, L. Lim, C. Farmakidis *Cough syncope* Respiratory Medicine (2014) 108, 244e25; Chih-Ping Chung et al. *Jugular venous reflux and plasma endothelin-1 are f*
2. Chih-Ping Chung et al. *Jugular venous reflux and plasma endothelin-1 are associated with cough syncope: a case control pilot study*MC Neurology 2013, 13:9
3. Naughton Trial 2 p2963, King Trial 2 p2866
4. e.g. Naughton trial 2 p3021, King Trial 2 p2868
5. Naughton Trial 2 p3006, p3021 King Trial 2 p2868, Steinfort Trial 2 p4488
6. Trial 2 p2902

provides a history that they witnessed someone coughing and then black out, that's very powerful evidence...'[7].

So the diagnosis of cough syncope relies on a patient recounting that they were coughing prior to blacking out, but confidence in the diagnosis is greatly enhanced by witnessed accounts. The different diagnoses provided in the testimony of the different experts seemed to reflect whether or not they believed the patient, Robert Farquharson, making the medical testimony very delicate in this case. It is not the role of the expert witnesses to decide whether or not Farquharson was lying, nor to decide the facts of the case. As I cannot tell whether Farquharson is lying, I collated his purported history of cough syncope, imagining Farquharson as a patient presenting to a doctor:

1. 30 August 2005: the patient reports a blackout after coughing in a car park. This was not witnessed but the story was relayed to a friend on September 1 2005.
2. 2 September 2005: the patient suffers a severe coughing fit leading to dizziness (a pre-syncope episode). Witnessed by his boss who helped him sit down.
3. 4 September 2005: the patient blacks out after coughing, resulting in his car running off the road. Not witnessed, this episode is an unverified claim of the patient.
4. 18 May 2009: the patient blacks out after coughing. Falls from chair to the floor and breaks leg. Witnessed by multiple people who say the patient remained unconscious for several seconds despite the broken leg. Sworn testimony to the veracity of these events was made in a court of law.
5. 11 June 2010: the patient blacks out after coughing, and collapses to the floor. Witnessed by sister, who is a nurse, and her husband. Sworn testimony to the veracity of these events was made in a court of law.
6. December 2011: the patient blacked out while standing, fell to the ground and hit his head hard enough to cut

---

7. Trial 1 p1611

forehead, resulting in quite severe bleeding. The patient now has a visible scar on his forehead. Incident was witnessed, and a sworn eyewitness account was made.

I will talk more about the reliability of eyewitness evidence later, and the care that must be taken with such evidence. However, taken as a whole, the eyewitness evidence pertaining to these episodes of cough syncope is strong, as it included multiple witnesses who corroborated each other on two of the occasions, and another eyewitness on a separate occasion. In terms of a typical diagnosis of cough syncope, this evidence is significant, or 'powerful' in the words of Professor Naughton.

The eyewitness statements and witness accounts of conversations are the existing evidence pertaining to whether Robert Farquharson has cough syncope. This evidence establishes a history of cough syncope and clearly favours Farquharson's story.

I know what some of you are thinking, especially those who are convinced of his guilt. He faked it! His sister is lying to get him off!

Yes, it is possible that Farquharson faked the history and faked the fainting spells to try to get himself off murder charges. Maybe his sister lied under oath with the support of her husband. However, there is no evidence for any of this. No witness said 'he looked like he might have been faking to me'. No one said 'his sister has told me she lied and he really faked it'. All the eyewitnesses said something along the lines of 'Farquharson had an infection at the time, he was coughing heavily, he fell unconscious, he dropped to the floor, he did not move'. In each case he had seen a doctor regarding a chest infection around the time, and there was significant evidence that he had an infection and had been coughing heavily.

The only way to conclude that Farquharson was faking is if other evidence in the case shows clearly that he is guilty, and therefore we can *infer* that he must have been faking. So far in the book, I have seen no evidence of guilt, but I have not covered all the evidence yet, so I will defer making an overall judgement.

However, the *possibility* that he is faking is not evidence. It is something we can conclude from the surrounding evidence, but it is not evidence. The eyewitness evidence of his episodes of fainting after coughing, that *is* evidence: and it clearly favours a diagnosis of cough syncope.

To find Farquharson guilty, it is necessary to explain away the eyewitness evidence of the cough syncope episodes. Thus, the prosecution spent considerable time implying that these episodes were faked, without presenting any evidence to support this, beyond pointing to some small inconsistencies between different second hand stories, that I will explore later in the book which did not amount to evidence.

It seems the normal roles were reversed: usually a defendant has a presumption of innocence. The prosecution then leads evidence that points to guilt, and the defendant tries to explain that evidence in a way that is 'possible' under the scenario of innocence, thus providing 'reasonable doubt'. In the Farquharson case, evidence pertaining to cough syncope points to innocence, and the prosecution had to somehow explain it in a manner that is 'possible' and is consistent with the scenario of guilt.

So, what was the prosecution's explanation of the first episode on my list? In that episode, Farquharson claims that he was in his car at a roadhouse when he started coughing. The next thing he remembers, his car had rolled around 15 metres into a stone barrier. Darren Bushell testified[8] that he saw Farquharson, by chance, in the week *prior to* Father's day 2005, and that Farquharson had told him this account of an apparent episode of cough syncope.

The prosecution claimed that Farquharson must have invented the story, 'This is a case of a man who relayed a completely phoney story to his friend Darren Bushell, possibly told in preparation for the events of Father's Day. Just a set up'.[9] According to this theory, Farquharson was establishing a false

---

8. Trial 2 p3299
9. Trial 2 p4990

history so that, after murdering his children, he could point to this history as proof that he suffered from cough syncope.

Next, seemingly as part of the plan, he faked a pre-syncope episode in front of his boss Sue Bateson. Episode two on my list. Bateson testified that Farquharson 'started having this really hard, dry, grabbing cough... It took... his breath away and I was just looking and then it was more the colour of his face. It was red...'[10]... 'It wasn't like just a continual or a sobbing cough, it was more like a gasping, continual... when we have the flu it like breaks but this appeared to me that it was like a ten second hold...'.[11]

Telling a friend of an episode during a chance encounter and then having a dizzy spell in front of your boss seems a pretty haphazard way to establish a history of cough syncope, for such a supposedly conniving individual. If Farquharson wanted to establish a history prior to Father's day 2005, why not fake a couple of episodes in front of several witnesses?

The other problem with this theory is that there is no evidence that Farquharson knew anything about cough syncope. For the prosecution theory to make sense, Farquharson needed to have known what cough syncope was, that it was diagnosed purely on history, that he fit the demographic of sufferers in terms of age and physical attributes, and that cough syncope typically caused unconsciousness for a matter of seconds.[12] Without all this, his allegedly fake story would have been exposed immediately.

However, there was no evidence of how Farquharson supposedly attained this knowledge. Firstly, there was no evidence that he went to a library. `I haven't been near no libraries.'[13] is the response that best sums an exchange with the prosecutor, who was suggesting that he looked up the diagnosis

---

10. Trial 2 p2851
11. Trial 2 p2852
12. Or, he got lucky with these details. See how hard it is to compare how desperately unlucky his accident was to the probability of him being a murderer? Because the latter requires, on top of all the other aspects, that he got very very lucky in his planning.
13. Trial 2 p 3938

of cough syncope in a library. There were no records of Farquharson ever having been to a library, but even if Farquharson did go to a library, the information pertaining to diagnosis by history and length of unconsciousness would not even be there,[14] as there is little in medical textbooks about cough syncope.[15] When he first wrote a report on the case and first gave evidence under oath, Dr. Naughton himself did not know that cough syncope was diagnosed by history, and nor did he know how long unconsciousness lasted.[16] So Farquharson purportedly knew more details about this medical condition than the expert witness, details that are not generally found in medical textbooks.

To find all the details he required, Farquharson would have had to scour medical journals, presumably online. However, this was 2005 and the internet was not what it is today. Farquharson had few computer skills, nor access to computers at the time. *'Did you have access to a computer in 2005 or 2004?*—No.' *Did you have any connection at all with an internet service provider back at that time?*—'No.' *Can I ask you did you have access if you wanted to in Winchelsea to a computer where you would be able to do a search on the internet?*—'I don't know where you'd go to do that. I don't know.' *Was there an internet café or anything like that?*—'Don't think so, no.' *What about in Geelong, back in 2005?*—'I wouldn't have a clue. I've never been there.' *Had you ever done a Google search by the time the year 2005 ticked around?*—'No.'[17] This evidence was bolstered by testimony by Farquharson's sister Carmen Ross.[18] When he was staying at their house in 2006 he wanted to search for cars, but needed his brother in law to turn on their computer, set it up and do the search.

The prosecution did lead evidence that Farquharson did a computer course in 2000, where he said he 'just learned how to write letters' and that 'I think it was just learning and

14. Trial 2 p3002
15. Trial 2 p3002
16. Voire Dire Trial 1 p47, p61
17. Trial 2 3939-3940
18. Trial 2 p4768

understanding what each key is and etc. like that, I think that's what it was'.[19]

Now, we can take this evidence with a grain of salt if Farquharson truly is a deceptive murderer and his sister is covering for him. However, in the second trial, his former wife Cindy Gambino was testifying for the prosecution. She had every opportunity to contradict his claims, and reveal that he actually did have the computer skills to find the information. She did not. Even more compelling is that the Farquharson family computer was forensically inspected. Farquharson's claim that he did not use the internet would be pretty easy for police to disprove by simply searching the computer and looking in the history for searches for cars, or for his favourite footy team, the Bombers, or even for porn. Internet searches leave a readily discernible fingerprint. It is far from easy to use the internet without leaving a trace, particularly as private browsing was not available in 2005,[20] and even if it were, evidence of the search history would still be found during a forensic analysis of the computer.[21] No evidence of Farquharson browsing the internet, let alone searching for cough syncope, was ever presented.

So the prosecution theory for explaining away the first cough syncope episode seems far-fetched, and is not supported by any evidence, evidence that one could readily expect to be available.

On the other hand Cindy Gambino testified that Farquharson often had very bad coughs, but in more than 10 years of living together she had never before seen him cough and then fall unconscious.[22] Isn't it a coincidence that Farquharson's first episode of cough syncope happened only shortly before Father's day of 2005? Naughton mentioned this lack of a history as one reason why he thought it *extremely* unlikely that Farquharson had cough syncope.[23] However, cough syncope occurs almost

---

19. Trial 2 p 3986
20. https://en.wikipedia.org/wiki/Privacy_mode
21. Ohana, D. J. & Shashidhar, N *Do Private and Portable Web Browsers Leave Incriminating Evidence?* 2013 IEEE Security and Privacy Workshops
22. Trial 2 p1207
23. Naughton report in appendix C, also see Trial 2 p3010

exclusively in middle age. Farquharson was 36 years old, an age where one may well expect the first episodes of the condition to occur. What is the relevance of his not having cough syncope during the time he was married to Cindy, in his twenties and early thirties?

Episode three on my list is the claim by Farquharson regarding the night the car went into the dam. Asking whether this episode is credible is the same as asking whether Farquharson is guilty, so needs to be answered by looking at all the remainder of the evidence. It should be noted though, that claiming cough syncope would seem an obscure option for covering up a murder. Farquharson had worked very early that morning, it had been a long day, and he had been sick. Why not just claim to have fallen asleep at the wheel? No medical history would be required for such a claim. Further, the questions about where he got the knowledge about cough syncope apply again to this episode.

What about episode four in which Farquharson coughed, and then fainted in front of several witnesses? This one happened in prison. Michael Eames testified that he 'saw Mr Farquharson, who was on my right, starting to cough... I could see it out of the side of my eye, his head was sort of coming towards my shoulder... and...the next thing I heard was a thud which sounded very much like to me a head hitting the concrete. I turned around and stood in my seat and I give him a sort of a thump... and he didn't seem to move... he was red in the face and he did not seem to be breathing at this stage...I thought at that stage he was unconscious... so I lifted his head up and cleared the tongue in his mouth, I didn't want the fellow to choke... I believe it was probably only a few seconds, maybe seven, could have been 10 or 12, but definitely no more' before Farquharson opened his eyes and 'said words to the effect of "What happened, mate?"'. Several other witnesses also saw this, so there was no doubt that Eames was telling the truth.

Of course, Farquharson could have been faking. Could Farquharson pull off such a fake of dropping to the floor and then remaining unresponsive, with a broken leg? Well, it may be possible. And maybe none of the multiple witnesses who were there could spot true unconsciousness from faked.

However, then there is episode five in Carmen Ross's living room. Carmen is a nurse who has witnessed plenty of fainting episodes. It would presumably be a little more difficult to fool a nurse. She described how he had a continuous cough, so she told him to go and sit down, he took a few steps and 'just dropped like a bag of spuds, so I got such a fright... he was on the floor... his eyes were open, he was just staring, so I got down on the floor and I grabbed his wrist and I couldn't feel his pulse, so I stuck my hand inside his T-shirt so I could feel his heart beat and I could feel his chest rising, he was very clammy, he was pale, and there was no, no response, no recognition when he was looking at me, so, I started to shake him and I'm going 'Rob, Rob', and then he seemed to sort of slowly – his hands started to twitch and his head sort of started to move from side to side and his eyes were open and then all of a sudden they started to blink '[24].

Ok, maybe he faked it again? He fooled her too? Or maybe she is lying? Under oath? And her husband is backing her up? Well, that is also possible. And isn't it suspicious that this occurred while he was still appealing his sentence?

Ok, what about the next episode in prison, which occurred after all avenues of appeal were exhausted? Again, this was witnessed, and Farquharson this time hit the floor face first, hard enough to cause a deep cut in his forehead that has left a visible scar. Corrado Motta said that Rob was going to join him in his cell, when he 'heard a loud noise come from Robert's cell, through the wooden door... I called Robert's name a number of times. I heard no response so I pulled the door open, I saw Robert on the floor of his cell... Robert slowly came to. I told him we must push the emergency button as blood was dripping profusely'. Again, expert faking that was not affected by pain. Or maybe Motta is lying. He is a convicted criminal after all. We do know that Rob was treated for his head wound, but maybe that was inflicted by Motta as part of the plan. I am just not sure

---

24. Trial 2 p4758-4759

what the plan was trying to achieve when there was no avenue for appeal, and at no stage did Farquharson contact his lawyer to inform him of this latest episode.

All this covert researching, planning, lying and faking is certainly a possible way to explain the eyewitness evidence surrounding Robert Farquharson's history of cough syncope. However, it has started to remind me of Richard Feynman's explanation of the scientific method and it's relation to the possible and impossible. Feynman tells the following anecdote: 'Some years ago I had a conversation with a layman about flying saucers... I said "I don't think there are flying saucers". So my antagonist said, "Is it impossible that there are flying saucers? Can you prove that it's impossible?" "No", I said, "I can't prove it's impossible. It's just very unlikely". At that he said, "You are very unscientific. If you can't prove it impossible then how can you say that it's unlikely?" But that is the way that is scientific. It is scientific only to say what is more likely and what is less likely, and not to be proving all the time the possible and impossible. To define what I mean, I might have said to him, "Listen, I mean that from my knowledge of the world that I see around me, I think that it is much more likely that the reports of flying saucers are the results of the known irrational characteristics of terrestrial intelligence than of the unknown rational efforts of extra-terrestrial intelligence." It is just more likely. That is all.'[25]

Yes, it is possible that Robert Farquharson knew what cough syncope was, read specialized medical journals on the condition online or in a library, managed to cover all tracks of such endeavours, planned the murder by lying to a random friend who he met by chance in the street, telling him that he had recently blacked out after a coughing fit, and then successfully faked a series of fainting episodes, fooling multiple people with an ability to remain totally unresponsive despite a broken leg and gashed forehead that was streaming blood. It is possible that his sister lied under oath with the support of her husband. It just seems

---

25. *The Character of Physical Law*, Cornell University Messenger Lectures (1964)

more likely, at least to me, that he had cough syncope. A very simple explanation for the evidence.

It is the same explanation that was reached by the two doctors who actually examined Farquharson, firstly Dr. Bartley at the hospital on the night of the incident,[26] and later Dr. Steinfort. Whilst Dr. Bartley has called his diagnosis 'preliminary', Steinfort saw Farquharson on multiple occasions, and put him through a large range of tests including induced pre-syncope episodes captured on video. Steinfort maintains to this day that Farquharson had 'classical cough syncope'.

At this stage I was starting to think that this really was a horrible accident. However, I again wanted to challenge my own conclusions. Had I become biased towards Farquharson? I decided to contact an expert on cough syncope, someone who really knew the topic. I honed in on the author of the 2014 review paper on cough syncope, referred to above. Peter Dicpinigaitis is Professor of Medicine at the Albert Einstein College of Medicine, in New York. He is triple-board-certified in Internal Medicine, Pulmonary Diseases, and Critical Care Medicine. He serves as the Site Director of Critical Care Medicine at the Einstein Division of the Montefiore Medical Center, and is the founder and director of the Montefiore Cough Center, one of the few specialty centres in the world exclusively committed to the evaluation and management of patients with chronic cough. He really is an expert on cough, and has published a comprehensive review of all that is known about cough syncope.

I emailed Dicpinigaitis and he agreed to take a look at the report made by Prof Naughton, the one which concluded that it was 'extremely unlikely that Robert Farquharson suffered from cough syncope'. Dicpinigaitis expressed concerns about the quality of the report and the strength of the conclusion. He asked 'Do you know Mr F's height, weight (is he large, obese?), if he had a history of smoking, or diagnosis of COPD [Chronic obstructive pulmonary disease], asthma or other medical conditions?'. I sent

---

26. e.g. Trial 2 p2074

Dicpinigaitis this information, including that Farquharson had been diagnosed with a respiratory tract infection at the time and been witnessed coughing, and that his former wife had testified that he had severe coughs annually and his coughing would 'take his breath away'. Dicpinigaitis replied that 'His short, stocky build is classic for cough syncope. Furthermore, having a current/recent upper respiratory tract infection (common cold) can actually render someone transiently with hyper-reactive airways, thus creating a situation in the lungs equivalent to COPD or asthma'. Dicpinigaitis concluded that 'cough syncope becomes a very reasonable consideration.'

At this stage, Farquharson's story about cough syncope was not sounding like 'bullshit' or 'extremely unlikely'. It was sounding 'very reasonable'.

CHAPTER 12

BEARING FALSE WITNESS

During the first trial, prosecutor Jeremy Rapke stated that 'this is a case which at the end of the day rests upon forensic science and medical science'[1]. By this standard, the case against Robert Farquharson has collapsed. The evidence surrounding sinking cars indicates that his story is plausible; nothing indicates that the car was being steered by a conscious driver; cough syncope is rare but not as rare as filicide; Farquharson's short, stocky stature, history of smoking and drinking, and diagnosed respiratory tract infection make cough syncope a 'very reasonable consideration'; cough syncope is diagnosed purely on history, and there was significant witness evidence from which to conclude that Robert Farquharson suffered from the condition.

However, there is also witness evidence in the case, the most important of which comes from Winchelsea local Greg King. King's evidence pertains to a conversation he had with Robert Farquharson around three months prior to the death of the children. Before I discuss the witness evidence, however, I want to tell a story. It is a true story that illustrates some important issues that need to be considered when assessing witness testimony, and in particular, why witness evidence should be treated scientifically, like all other evidence.

In 1984, a man broke into the apartment of 22 year old college student Jennifer Thompson, put a knife to her throat, and raped

[1]. Trial 1 p521

her. During the ordeal, Thompson took the heroic decision that she would remember every detail of this man, to ensure that he was brought to justice. Thompson also used this exercise as an attempt to distance herself from the horrific event.

Several days later, Thompson was shown a set of mug-shots by police. She picked out two photos and looked at them for several minutes before pointing to Ronald Cotton 'Yeah. This is the one, I think this is the guy' she said. A detective asked, 'You 'think' that's the guy?' and she answered, 'It's him.' 'You're sure?'. 'Yes'. 'Did I do OK?' she asked, to which the detective answered, 'You did great, Ms. Thompson.' Later, a physical line up was done. Again, Thompson was not sure, and was considering suspect numbers four and five (Cotton). After considerable deliberation, she indicated that number five 'looks the most like him.' She was again asked if she was certain, and she said yes. Thompson recalls that 'When I picked him out in the physical lineup and I walked out of the room, they looked at me and said, 'That's the same guy...you picked out in the photos.' For me that was a huge amount of relief.'

When Thompson identified Ronald Cotton with 100% confidence during his trial, he was convicted and sentenced to life in prison.[2]

Whilst Cotton was in prison, another prisoner called Bobby Poole was serving time for breaking into women's homes and raping them at knife point. Poole bragged about perpetrating the crime for which Cotton was serving time. Cotton was granted a second trial during which his lawyers pointed to Poole as the perpetrator, emphasizing his record of committing similar crimes. But Jennifer Thompson was sure. 100% sure. It was Ronald Cotton who had raped her. She had never seen Bobby Poole in her life. Cotton was again convicted and was sentenced to life in prison plus 54 years.

Cotton maintained his innocence and in 1995 the DNA in the semen from the crime scene was tested. It matched Bobby Poole.

---

2. For details of this story see the book co-written by Jennifer Thompson, Ronald Cotton and Erin Torneo, *Picking Cotton*, publisher: St. Martin's Griffin, 2010

Faulty eye-witness testimony is the most common cause of miscarriages of justice, more common than all other causes combined.[3] This finding has led to a lot of research, trying to understand why eye-witness testimony is not as reliable as had long been assumed. Such research points to several errors made in the identification of Ronald Cotton. Firstly, neither the mugshots nor the physical line-up included the perpetrator, Bobby Poole, who was not a suspect at that stage. Witnesses should be informed that the perpetrator may not be included in the mugshots or in the line-up, as there is a tendency to assume that the police have a suspect.[4] 'When you're sittin' in front of a photo lineup, you just assume one of these guys is the suspect. It's my job to find it,' said Thompson.[5]. Witnesses choose the picture that *looks the most like* the perpetrator. This tendency also makes it important that the 'fillers' look at least somewhat like the suspect, or else the suspect will stand out.[6]

Another error was made when all the photos were shown at the same time. This leads witnesses to compare the photos to each other, promoting the tendency to choose the one that looks most like the perpetrator. Witness evidence is more accurate[7] when the photos are shown one at a time, because the witness will compare each photo directly to the memory they have of the perpetrator, rather than to the other photos.

After a witness makes an identification, the police should ask open ended questions regarding confidence, such as 'how confident are you in that selection?'. Instead they had pushed Thompson to be more certain, implying that she needed to be

---

3. e.g Borchard, *Convicting the innocent: Errors of criminal justice* 1932 Yale University Press ; Brandon, & Davies, *Wrongful Imprisonment* 1973 London, Allen & Unwin; Frank, , Frank & Hofmann, *Not guilty*, 1957 London; Gallancz; Huff, Rattner, & Sagarin, *Guilty until proven innocent*. 1986 *Crime and Delinquency*, 32, 518-544; The innocence project
4. e.g. Malpass and Devine 981 Eyewitness identification: Lineup instructions and the absence of the offender. Journal of Applied Psychology, 66, 482-489
5. 60 minutes, CBS, Eyewitness: how accurate is visual memory March 6 2009
6. e.g. Lindsay and Wells (1980); Wells, Rydell, and Seelau 1993
7. E.g. Lindsay and Wells 1985; Cutler & Penrod, 1988; Lindsay, et al. 1991a; Lindsay, Lea, Nosworty, Fulford, Hector, LeVan, & Seabrook, 1991; Sporer, 1993

sure by asking 'You're sure?', to which she could respond yes or no. The interviewers gave positive re-enforcement 'you did great', 'that is the same guy', increasing Thompson's confidence that the selected person was the perpetrator.[8]

The fact that Thompson took several minutes looking at two photos, and took considerable time pondering two people in the physical line-up, should have been taken as an indication of uncertainty. 'Recognition memory is actually quite rapid.' according to memory researcher Gary Wells, 'If somebody's taking longer than ten, 15 seconds, it's quite likely that they're doing something other than just using reliable recognition memory.'[9,10]

Finally, the police conducting the line-up knew that Cotton was the suspect that Thompson had picked from the photos. When the police have a particular suspect in mind, they may 'signal' the correct choice to the eyewitness, even unintentionally.[11] To avoid this tendency, the police conducting the line-up should not know who the suspect is,[12] i.e. they should

---

8. e.g. Semmler C, Brewer N, Wells GL. *Effects of postidentification feedback on eyewitness identification and nonidentification confidence.* Journal of Applied Psychology. 2004;89:334–345. [PubMed] ; Wells GL, Bradfield AL. *"Good, you identified the suspect": Feedback to eyewitnesses distorts their reports of the witnessing experience.* Journal of Applied Psychology. 1998;83:360–376.; Bradfield AL, Wells GL, Olson EA. *The damaging effect of confirming feedback on the relation between eyewitness certainty and identification accuracy.* Journal of Applied Psychology. 2002;87:112–120. [PubMed]; Luus CAE, Wells GL. *The malleability of eyewitness confidence: Co-witness and perseverance effects.* Journal of Applied Psychology. 1994;79:714–723
9. *60 minutes "Eyewitness testimony"* CBS, March 8, 2009
10. see also e.g. Brewer, N., & Wells, G. L. (2006). *The confidence–accuracy relationship in eyewitness identification: Effects of lineup instructions, foil similarity, and target-absent base rates.* Journal of Experimental Psychology: Applied, 12(1), 11–30; Sauerland, M. & Sporer, S. L. (2009). *Fast and confident: Postdicting eye-witness identification accuracy in a field study.* Journal of Experimental Psychology: Applied, 15, 46–62
11. e.g. Fanselow & Buckhout, 1976 *Nonverbal cueing as a source of biasing information in eyewitness identification testing.* Centre for Responsive Psychology Monograph No. CR-26.. New York: Brooklyn College CUNY, Wells and Seelau, 1995 *Applied eyewitness research: The other mission.* Law and Human Behavior, 19(3), 319-324.
12. E.g. Wells G. L., Small M. , Penrod S., Malpass R. S., Fulero S. and Brimacombe C. A. E. *Eyewitness Identification Procedures: Recommendations for Lineups and Photospreads* Law and Human Behavior Vol. 22, No. 6 (Dec., 1998), pp. 603-647

employ the 'double-blind' procedure used in science. Computer software has been developed that will unemotionally take the eyewitness through the identification process.

By the time of the trial of Ronald Cotton, Jennifer Thompson was 100% sure in her identification of Ronald Cotton, even though she had been relatively unsure selecting from the mugshots and the line-up. Once Thompson had completed the line-up, with positive reinforcement from the police officers, she had Ronald Cotton's face in her head. Her memory of the horrific events had updated to include the face that she had selected, the face of Ronald Cotton, as the perpetrator. Her memory was wrong, but it felt real, as real as her other memories of the events. She was able to identify Cotton with 100% confidence and with 100% honesty. Thompson made a very strong, highly credible witness.

Memory research and the implications for eyewitness testimony have been intimately linked since the pioneering work of Elizabeth Loftus, beginning in the 1970s. We have steadily moved away from a model of memory as a digital recorder, replaying the same images and sounds time after time. Memory is now largely considered a *process*.[13,14] Memories can be corrupted during encoding, storage, and retrieval. Memory is full of gaps, it is malleable, it can be contaminated, it is susceptible to suggestion, and it is influenced by our expectations and beliefs about how the world works.[15] 'Memory works like a Wikipedia page: you can go in there and change it, but so can other people'[16] according to Loftus.

Loftus showed that suggestive interviewing techniques could lead to errors in eyewitness testimony.[17] In one study,

---

13. Blank 2009 *Remembering: A theoretical interface between memory and social psychology.* Social Psychology, 40, 164–175
14. Nash, A. & Ost, J. *False and Distorted Memories*, Current Issues in Memory 2016 eds. Nash and Ost, Psychology Press
15. e.g. Alba & Hasher, 1983 *Is memory schematic?* Psychological Bulletin, 93, 203–23; Brewer & Treyens, 1981 *Role of schemata in memory for places.* Cognitive Psychology, 13, 207–230
16. Shaw, Julia. The Memory Illusion: Remembering, Forgetting, and the Science of False Memory (Kindle Locations 55-57) 2016. Random House.

participants were asked to watch a simulated car accident, and answer a series of questions. The participants were split in two. In an early question, half the participants were asked about the speed of a car when it 'turned right' while the other half were asked about the speed of the car when it 'passed the stop sign'. A later question asked whether participants had seen a stop sign. 35% of the group asked about the speed when the car turned right could remember seeing a stop sign, compared to 53% of those who were asked about the speed when the car passed a stop sign.

Participants were later asked to estimate the speed at which the cars 'contacted' or 'smashed' each other.[18] The participants who were asked to estimate the speed of *contact* gave lower estimates than those who were asked to estimate the speed of the *smash*, even though they had watched the exact same video.

When the presence of a barn in the video was suggested, 17% of participants later recalled a barn, even though none existed in the scene.

Small differences in the ways that questions are asked can lead to different responses from witnesses. Recollections are influenced by the presence of new information that was introduced during questioning. These types of studies highlighted the fact that law enforcement officers need to be very careful when attaining and processing eyewitness information.

The *misinformation effect* is the term given to the tendency to incorporate new information into our memories[19] in the way

---

17. e.g. Loftus E. F. & Palmer J. C. 1974, *Reconstruction of auto-mobile destruction: An example of the interaction between language and memory*. Journal of Verbal Learning and Verbal Behavior, 13, 585-589; Loftus E. F. 1975 *Leading Questions and the Eyewitness Report*, Cognitive Psychology 7(4):560-572; Loftus E.F., Miller D.G. & Burns H.J.1978, *Semantic integration of verbal information into a visual memory* Journal of experimental psychology: Human learning and memory 4 (1), 19

18. Loftus & Palmer 1974 actually trialed *contacted, hit, bumped, collided* and *smashed*, with the estimated speeds increasing in order of the listed word, so *contacted* and *smashed* were the extreme cases.

19. e.g. Hyman, Husband, & Billings, 1995 *False memories of childhood experiences*. Applied Cognitive Psychology, 9, 181-197; Porter, Yuille, & Lehman, 1999 *The nature of real, implanted, and fabricated memories for emotional childhood events: Implications for the recovered memory debate*. Law and Human Behavior, 23, 517-537; Strange, Sutherland,

that Jennifer Thompson had incorporated Ronald Cotton into the memory of her rape. One study of the *misinformation effect* involved U.S. Navy personnel who were being subjected to a mock prisoner of war camp, designed to reproduce realistic environments that would test the physical and mental abilities of these elite soldiers. The army allowed access to memory researchers, wanting to know the reliability of information the soldiers recalled when returning from these situations. The soldiers were interrogated whilst they were held in mock captivity, and the research tested their ability to identify their interrogators. Whilst held in the mock prison, one hour after the interrogation, some soldiers were shown photos of a person who was not their interrogator, and simultaneously asked a series of questions regarding their interrogation. Later, during their debrief, 84% of those who had been shown this misinformation falsely identified the person from the photo as being the interrogator.

When new information is mixed in with other memories, the *source* of information becomes unclear. Information leading to *source confusion* can come from conversations, newspaper articles or television. In 1974, Australian psychologist and researcher Donald Thomson was questioned by police as a suspect in a rape case, as he matched the description provided by the rape victim. But Thomson had an alibi. Incredibly, at the time of the rape, he was doing a live television interview about the fallibility of eyewitness testimony. The victim had been watching Thomson on TV just prior to the rape, and had confused her memory of Thompson with that of the rapist.

Not only can the wrong person be incorporated into the memory of an existing event, but whole events that did not occur at all can be incorporated into memory. By using suggestive techniques, including leading questioning and encouraging visualization of the events, researchers are able to implant false

& Garry, 2006 *Event plausibility does not determine children's false memories.* Memory, 14, 937–951; Laney, C., & Takarangi, M. K. T. 2013. *False memories for aggressive acts.* Acta Psychologica, 143, 227–234; Shaw, J. & Porter, S. 2015 *Constructing Rich False Memories of Committing Crime* (2015) Psychological Science, Vol. 26(3) 291–301

memories of events that never occurred into the minds of participants, including tipping a punch bowl on a parent of the bride at a wedding,[20] being the victim of a serious animal attack[21], cheating,[22] having a ride in a hot air balloon[23] and committing assault[24].

Research[25] has also shown that *false* memories are essentially indistinguishable from accurate memories, both from a psychological and a physiological perspective: neuroscientists cannot distinguish the brain activity of people who are recounting accurate memories from false ones.

The implications for the legal system are profound and far reaching: eyewitness evidence can be tainted during the process of taking statements, and can get corrupted by information that the witness encounters between the time of the event and the time they provide a statement to police or testify in court. 'Memory evidence is easily distorted' and 'should be treated in similar ways to biological evidence; protected from any distorting or contaminating influence at every step of the judicial process'[26] according to memory researcher Deryn Strange. The lead detective on the Ronald Cotton case, Mike Gauldin, agrees, 'law enforcement wasn't schooled in memory. We weren't schooled in protecting memory, treating it like a crime scene,

20. Hyman, Husband, & Billings, 1995 *False memories of childhood experiences*. Applied Cognitive Psychology, 9, 181–197;
21. Porter, Yuille, & Lehman, 1999 *The nature of real, implanted, and fabricated memories for emotional childhood events: Implications for the recovered memory debate*. Law and Human Behavior, 23, 517–537
22. Russano, M. B., Meissner, C. A., Narchet, F. M., & Kassin, S. M. (2005). *Investigating true and false confessions within a novel experimental paradigm*. Psychological Science, 16, 481–486
23. Strange, Sutherland, & Garry, 2006 *Event plausibility does not determine children's false memories*. Memory, 14, 937–951
24. Shaw, J. & Porter, S. 2015 *Constructing Rich False Memories of Committing Crime* (2015) Psychological Science, Vol. 26(3) 291 –301
25. For a review see Bernstein, D. M. & Loftus, E. F. *How to tell if a particular memory is true of false*, Perspectives in Psychological Science 2009, Vol 4, No. 4 pp 370-374 ; see also Brandon, S. et al. *Recovered memories of childhood sexual abuse: implications for clinical practice*, British Journal of Psychiatry, April 98, p. 304
26. At the 11th International Chamber of Commerce (ICC) New York *Conference on International Arbitration* on September 14, 2016.

where you're very careful and methodical about what you do and how you use it.'[27]

Researchers continue to carry out experiments that examine the factors that improve or worsen the accuracy of memories.[28] Indeed, the protocols of many police departments have changed[29], working with memory experts to create optimal procedures for attaining eyewitness evidence that is as accurate as possible. Correct procedures for taking eyewitness statements do not guarantee accuracy, but they can *increase the likelihood* that the eyewitness evidence is accurate.

Eyewitness evidence plays a very important role in our justice system. We therefore need to be careful in how we process it and how we assess it. 'We need eyewitnesses. I mean, if we couldn't convict based on an eyewitness, that's giving a lot of comfort to criminals' said researcher Gary Wells. 'We have no choice. We have to find ways to make this evidence better.'[30]

---

27. *60 minutes* CBS, Eyewitness: how accurate is visual memory March 6 2009
28. for a review see e.g. Nash, R. A., Hanczakowski, M., & Mazzoni, G. (2015). *Eyewitness testimony*. In J. D. Wright (Ed.), International encyclopedia of the social and behavioral sciences (2nd ed.) (Vol. 8, pp. 642-649). Oxford: Elsevier.
29. e.g. Tudor-Owen & Scott, J *Interviewing Witnesses in Australia*, 2016 pp 74-86; *Eyewitness Evidence: A Trainers Manual for Law Enforcement*, Department of Justice Response Center 2003; *A National Survey of Eyewitness Identification Procedures in Law Enforcement Agencies* Police Executive Research Forum 2013
30. 60 minutes, CBS, Eyewitness: how accurate is visual memory March 6 2009

Chapter 13

MEMORIES OF A KING

I was down at the Winchelsea fish and chip shop one Friday night my kids went into the shop to wait for our order. Robbie was in there with his kids. He saw my kids come in and looked out the window and saw me, he came out. He stood beside my driver's side door window. We were talking away, I don't remember what about. But he seemed down in the dumps. Then Cindy pulled up, she got out of her car and said hello Greg and Robbie. I said hello Cindy, Robbie said nothing. I looked at Robbie and said I have to say hello, he said no you don't and got very angry. I said come on Robbie you have to move on. He said move on how, I've got nothing. Then he said. NOBODY DOES THAT TO ME AND GETS AWAY WITH IT, ITS ALL HER FAULT. I said what is. He said take that sports pack car I paid $30,000 for. SHE WANTED IT. And they are fucking driving it. Look what I'm driving the fucking shit one. Then he started on about the house and said that she wanted the best of every thing and we couldn't afford it. Now it looks like she wants to marry that fucking dick head. There is no way I'm going to let him and her and the kids fucking live in my house together and I have to pay for it. Also pay fucking maintenance for the kids no way. Then he said I'M GOING TO PAY HER BACK BIG TIME. I asked him how he then said. I'LL TAKE AWAY THE MOST IMPORTANT THING THAT MEANS TO HER. Then I asked him what's that Robbie. He then nodded his head towards the fish and chip shop window, where the kids were standing with Cindy and my kids. I then said what the kids HE SAID YES. I asked him what would you do, would you take them away or something. HE THEN JUST STARED

AT ME IN MY EYES AND SAID [KILL THEM] I said bullshit that's your own flesh and blood Robbie, He said so I hate them. I said you would go to jail. He said no I wont I will kill myself before it gets to that. Then I asked him how, he said it would be close by; I said what, he said an accident involving a dam where I survive and the kids don't. He then said it would be on a special day I asked him what day. He said something like fathers day so every body would remember it when it was father's day. And I was the last one to have them for the last time NOT HER. THEN EVERY FATHERS DAY SHE WOULD SUFFER FOR THE REST OF HER LIFE. Then I said you don't even dream of that Robbie. Nothing was said my kids started to come out of the shop and then I said to him you deserve to get caught. Then we went home. I told my wife about the conversation, We didn't do anything about it because we thought he was only bull shitting like he did a fair bit.

This is the signed statement of Greg King, outlining a conversation with Robert Farquharson outside the Winchelsea fish 'n chip shop a few months before Farquharson drove the three boys into the dam.

King and Farquharson were friends who had worked together for the council, and socialized at the local footy club and at the pub. King was now working as a school bus driver and had a young family of his own. Upon hearing of the death of the three Farquharson boys, King became very distressed.[1] For the following days, he was crying constantly, wracked by his conscience, struggling to remember the details of the conversation he had with Farquharson out the front of the fish 'n chip shop, that he thought may be linked to the boy's deaths.[2]
King was having nightmares and waking visions of the deaths.[3] In these visions, Robert Farquharson was responsible for the deaths.[4] He was guilty. In these visions, Farquharson was telling King of his plans to kill the children in order to hurt Cindy.[5] King

1. Trial 1 p1383
2. Trial 1 p1400
3. Trial 1 p1400
4. Trial 1 p 1399
5. Trial 1 p1400

was not sleeping due to the nightmares and could not control the waking visions.[6]

Seeing the distressed state of King during the week, his boss, an ex-policeman, thought that King may have some relevant information and contacted police[7], who contacted King. Greg King made his first statement to police five days after the deaths, alleging that Farquharson had told him Cindy 'was going to pay, big time' and that 'I'll take away the most important thing that means to her.'

King continued to have nightmares and waking visions,[8] and three days later he returned to the police to add to his statement. When Farquharson said he would take away the most important thing to her, King added, he had nodded his head toward the fish 'n chip shop where the children were, and that 'I have a recollection that at the same meeting something was said by Robert about a dream – an accident – he got out and the kids don't.'

Whilst making these two statements, King explained that he was struggling to recall the details of the conversation, as 'I was under too much stress, I was traumatized',[9] telling police that 'it has been going over and over in my head',[10] 'I can't put it all together',[11] 'there is so much going on in my head',[12] 'it's coming back to me in bits and pieces',[13] 'I ask the question every day, what's he told me?'[14]

The police asked King to wear a wire, and confront Farquharson with the details of what was said at the fish 'n chip shop, so they could monitor Farquharson's response. Eleven days after the deaths of the boys, King confronted Farquharson, reminding him of his pledge to 'pay back' Cindy 'big time'.

---

6. Trial 1 p1400
7. Trial 1 p1383
8. Trial 1 p1400
9. Trial 1 p1415
10. Trial 1 p1447
11. Trial 1 p1415
12. Trial 1 p1415
13. Trial 1 p1415
14. Norris, M. *On Fathers Day* kindle location 2803

Farquharson agreed that he had made angry comments about Cindy and Stephen Moules, but said they were 'just a figure speech of me being angry' and that he meant that he was determined to show Cindy that he could make a success of himself, to make her regret leaving him. Farquharson protested against any relation between his comments and what had happened to the boys, and vehemently proclaimed his innocence.

Four weeks later, King was asked to confront Farquharson with more details of the conversation. King was again wired up to make a second secret recording and again confronted Farquharson with the 'pay back' comment. Again Farquharson claimed that it was not a threat and had nothing to do with the death of the boys. Farquharson expressed his dismay that King thought he could have killed them, again emphatically denying it. King then confronted him with the alleged comment that referenced the children, putting to Farquharson that he had said he would 'take away the most important thing that meant to her', to which Farquharson protested 'Not that. Not that. No way known. No not that. I didn't mean anything like that.' King went further 'Rob, ya said to me... Funny what you say about dreams, I have an accident, and survive it, and they don't' to which Farquharson again responded with vigour 'I never, never said that. I never said that... No, no. no, you're getting it all wrong, you're getting it all twisted'.

Farquharson did say he was angry at the time, but that it was early in the break up and that things had got better after that. He said that he was mainly angry about Stephen Moules 'I was just pissed off that I had this really good car and that cunt was driving it, that is what I was angry about'. He also said that he was angry with the way Moules had spoken to Jai, the eldest boy. He said that King had 'misinterpreted the anger and how it's placed', and that it was 'just idle bullshit talk of being upset.'

After that conversation, during his recorded debrief, King told police 'I don't know. I don't know. I keep telling myself, ever since this happened, am I right or am I wrong? I mean I've gotta know... I'm only 80% sure...am I right or am I wrong?'

The lead investigator, Detective Clanchy, encouraged King to continue trying to recall the details of the conversation and to jot down notes of what he could recall, as memories came back to him. Clanchy phoned him intermittently to check on his progress. Over the next few weeks, as he continued to have nightmares and waking visions of the deaths of the children, King made several jotted notes and then 'put it all together'[15] into a statement that he typed on his computer. 'I started typing it, but the conversation is all coming back in bits and pieces after that last taping'[16] 'I knew he'd done it, right, so I put it all together and put it in the way he said it...I had a lot going around my head so I put it together.'[17] King was getting very little sleep as he tried to get the conversation accurate in his head 'I was trying. I was distressed, traumatised. I was scared'.[18] King's final statement was completed in early December, three months after his first statement and 5-6 months after the conversation.

King was now claiming that Farquharson had told him of his plan to kill his children in full detail, including the exact date that it would occur, how he would do it, and how he would make it look like an accident. King also became increasingly confident in his recollection since the last secret taping on 13 October, stating that 'after that conversation, that last taping, I was 100 per cent sure'.[19]

How should the statements of Greg King be assessed in light of what is known about memory?

Memory for what was said during conversations is astonishingly poor. The inability to recall *verbatim* details of conversations has been consistently demonstrated[20] over many decades. In 1974, for example, research[21] showed that 80 seconds after hearing short conversations, participants are unable to

---

15. Trial 2 p 207
16. Trial 1 p1474
17. Trial 2 p203-204
18. Trial 1 p1393
19. Trial 1 p1394
20. e.g. Ackerman, 1982; Bransford & Franks, 1971; Brewer, 1977; Jarvella & Collas, 1974; Kemper, 1980; Sachs, 1967, 1974; Wanner, 1974; Miller, deWinstanley, & Carey, 1996; Ross & Sicoly, 1979; Stafford, Burggraf, & Sharkey, 1987; Stafford & Daly, 1984; Stafford et al., 1989

distinguish original sentences from paraphrases that capture the meaning but use different wording. Unless memory techniques are employed,[22] as with actors learning scripts, verbatim memory for conversations lasts only a matter of seconds.[23] Instead, 'sentences are quickly transformed into an underlying abstract meaning and... the original surface structure is lost'.[24] People remember the *gist* of what was said, but do not remember the *actual sentences* used. This understanding of memory for conversations is old,[25] it has been extensively researched and it is 'one of the most robust findings in psycholinguistics'.[26]

Memories for conversation are more a case of 'she said *something like....*' than 'she said... *exactly these words*'. Any recall of actual sentences from conversations is done by reconstructing what was said from the remembered gist. When conversations are purportedly recalled verbatim the specific words are, with few exceptions, false memories. We can safely say that the particular sentences spoken in the conversation according to Greg King's statement are not accurate.

There is an exception that should be considered here. Key words[27] may be recalled, while figures of speech, jokes, and insults[28] may also stick in the mind. Gist memories may then be

---

21. Sachs, J. S. *Memory in Reading and Listening to Discourse*, 2 MEMORY & COGNOrrON 95, 97-98 (1974).
22. e.g. Noice, H. *Effects of Rote Versus Gist Strategy on the Verbatim Retention Of Theatrical Scripts,* Appl. Cognit. Psychol., 7: 75–84
23. see also Toglia, M. P. Shlechter, T. M. and Chevalier, D. S. *Memory for directly and indirectly experienced events* Applied Cognitive Psychology, 1992 6 (4), 293–306;
24. Holtgraves, T. Memory & Cognition (2008) 36: 361.
25. Binet and Henri 1894 as translated in Nicolas, S. et al. Consciousness and Cognition 20 (2011) 399–400; see also Bartlett, F. C. (1932). *Remembering: A study in experimental and social psychology.* New York, NY, US: Cambridge University Press.
26. Loebell, H., & Bock, K. (2003). Structural Priming across Languages. Linguistics, 41, 791-824
27. e.g. Hjelmqvist & Gidlund *Free recall of conversations.* 1985 Text, 5, 169-185; Hjelmqvist, E. *Recognition memory for utterances in conversation*, Scandinavian Journal of Psychology, 1989, 30, 168-176
28. Keenan, J. M., MacWhinney, B., & Mayhew, D. (1977). Pragmatics in memory: A study of natural conversion. *Journal of Verbal Learning & Verbal Behavior, 16*(5), 549-560; MacWhinney, B., Keenan, J.M. & Reinke, P. Mem Cogn (1982) 10: 308.

used to reconstruct sentences based around the keywords.[29] A sentence such as 'I will kill them', or at least the key-word 'kill', may well be such a case. Similarly, 'I hate them' may stick in the mind when it is a father referring to his children. However, in King's case he did forget; these words did not stick in his mind. He did not recall them at all when giving his first statement. He did not recall them when giving his second statement. It 'came back to him' during the following months. Yet evidence shows that we tend to remember fewer and fewer details of an event as time passes,[30] not more, and memories for conversations are no exception.[31] There is no research that suggests that memories are forgotten and then accurately recalled later in 'bits and pieces', as Greg King described.

What about memories that are repressed due to trauma? Doesn't that occur? Maybe King had repressed the memory and it came back to him later?

Memory repression was a notion invented by Sigmund Freud, who was not a scientist.[32] Psychoanalysis is pseudo-science[33] and Richard Feynman referred to psycho-analysts as 'witch doctors'. Freud was a fraud[34] and 'there is literally nothing to be said, scientifically or therapeutically, to the advantage of the entire Freudian system or any of its component dogmas'.[35] The

---

29. e.g. Hjelmqvist & Gidlund *Free recall of conversations*. 1985 Text, 5, 169-185; Hjelmquist, E. *Recognition memory for utterances in conversation*, Scandinavian Journal of Psychology, 1989, 30, 168-176
30. e.g. Peterson and Peterson 1959; Berman M G, Jonides J, Lewis R. *In search of decay in verbal short-term memory* Exp Psychol Learn Mem Cogn. 2009 Mar;35(2):317-33.The issue of whether time alone, or interference, is the dominant factor in memories becoming worse with time is not addressed in this book. This is an ongoing question that does not affect the fact that memories tend to get worse rather than better over time.
31. Stafford, Burggraf, & Sharkey *Conversational Memory The Effects of Time, Recall, Mode, and Memory Expectancies on Remembrances of Natural Conversations* 1987 Human Communication Research 14(2) ; Kintsch & Bates 1977
32. Crews, F. *The verdict on Freud* Psychological Science March 1, 1996 and references therein; Pomeroy, R. *Why Freud Was Not a Scientist* Realclearscience, April 23, 2015
33. e.g. Derksen, A.A. Journal for General Philosophy of Science (2001) 32: 329.
34. see e.g. Sulloway, F. *Reassessing Freud's Case Histories* 1991 ISIS, 82 pp. 245-275
35. Crews, F. *The verdict on Freud* Psychological Science March 1, 1996

vast majority of people who experience traumatic events can recall them[36,37] and research now centres more on memory *suppression*[38], whereby victims of trauma attempt to push the memories out of their consciousness.

It remains an ongoing debate as to whether memory repression has validity.[39] This debate was the centre of what are now called the 'memory wars' between researchers and therapists[40] during the 1990s, largely centered on memories of child abuse that were repressed and then 'recalled' many years later during therapy. During the 1980s and 1990s, a spate of false accusations of satanic ritual child abuse at day-care centers resulted in a number of convictions, based on recalled memories that purportedly had been repressed. Therapists at the time were using 'memory recovery' techniques such as guided imagery to promote recall of their patient's lost memories, but these are precisely the types of activities that lead to false memories.[41] There is more scientific evidence for false memory creation than for memory repression.[42]

Some of these recalled memories were so extreme, including systematic ritualised satanic abuse, gross acts of sexual perversion, cannibalism, and human and animal sacrifice on massive scales with no corroborating evidence, that in some cases it defied belief that prosecutions were made. However the

---

36. e.g. McNally RJ. *Remembering Trauma* Cambridge, MA: Belknap Press/Harvard University Press; 2003
37. Pope HG Jr, Oliva PS, Hudson JI. *The scientific status of repressed memories*. In: Faigman DL, Kaye DH, Saks MJ, Sanders J, eds. Modern Scientific Evidence The Law and Science of Expert Testimony V 1 St Paul, MN: West Publishing; 1999 p115
38. e.g. Hulbert. J, Henson R. *& Anderson, M Inducing amnesia through systemic suppression 2016 Nature Communications 7, 11003*
39. e.g. Nally, RJ *Dispelling confusion about traumatic dissociative amnesia.".* Mayo Clinic Proceedings. 2007 **82** (9): 1083–90.
40. Some researchers did advocate for repression but it was mainly therapists.
41. e.g. Gary M., Manning C., Loftus E. & Sherman S. *Imagination Inflation: Imagining a Childhood Event Inflates Confidence that it Occurred* Psychonomic Bulletin & Review 1996, 3 (2), 208-214;
42. e.g. McNally, R. J. *Remembering Trauma* 2005 Harvard University Press; French, C *Explainer: what are false memories?* in The Conversation Oct 22 2015; McNally RJ *Searching for repressed memory* 2012 Nebr Symp Motiv 58:121-47.

community, fuelled by a rampant, unrelenting media,[43] were outraged and wanted retribution. This 'satanic panic' spread[44] through the U.S., U.K.,[45] Australia,[46] New Zealand,[47] Canada[48] and Italy[49] amongst other places and resulted in miscarriages of justice, and more commonly the destruction of families and lives resulting from false memories induced by misguided, well-meaning therapists.

Regardless of the debate surrounding repression of traumatic memories, the conversation at the fish 'n chip shop was not a traumatic event for Greg King at the time it occurred, nor did it seem particularly important. King had not taken Farquharson's statements seriously.[50] So there was no reason for King to dissociate or to suppress or even repress these memories. King believed that Farquharson was 'talkin' shit like he used to a fair bit',[51] 'I just thought he was talking crap'.[52]

This initial reaction of King seems incongruous with his final statement, in which Farquharson had told him of a detailed plan to kill his own children. Does the Australian vernacular 'talkin shit' apply to situations where a person says that they hate their children and are planning to kill them, and then provides a detailed plan of how and when it will happen?

Memory researchers advise looking for corroborating evidence when memories are used as evidence.[53] King claimed

43. see e.g. Romana, A, *The History of Satanic Panic in the US-and why it is not over yet*. Oct 30, 2016, Vox
44. e.g. Grometstein, R. *Wrongful Conviction and the Moral Panic About Organized Child Abuse: National and International Perspectives* 2006 Wrongful Conviction: International Perspectives on Miscarriages of Justice, ed. C. Huff and M. Kilias, Temple University Press.
45. e.g. *Miscarriage of Memory – Historic Abuse Cases: A Dilemma for the Legal System* 2010 Eds William Burgoyne and Norman Brand, BFMS
46. e.g. Wood, Justice R. *Royal Commission into the New South Wales Police Service* 1997
47. e.g. Hood, L. *A City Possessed: The Christchurch Civic Creche Case* 2001 Longacre Press
48. e.g. *Settlement details released for Sask. couple accused of child abuse*. CBC News. 19/11/2004
49. e.g. Lucia Bellaspiga, *Il caso. Pedofilia, assolti dopo 16 anni*, Avvenire, 5 Dec 2014
50. Trial 2 pp3089, 3090
51. Trial 2 p3087
52. Trial 1 p1476

that he had told his wife, Mary, about the conversation when he arrived home from the fish 'n chip shop, and that they had discussed it in detail.[54] Yet his wife gave evidence that she had no recollection of such a conversation.[55] If King had said anything to his wife that night, it had not made a lasting impression.

---

53. E.g. Shaw, J. *The Memory Illusion* Kindle Location 3704
54. Committal Hearing p187
55. Mary King evidence in Trial 2 p3241-3246

Chapter 14

THE GIST OF IT

Could Greg King's mind so severely distort the details of the conversation to create false memories that are so damning to Farquharson? Could research about false memories provide a plausible explanation for how his statement, and presumably his memories, evolved so dramatically from the first statement to the last?

Just like photographs or television images can be confused with being memories, imagined events can be confused for real ones.[1] When implanting false memories in her studies, Julia Shaw[2] asks participants to visualize an event, to close their eyes and imagine what the event would look like, accessing their imagination rather than their memories. She encourages them to continue to visualize the event at home, before returning for the next session. The goal is to create source confusion, whereby the imagined event becomes confused with a memory.

Was Greg King remembering the conversation, or the waking visions which so tormented him and which he was unable to control?

Research[3] shows that people with higher imagery abilities are

---

1. see also Garry, Maryanne; Polaschek, Devon L.L. (2000). "Imagination and memory". *Current Directions in Psychological Science.* **9** (1): 6–10
2. see Shaw, Julia. The Memory Illusion: Remembering, Forgetting, and the Science of False Memory 2016. Random House
3. e.g. Lee, Kerry (2004). "Age, Neuropsychological, and Social Cognitive Measures as Predictors of Individual Differences in Susceptibility to the Misinformation Effect". *Applied Cognitive Psychology.* **18** (8): 997–1019; Dobson, M., & Markham, R., M;

more susceptible to source confusion and the misinformation effect, and therefore the creation of false memories, than those with lower imagery abilities. Greg King's waking visions indicate that he may be particularly prone to incorporating new information into his memories.

There are other aspects in Greg King's process of recollection that should also be considered in terms of the evolution of his statement.

Firstly, long time lapses between events and their recall not only decrease the accuracy with which the events are remembered, they also increase the rate of source confusion and of false memories associated with the events.[4]

Secondly, during the period that King was trying to recall the details of the conversation, he already believed that Farquharson was guilty. King 'knew he'd done it'.[5] This provided a *schema* for the events, an outline of what must have occurred in the planning and execution of the presumed murder. False memories are more likely to occur when they fit within an already existent *schema* of what is believed.[6] In fact, false memories that fit within a schema may be *more* readily 'remembered' than true memories that fall outside the schema.[7] This is closely related to the cognitive biases that were addressed earlier in the book, and the tendency to accept information that is consistent with already held beliefs, but reject information that contradicts those beliefs. Just like other information that our brains process, our memories are strongly influenced by motivational biases.[8]

Markham, R (1993). "Imagery ability and source monitoring: implications for the eyewitness memory". *British Journal of Psychology*.

4. Payne .D.G.,Elie C,.].,Blackwell J ,& Neuschatz, J.S *Memory Illusions: Recalling, recognizing, and recollecting events that never occurred.* 1996 Journal of Memory and Language, 35, 261-285; McDermott, K. B. *The persistence of false memories in list recall* 1996 New Haven CT, Yale University Press
5. Trial 2 p203
6. e.g. Brewer W. & Hay, A. *Reconstructive Recall of Linguistic Style*, 1984 23 J. Verbal Learning & Verbal Behav. 237; Hyman, I. E., & Pentland, J. 1996. The role of mental imagery in the creation of false childhood memories. Journal of Memory and Language, 35, 101–117
7. Brainerd, C. J., & Reyna, V. F. (1998) *When things that were never experienced are easier to "remember" than things that were.* Psychological Science, 9, 484-489

A further issue occurs when police and lawyers actively try to 'coax witnesses to assent to things that they cannot clearly remember',[9] encouraging them to 'go beyond what they explicitly remember and recollect things that could or should have happened to them on the basis of belief'[10]. When witnesses do not have clear recollections of details, they are *encouraged* to fill in the gaps, and as above, they will tend to do so in a manner that fits within their beliefs, beliefs that can be re-enforced and encouraged by the police and/or lawyers.

Was King's initially uncertain belief in Farquharson's guilt given positive reinforcement by the police? Recall that Detective Clanchy had stayed in contact with King, encouraging him to jot down details of the conversation as they 'came back to him', encouraging him to fill in the gaps of the conversation that he had not been able to recall. What did Clanchy say during these phone calls to King? When asked in trial, neither Clanchy nor King could recall any details of the calls. We have already seen that Clanchy provided Professor Naughton with police files that purported to prove guilt, and King was aware that the police believed, or at least strongly suspected, that Farquharson was guilty.

As with forensic evidence, influence and biases can have subtle effects on memory evidence. In one study,[11] participants who were asked to identify a culprit in a mock crime were more likely to select a particular person from a line-up if they were told that person had confessed, regardless of whether it was the culprit. If courts are going to rely on memory evidence, then all interactions with witnesses need to be recorded, so that any potential influence can be assessed. If this was eyewitness

---

8. e.g. Neisser, U. *John Dean's Memory*, 2000 in Memory Observed: Remembering In Natural Contexts 263   Neisser, U & Hyman, I. Jr., eds., 2d ed..
9. Brainerd, C. J., & Reyna, V. F. (1998) *When things that were never experienced are easier to "remember" than things that were*. Psychological Science, 9, 484-489
10. Brainerd, C. J., & Reyna, V. F. (1998) *When things that were never experienced are easier to "remember" than things that were*. Psychological Science, 9, 484-489
11. Lisa E. Hasel, Saul M. Kassin *On the presumption of evidentiary independence: can confessions corrupt eyewitness identifications?* Psychol Sci. 2009 Jan; 20(1): 122–126.

identification memory evidence, the interactions between Clanchy and King would be considered as polluting the evidence. The same reasoning should apply to memories for conversation.

Rapport building is an effective interviewing tool[12] and is used extensively, for good reason: psychologists agree that rapport encourages full and honest accounts of events from witnesses.[13] Detective Sergeant Clanchy understood this, and he built strong rapport with the witnesses. Greg King referred to Clanchy as 'Gerard' and even 'Gerry' from the witness stand, displaying an air of familiarity. However, rapport building also runs the danger of influencing witnesses.[14] According to research, the combination of rapport building and motivated reasoning is particularly powerful in influencing witness statements,[15] and people in authoritative positions such as police are particularly influential[16].

Personality traits can also influence the way that words, and presumably conversations, are remembered. People with aggressive personality traits have a tendency[17,18] to interpret

---

12. Clarke, C, Milne, B & Bull, R 2011, 'Interviewing suspects of crime: the impact of PEACE training, supervision and the presence of a legal advisor', *Journal of Investigative Psychology and Offender Profiling*, vol. 8, no. 2, pp. 149-162; Oxburgh, G & Ost, J 2011, 'The use and efficacy of empathy in police interviews with suspects of sexual offences', *Journal of Investigative Psychology and Offender Profiling*, vol. 8, no. 2, pp. 178-188; Walsh, D & Milne, B 2008, 'Keeping the PEACE? A study of investigative interviewing practices in the public sector', *Legal and Criminological Psychology*, vol. 13, no. 1, pp. 39-57; Dando, C, Wilcock, R & Milne, B 2008, 'The cognitive interview: inexperienced police officers' perceptions of their witness/victim interviewing practices', *Legal and Criminological Psychology*, vol. 13, no. 1, pp. 59-70.
13. Centre for Investigative Skills. (2004). Practical guide to investigative interviewing (4th ed.). published by CENTREX (now the National Policing Improvement Agency in England and Wales); B Milne, G Shaw, R Bull - Applying psychology to criminal justice, 2007
14. e.g. Wright, D. Nash., R. & Wade, K. *Encouraging eyewitnesses to falsely corroborate allegations: effects of rapport-building and incriminating evidence*, Psychology, Crime & Law, 2015Vol. 21, No. 7, 648–660
15. ibid
16. e.g. Shawyer, A. Milne, B., Ball, R. *Investigative Interviewing in the U.K.* in International Developments in Investigative Interviewing eds Tom Williamson, Becky Milne, Stephen Savage 2013 Routledge
17. Nasby, W., Hayden, B., & DePaulo, B. M. 1980 *Attributional bias among aggressive boys*

ambiguous words and behaviours as having a hostile intent, referred to as *hostile attribution bias*. The fact that such biases extend to our memories highlights the intimate link between our memories and ourselves.

Greg King often got into fights after drinking.[19] A Swedish study[20] has shown that people who suppress feelings of anger when they are sober are disposed to fight when they are drunk. Could Greg King have aggressive personality traits? Did this bias him towards remembering and interpreting the conversation at the fish 'n chip shop in a violent manner?

Finally, a relevant general problem is that witnesses are often asked to repeat their evidence multiple times during police interviews, interviews with lawyers, committal hearings and trials, not to mention the repetition of the story to family and friends. 'Repeatedly questioning a witness tends to increase their confidence in both correct and mistaken answers'.[21] Repeated recollections strengthen memories, whether they are true or false.[22] Greg King retold this story many times over a period

---

to interpret unambiguous social stimuli as displays of hostility. Journal of Abnormal Psychology, 89(3), 459; Dodge, K. A. 1980 *Social cognition and children's aggressive behavior*. Child Development, 162-170; Dodge, K. A. 2006 *Translational science in action: Hostile attributional style and the development of aggressive behavior problems* Development and Psychopathology, 18(03), 791-814.
18. Takarangi, M. Polaschek, D. Hignett, A. & Garry, M. *Chronic and Temporary Aggression Causes Hostile False Memories for Ambiguous Information* 2008, Applied Cognitive Psychology 22(1):39 – 49; see also Copello & Tata, 1990; Tiedens, 2001; Kirsh and Olczak 2002
19. Trial 2 Voir Dire p. 193
20. Norström, T. and Pape, H. *Alcohol, suppressed anger and violence*. 2010 Addiction, 105: 1580–1586.
21. Professor Tim Valentine from the University of London, quoted in French C. *False memories of sexual abuse lead to terrible miscarriages of justice*, 25 November 2010, The Guardian
22. see also e.g. Register, P.A., & Kihlstrom, J.F. *Hypnosis and interrogative suggestibility* 1988. Personality and Individual Differences, 9, 549-558; Roediger, H. L., Jacoby, J.D., & McDermott, K. B *Misinformation effects in recall: Creating false memories through repeated retrieval* Journal of Memory and Language 1996 35, 300-318; Henkel, L. A. *Erroneous memories arising from repeated attempts to remember* 2004 Journal of Memory and Language, 50, 26-46.

during which he significantly increased his level of certainty in his memory of the conversation.

Despite the unreliable nature of Greg King's memory evidence in terms of how and when it was retrieved, several factors potentially made it appear far more compelling than it warranted.

Firstly, the majority of people believe that memory *does* work like a video recorder,[23] and over-estimate the abilities of their own memories,[24] elevating their expectations of the memories of witnesses. People believe that they only forget details when they are just not trying hard enough, but that witnesses are motivated to recall accurate details.[25] The reality of how memory works is lost on us because when we update our memories, it is not something we notice, we just think that the new memory is the original 'video tape'. So King's ability to 'see' and 'hear' the conversation that occurred several months earlier may seem more credible to a jury than is suggested by research.

This is not to say that people accepted Greg King's final 'extreme' version of the conversation. The judge in the second trial, Lex Lazry, explicitly stated that he was 'not satisfied beyond reasonable doubt' that King's third, extreme, version of the conversation 'was actually said ... in the terms that he described.'[26]

It seems that it was the first version of King's statement that was more generally accepted, and that played a role in the outcome of the case. The Court of Appeal stated that 'the version of the Mr King conversation which the applicant [Farquharson] accepted was itself very significant because it disclosed — at a time relevantly proximate to the death of the children — the intensity of the applicant's animosity towards Ms Gambino and,

---

23. e.g. Simons DJ, Chabris CF (2011) What People Believe about How Memory Works: A Representative Survey of the U.S. Population. PLoS ONE 6(8): e22757.
24. e.g. Kornell, Nate & Bjork, Robert A. (2009). A stability bias in human memory: Overestimating remembering and underestimating learning. _Journal of Experimental Psychology: General_ 138 (4):449-468.
25. S Kassam, Karim & T Gilbert, Daniel & Swencionis, Jillian & Wilson, Timothy. (2009). *Misconceptions of Memory The Scooter Libby Effect*. Psychological science. 20. 551-2.
26. R v Farquharson [2010] VSC 462 Lasry sentencing

in particular, the applicant's use of language conveying an intention to seek revenge.'[27]

Yet Farquharson did not accept that he had conveyed an intention of seeking revenge. He had denied that as the *gist* of the conversation. The Court of Appeal seems to be referencing the particular language used by King, rather than the gist. It becomes apparent in what the Court of Appeal says next that this is precisely what they have done: 'put another way, what was most important about Mr King's evidence was the extent to which it was confirmed by the applicant, both in the covertly-recorded conversations and in his evidence at the trial. Given the difficulties of recollection, which were such a prominent feature of the applicant's answers under cross-examination, that confirmation was capable of being viewed as adding strength to the prosecution case. So, too, was the implausibility of the applicant's attempts to give a benign explanation for his threat to "pay her back big time"'.[28]

The Court of Appeal had tested Farquharson's version of the gist against the specific wording 'pay her back big time'. However, these specific words were created by King to reflect his memory of the gist of the conversation. So of course they are a better reflection of King's version of the gist than they are of Farquharson's version. If Greg King's memory of verbatim words could be relied upon, then indeed Farquharson's version of the gist would seem less plausible than King's. But it cannot. What if Farquharson had actually said 'I'll show her!' or 'I am going to make her regret it'? Such a statement is even more ambiguous and could be interpreted as meaning *pay her back* in terms of taking revenge, i.e. King's version of the gist. Or it could just as easily be interpreted as *She is going to regret leaving me for that dickhead Moules*, Farquharson's version of the gist.

Indeed, it is Farquharson's version of the gist that has some corroborating evidence. At the time, Farquharson's counsellor Peter Popko had been encouraging him to focus on his future, on

---

27. Farquharson v The Queen [2012] VSCA 296 p11
28. ibid

making something of his own life.²⁹ 'Peter was directing me as a single man, or as a single parent... and it was me not thinking of me all the time. I never thought of me, everything was about the kids, everything. He said to me "Rob, you've got to think about you"'. What if Farquharson's rant at the Fish n Chip shop simply incorporated this advice in the most straight forward manner? He was expressing that he had been thinking about how to make something of himself? Maybe he gained extra motivation for following Popko's advice by imagining himself making Cindy have regrets about leaving him for his bitter rival Moules?

Not only did the Court of Appeal resolve the dispute of which version of the gist was more likely by referencing a particular verbatim sentence that had been recalled by King, they explicitly commented on the Farquharson's 'difficulties of recollection',[30] as though he should have been able to 'recall' sentences, as did King. Farquharson could not be expected to deny the use of specific words because he could not be expected to recall the conversation *verbatim*. Farquharson *had* recalled the conversation and presented his version of the gist. The fact that King recreated specific sentences that reflected his recollection of the gist should not add credibility to King's version of the gist over Farquharson's.

The second reason that King's evidence made an impact in the case is that he seems to have believed these memories, whether they were true or false. As false memories cannot be distinguished from true ones,[31] King made for a determined witness.

Thirdly, King was a friend of Farquharson, so 'why would he lie?' Of course, if King really had formed false memories, then in his mind he was not lying, he was telling the 'truth' as he knew it. He was doing the right thing.

---

29. Trial 2: Popko testified that part of his role was to 'establish future goals' (p 2828) and that by June 'he seemed to be less preoccupied with going over what had happened in the past and more focused on future goals and future prospects' (p 2837).
30. Farquharson v The Queen [2012] VSCA 296 p11
31. Or at the least false beliefs as explained in the previous chapter.

Don't get me wrong, Greg King's recollection of a conversation with Robert Farquharson out the front of the fish' n chip is relevant evidence in the case. The question is how to interpret the evidence, which of his versions to consider, and how much weight to give it. At its best, when provided immediately after an event and following strict protocols, memory evidence can be strong,[32] although flaws in memory mean that it needs to be treated with appropriate caution. The long time lapses between the conversation and Greg King's recalling of it, the vast changes from the first statement to the last, and the numerous ways that his memories could have become contaminated, mean that there is significant uncertainty as to what was said during the fish 'n' chip shop conversation, and even more uncertainty as to what was in Farquharson's mind at the time. Was Farquharson declaring a murderous intent, an outline of his plans for filicide, or was it just the bluster of a wounded male, whose wife had left him and taken up with another man, trying to salvage some pride and status amongst his peers?

---

32. e.g. Wixted, J & Mickes, L. *Eyewitness Memory Is a Lot More Reliable Than You Think* Scientific American 13 June 2017

CHAPTER 15

A FALSE DAWN

On father's day of 2005, Dawn Waite took her teenage daughter Jessica, and Jessica's friend Samantha on a shopping trip to Melbourne's largest mall. Waite lives in Victoria's south east, and the long homeward route took them along the Princes highway. The night was dark by the time they approached Winchelsea, right around the time Robert Farquharson and his three sons were returning from KFC in Geelong.

When Waite saw Farquharson's car being pulled from the dam on the tv news the following night, she recalled a car she had overtaken on the trip back from Melbourne, a car that had been driving erratically. She was sure it must have been Farquharson they had passed, and she said so to Jessica. Jessica, who had been in the front passenger seat, told her mother that she had 'got it wrong',[1] that the car was the wrong colour.[2]

At least, that is Dawn Waite's memory of events. Jessica couldn't remember much of any of this, including seeing the car on the tv news nor her own comments that her mother had got it wrong. Nor could the other passenger, Samantha, recall anything about passing the car.[3] This is understandable, because they were being asked about passing a car, in the dark, on an unremarkable stretch of highway four years earlier. Waite had

1. Trial 2 p54
2. Trial 2 p54
3. Trial 2 p87

only come forward after Farquharson won his appeal, so her statement was taken more than four years after the incident.

Waite told police that they passed the Farquharson car that night, and that she had been the last person, other than Robert Farquharson, to have seen the children alive. Her evidence was deemed crucial to Farquharson's conviction in the second trial[4,5,6].

Waite claimed that, as they approached from behind, Farquharson's car was driving slowly, varying his speed,[7] and veering across his lane.[8] As she slowed down, preparing to overtake, the driver in front 'kept on looking out to his right',[9] his 'head kept on turning to the right'.[10] Then 'as I went past the car I noticed that there was a fair-headed boy in the backseat behind the driver'[11] along with at least two other children, and that they 'looked all squashed in the back'[12] seat. Waite repeated it multiple times, the fact that the children were 'squashed in the back seat'.[13] As she continued to drive alongside the car, she also managed to look at the driver, who was 'in his late 30s',[14] 'dark hair',[15] 'clean-shaven',[16] 'caucasian'[17] 'no facial expression at all',[18] 'I only saw his profile because at no time would he make eye contact with me'[19] and he 'kept on looking to the right, but funnily enough not, not

---

4. Media Watch Episode 10, 11 April 2011
5. Little, J. and Tyson, D. *Filicide in Australian Media and Culture In Oxford Research Encyclopedia of Crime and Criminal Justice; Crime, Media, and Popular Culture.* New York: Oxford University Press at p10
6. Farquharson v The Queen [2012] VSCA 296 p7 & p 17
7. Trial 2 p82
8. Trial 2 p25
9. Trial 2 p1615
10. Trial 2 p1615
11. Trial 2 p1616
12. Trial 2 p1621
13. Trial 2 p1662
14. Trial 2 p1617
15. Trial 2 p1617
16. Trial 2 p1617
17. Trial 2 p1617
18. Trial 2 p1620
19. Trial 2 p1617

at me'.[20] She also testified that there was no indication that he was coughing or indisposed.

As she pulled ahead Waite says that she looked back in her rear view mirror and saw Farquharson's car as it came down the overpass, and that it was 'veering right'.[21] Waite was questioned extensively on this, and was very clear that the car 'veered right',[22] it was 'just a smooth movement off to the right',[23] a 'gradual turn to the right, it wasn't sharp or anything, just gradually'.[24]

How much of these memories of Waite should we rely upon? Not much according to memory research. Four years is a long time, and this high profile case had significant media exposure, and was talked about a lot especially in the region where Waite lived. The risk of the misinformation effect and source confusion was very high. Was she describing the man she passed in the car or the man she had seen on tv? And then there are the motivational aspects, with Waite coming forward only after Farquharson won his appeal.

Let us look at some of the details of Waite's memories.

Waite's recollection that she saw the three boys 'squashed up in the back seat' went against the accepted facts of the preceding four years, which is that Jai was in the front, Tyler in the middle in the rear and Bailey was in his baby seat on the rear passenger side. This is how the children always sat, it is how they were seen[25] when leaving Farquharson's sister's house fifteen minutes prior to the car going into the dam, and it was where the children were found when police extracted the car from the dam. Jai in the front, Tyler and Bailey in the back.

During the *voir dire*, Waite herself suggested a possible explanation for the discrepancy, pointing out that 'I saw a photo of three children in the telly and there was a car seat'.[26] However,

---

20. Trial 2 p1619
21. Trial 2 p1625
22. Trial 2 p1622
23. Trial 2 p1647
24. Trial 2 p1647
25. Trial 2 p1583
26. Trial 2 p36

there was *never any photo of the children on telly that showed any child in a car seat*. Dawn Waite had incorporated a car seat,[27] which comes from knowing that this was a car accident, into her memory of what she saw on the television news, 'when the photo was shown up on the screen I thought there was a child in the car seat'.[28] This is a clear case of the misinformation effect.

This image of Jai, Baily and Tyler (left to right) squashed together on a sofa has been widely shown in the media. No image of the boys in a car seat, which was what Dawn Waite recalled seeing on telly, was shown in any media.

Shown above is a photo of the children on a sofa, which was widely shown in the media coverage of the events. Given that Waite incorporated a car seat into her memory of what she saw on telly, could she have, in turn, incorporated the image of the three boys on the sofa, that she saw on telly, into her memory of what she saw in the car? Is this why she has such a vivid memory of three children 'squashed up' in the back seat? With a blond boy on the seat behind the driver? Isn't she describing the picture of the boys squashed up on the sofa, the one she saw on telly?

27. Trial 2 1652
28. Trial 2 1652

Was this again the misinformation effect, a case of source confusion?

This explanation seems more likely than the alternative, which would involve Farquharson leaving his brother-in-law's house with Jai in the front, then stopping somewhere and convincing Jai to move from the front seat to the back seat, climbing over his brothers. Jai would have been reluctant as he liked the front seat, but it is possible that Farquharson convinced him. Then, Jai would have had to climb from the back to the front as the car was sinking, again possible but this would not have been easy. And it would also mean that Farquharson lied about the seating position of the boys, although it is not totally clear why he would lie about that particular aspect if he were guilty, especially if he had been passed by a car as Waite claims, as there would have been a possibility of his lie being exposed.

The issues surrounding the misinformation effect and source confusion in Waite's account are precisely why it is so important to take witness statements early, and why statements made years after events need to be treated with a large amount of caution.

The reliability of four year old memories is not the only thing that baffles me about the importance of Dawn Waite's evidence. Even if she remembers correctly, how does her evidence point to Farquharson's guilt? Waite's description of Farquharson veering to the right fits very well with the defence expert's testimony regarding the path of the car. It fits with the claim that the driver was unconscious, with the car following the slope, veering toward the dam.

There has been some suggestion that Farquharson was driving slowly, and pulling to the left, to allow Waite to pass and to drive ahead, so that the road was clear of any witnesses when he drove into the dam. But Waite stated that she was only 'a few car lengths'[29] ahead when she saw his car veer right. If it was Farquharson that she passed, then he had *not* waited for the road to be clear and his veering off the road *was* witnessed.

Even if Farquharson was driving slowly and had pulled over to

---

29. Trial 2 p.1647

the left of his lane at some stage on his journey, couldn't he have been coughing? Slowing down and pulling toward the left of the road whilst he regained his composure? He always claimed the coughing fit that led to the blackout had not commenced until the overpass, but he was coughing a lot during that period of time. Whilst driving back from Geelong, why wouldn't he have coughed?

And then there was the claim that Farquharson kept 'looking to the right'. How did Waite see inside Farquharson's car as she approached from behind? It was a very dark night. In the pre-trial hearing, she said that she had 'flicked'[30] her high beam headlights on to make sure the driver was aware that she was about to pass, and 'that's when I noticed that there was no adult head in the front seat of the passenger side... there was only one head in the front seat'.[31] However, she could not be sure whether what she had seen on the driver's side was a head, or rather a head-rest,[32] because she only saw it during the 'split second'[33] flick of the lights. This makes sense, especially considering that Farquharson is so short, so his head does not extend above the head rest.

Waite was asked whether she had seen the blinds at the back of the car she passed, and testified that she had not.[34] Nor did the car have tinted windows, from what she recalled.[35] The fact that Farquharson's car had blinds and tinted windows is not particularly damning of Waite's evidence, we can't expect Waite to accurately recall details of a car she passed on the road 4 years earlier. Which really is the point. However, the blinds and the tinted windows on Farquharson's car (shown in the image) do have relevance when assessing how well we may expect Waite could see into Farquharson's car, assuming that it was his car that Waite passed.

30. Trial 2 p24
31. Trail 2 p23
32. Trail 2 p24
33. Trail 2 p24
34. Trial 2 p83
35. Trial 2 p1659

Farquharson's car that was retrieved from the dam. Note the tinted windows, the blinds and the various items on the back dashboard, all of which would limit viewing into the car.

Farquharson's car that was retrieved from the dam is shown in the picture above. Note the tinted windows, the blinds and the various items on the back dashboard, all of which would limit viewing into the car

By the time of the trial two months later, Waite claimed that she had 'left the lights on full beam to see the way clear for me to pass the vehicle'[36] and that this allowed her to see inside the car where the driver, purportedly Farquharson, 'kept on looking out to his right'.[37] So she now claimed that she had turned her lights to high beam while she was still behind the car,[38] allowing her to see Farquharson who kept turning his head to the right.

Let us assume this new version is correct, that Waite had turned on her high beams whilst still behind the car, long enough to witness someone in the car in front turn their head, look straight, turn their head again, look straight, then turn their head again. So Dawn Waite's testimony implies that she illegally[39] drove close behind the car with her high beams on for a significant amount of time. What is the driver of the leading

36. Trial 2 p1664
37. Trial 2 p1615
38. Waite's testimony from the *voire dire* and trial can be found in Appendix D, where you can compare them.
39. Victorian Road Rule 218 states that 'drivers must not use the high beam headlights when driving less than 200 metres behind a vehicle travelling in the same direction'

car going to do in such a situation? He cannot look into the rear vision mirror when someone is up his ass with their high beams on. Highly likely, he will look to the right side mirror, waiting for the car to drive past. In fact, when Waite is again asked about his looking rightwards as she passed, she said 'it was almost like he was looking into his [side] mirror... on that angle.'[40] So even if we assume Waite's new version of events, and that indeed it was Farquharson's car that she passed, it is hardly damning evidence. What was he meant to be looking to the right for anyway, that would imply guilt? Was he supposedly looking for a dam? While someone was up his ass with their high beams on? When everything around was pitch black? Besides, didn't he know where the dam was? Didn't he have a plan? Or was he now randomly searching for a dam? In the pitch black?

The next part of Waite's testimony has her looking into the Farquharson car as she passed. They were driving on a single lane highway, so Waite was now in the wrong lane, and she testified that she was 'going approximately ... the same speed as the Commodore was because I was level with him for a couple of seconds',[41] and at this time she was 'only about half a car length away... very close...'[42] So according to this testimony, Waite slowed down during the passing manouvre and was illegally[43] and dangerously driving on the wrong side of the road along-side Farquharson.

So if we are to believe Waite's trial testimony she was firstly driving closely behind someone with her high beams on, and then as she passed on the wrong side of the road she slowed down to drive alongside the car. Her daughter Jessica did describe her in court as a 'road rager',[44] but this description of

---

40. Trial 2 p1620
41. Trial 2 p1619
42. Trial 2 p1619
43. According to Rodney Blythe, Senior Policy Analyst at VicRoads *'If a car slowed down and paced the vehicle they were overtaking I would suggest that they were not overtaking safely and that would be the offence.'*
44. Trial 2 p76

dangerous and illegal driving sounded like she was trying to find ways of explaining how she managed to see so much.

Whilst passing, Waite claimed that 'my lights were on high beam, so, I could see very clearly into the vehicle'.[45] If she is level with Farquharson and looking into his car, her high beams are pointing forwards. So how did she so clearly through the tinted windows and into his car? This question was pursued by the defence[46] but it never became particularly clear. One suggestion made by the prosecutor was that Farquharson was illuminated by the 'dashboard lights'.[47] Regardless, Waite testified that she could see into Farquharson's car as she passed.

The four years timespan of between the events and Dawn Waite's statement, the fact that it gained no corroboration by two other people who were with her at the time, the amount of information and images shown on the media, the fact that her testimony in the trial contradicted the testimony she gave in the voir dire, and the implausibility of some the things she describes means that it is very weak evidence, it carries very little weight. It is quite extraordinary that the police and prosecution even presented such evidence, as they are well aware of the degrading effects of time on witness evidence, and the possibility of people incorporating information about high profile cases from the media into their memories, placing themselves into the story. Whatever little weight Waite's evidence does carry, it is just as supportive of Farquharson being innocent as of him being guilty. Any interpretation that she gave important evidence pointing to guilt looks very much like confirmation bias.

---

45. Trial 2 p1620
46. Trial 2 p1679
47. Trial 2 p4923

Chapter 16

STRANGE BEHAVIOUR

Cindy had taken the boys to Farquharson's house at around 3pm. It was father's day and they had bought a present for him, a framed photograph of the three boys, the one showing them squashed together on the sofa, grins on their faces. When she asked the boys if they wanted to stay with their father for dinner, Jai and Tyler jumped at the chance, knowing it would mean Kentucky Fried Chicken. Cindy proposed that Farquharson drop them home at 7.30pm. To Cindy, Farquharson had 'seemed quite normal',[1] 'He was very tired because he hadn't been well. A little emotional but nothing I didn't expect'.[2]

Around 4pm, Farquharson visited Michael Hart, to see if he and his son Dean wanted to come to KFC. Hart did not fancy the drive to Geelong and suggested they have a barbeque instead, but the boys had their hearts set on KFC. The Farquharsons headed for Geelong. After eating a bucket of chicken and some chips, they stopped off at Kmart where Rob's sister Kerri worked, buying each of the boys a small gift. He was 'just the normal Rob'[3] according to Kerri. On the way back, Farquharson and the boys stopped at Kerri's house to collect a football that Tyler had left there recently. Kerri's husband Gary Huntington was home with his daughter. The Farquharsons stayed around 10-15 minutes and left just 20 minutes prior to running off the road and into the

---

1. Committal Proceedings p17 and confirmed Trial 2 1255, and trial 2 p1188
2. Committal Proceeding p17
3. Trial 1 p1025

dam. According to Huntington, Farquharson 'seemed fine and just his usual self'.[4]

Tony McClelland and Shane Atkinson were the next people to see Robert Farquharson, who was waving them down on the Princes Highway with 'water dripping off him'.[5] 'He was mumbling a lot. And just very confused',[6] 'he was just sort of panicky, he was just upset…he couldn't really talk',[7] 'he was puffing and panting, sort of crying and then he started raving on',[8] 'He wasn't really making sense',[9] he was 'a babbling mess[10]…he was just swearing, like, 'Oh no, fuck, what have I done? What's happened?'. We couldn't get no sense out of him',[11] 'He wasn't really making sense',[12] 'he'd mumble and make attempts to talk.' 'He just didn't seem to be with it. He'd start talking about one thing and then he'd change in midstream and talk about something different.' 'He seemed to be muddled up.' 'He was hard to understand because he was mumbling and muttering. He was incoherent.' 'He kept chopping and changing the topic.',[13] 'It appeared … like he was in shock'.[14]

Several details differed between the testimony of McClelland and Atkinson regarding exactly what happened that night. They did, however, agree on the state of Farquharson when they found him. Cindy Gambino also agreed. When Farquharson arrived at her house, he 'was rambling; he was hysterical',[15] 'he was soaking wet and he was rambling, yes, hysterically',[16] 'he was saturated and delirious. He was very hysterical'.[17]

4. Trial 2 p1591
5. Shane Atkinson statement at 7.42pm 06/09/2005 to Det. Sgt. Brett Gallaughar at Winchelsea
6. Trial 2 p1829
7. Trial 1 p395
8. Trial 1 p408
9. Trial 2 p1795
10. Trial 2 p1823
11. Trial 1 p360
12. Trial 2 p1795
13. Trial 1 p409-410
14. Trial 1 p400
15. Trial 2 p1264
16. Trial 2 p1264

Cindy and Robert rushed back to the dam, with Stephen Moules arriving soon after with his cousin, followed by Brent McCallum and Kiri Fausett, then the fire brigade and the State Emergency Services (SES). The focus of these people was finding the car and the children, and they did not really take much notice of Farquharson.[18,19] Carolyn Fausett was one of the next to arrive at the scene, several minutes behind her husband Kiri who by this time was diving into the freezing water. When she saw Farquharson, 'I walked over and we hugged and he put his head on my shoulder and we cried'.[20]

Tony McClelland and Shane Atkinson also returned to the dam. McClelland saw Farquharson 'sort of crying and murmuring, but I couldn't understand what he was saying or – the only response that I could recognise was asking for a cigarette...it was just a general noise, just appeared to be like crying, just murmuring'.[21] Atkinson saw him 'pacing up and down the road, he was crying as well, he was very upset'.[22]

Farquharson was taken from the scene to a room at Geelong hospital, where his sister Carmen entered to see him 'laying on a stretcher bed covered in foil, he was shaking uncontrollably, he didn't recognize me, he couldn't speak'.[23] Police sergeant Brendan Bosely arrived to ensure that a blood sample was taken, and 'heard Farquharson a number of times thump the bed under the blankets and he appeared distraught'.[24] Farquharson's friend Darren Bushell visited at around 9.30pm and Farquharson 'just said, 'I've killed my kids'. That was it. He was just shaking...'[25] Sergeant Smith, who interviewed Farquharson in the hospital that night, told reporters at the scene that Farquharson was 'as

17. Trial 1 p980
18. Moules Trial 1 p1008 p, Trial 2 p1482
19. Fausett Trial 2 p1866
20. Trial 2 p 1880
21. Trial 2 p1847
22. Committal Hearing p78
23. *Across the Night Sky* 28 March, 2011 Australian Story ABC TV
24. Trial 2 p2278
25. Trial 1 p1690

you'd imagine, you know, I mean, he's speechless, he doesn't know what's going on'.[26]

The next morning when grief councillor Leona Daniel entered Farquharson's hospital room, he was 'thrashing about from side to side'.[27] As Daniel tried to comfort him, 'his head was still going from side to side. He was clearly in great anguish',[28] 'he was tremendously flushed. He at one point was coughing and he was sweating. Very disheveled. The bedclothes were everywhere'.[29] Farquharson told her 'I should be with them... I shouldn't be here.'[30] Importantly for memory evidence, Daniel had taken notes on the day of the visit, writing that 'he was in absolute anguish about his children'.[31] A couple of days later, Daniel visited Farquharson a second time, and he was 'very confused, very distressed.'[32]

Two days later, Farquharson's sisters Kerri and Carmen took him to visit Cindy in hospital. Farquharson 'was making twitching movements, he was unable to speak'[33] according to Cindy. 'He was racked with involuntary jerking, his arms thrashing around and his head and body twitching in a way she found too disturbing to watch...Every few minutes, Kerri would grab his hand, repeating his name and telling him to stop.'[34] To Cindy, he seemed as traumatized as she was[35] as she 'reflected on how terrible it must be for him – the sole survivor of a freak accident that had claimed their children's lives.'[36] Footage of Farquharson leaving the hospital was shown on television

26. e.g. report of Nicole Strahan on 10 news 05/09/2005
27. Trial 2 p4298
28. Trial 2 p4298
29. Trial 2 p4298
30. Trial 2 p4299
31. Trial 2 p4302
32. Trial 2 p4300
33. Trial 2 p1302
34. Norris, M *On Father's Day: Cindy Gambino's Shattering Account of her Children's Revenge Murders* 2013 (Kindle Locations 1330-1331). The Five Mile Press.
35. Norris, M *On Father's Day: Cindy Gambino's Shattering Account of her Children's Revenge Murders* 2013 (Kindle Locations 1330-1331). The Five Mile Press
36. Norris, M *On Father's Day: Cindy Gambino's Shattering Account of her Children's Revenge Murders* 2013 (Kindle Locations 1330-1331). The Five Mile Press

news, and the images accord with Cindy's description. Channel 10 news reported that 'clearly still traumatised by the events of the past few days, Robert Farquharson had to be supported as he left Winchelsea hospital'.[37]

The funeral for the boys was held a week later on Wednesday, 14th September 2005 and there was a large media presence. At the end of the funeral service, 'Cindy collapsed on Rob's shoulder…the two separated parents united in their grief, supporting one another through the nightmare. Cindy wept, and Rob's bottom lip trembled at the sight of the three small coffins being lowered into the ground' as they 'clung to one another in their mutual suffering'.[38]

There is no uniform, or 'correct' way to act in such horrific circumstances,[39] but these descriptions of Farquharson prior to, and after the deaths of his sons seem consistent with a person who has lost his children in a terrible accident.

So why did the prosecutor assert that Farquharson had a 'strange demeanour',[40] and that his 'strange behaviour after the drowning of his children'[41] pointed to his guilt?

The most important 'strange behaviour' was that Farquharson 'refused' to call emergency services from the scene and instead 'insisted' that he be driven to see his ex-wife Cindy. This was central to the case, with the prosecution,[42] the police[43] and many others[44] interpreting this as his desire to see Cindy's reaction when he told her the fate of her children, that this was his 'payback' for her leaving him.

---

37. Luke Waters Channel 10 News (VTS_05_1.VOB)
38. Norris, Megan . *On Father's Day: Cindy Gambino's Shattering Account of her Children's Revenge Murders* 2013 (Kindle Locations 2175-2176). The Five Mile Press. .
39. e.g. Grimm, A., Hulse, L., Preiss, M. and Schmidt, S. (2014), *Behavioural, emotional, and cognitive responses in European disasters: results of survivor interviews*. Disasters, 38: 62–83
40. Trial 2 p4901
41. Farquharson v R 2012 Court of Appeal
42. e.g. Trial 2 p5146
43. e.g. Sergeant Jeffry Smith on "Crimes that Shook Australia" states that he considers Farquharson wanted to be taken to see Cindy as evidence that he "did it".
44. e.g. Norris, M *On Fathers Day* Kindle Location 7611,

This type of 'payback' does happen. In 2011, Ramazan Acar killed his daughter Yazmina, then taunted his ex-partner, Rachelle D'Argent by posting on Facebook 'payback u slut'. The difference in the Farquharson case is that there is no evidence that he taunted Cindy when telling her what had happened, and no evidence that he taunted her at any stage afterwards, nor did he give any indication of gaining satisfaction at seeing Cindy suffer. During Farquharson's secretly recorded phone calls with Cindy, there was nothing said that indicates that Farquharson had done this to hurt her. The prosecution dismissed the lack of direct evidence that Farquharson had wanted to see Cindy suffer by saying that 'It would hardly have been in his interests in those days after the events to show his true feelings towards his wife'.[45]

The other difference between the cases is that Cindy had never felt at all threatened by Farquharson, or had any issue with leaving the boys in his care whilst D'Argent had restraining orders out on Ramazan Acar, who was violent, and had been very reluctant to allow Yazmina to go to the milk bar with him, fearing what would happen.

Let us explore, in the alternative, what we may expect of Farquharson's behaviour at the scene if he is innocent. In that case, we can presume that he was in shock and under immense stress when Tony McClelland and Shane Atkinson found him. A range of studies have shown that stress impairs the performance of tasks that require 'complex, flexible thinking, but that it could actually improve the performance of simpler and/or well-rehearsed tasks'.[46] These effects are physical, with neuroscience research showing that 'the types of tasks that were impaired by stress were those that required pre-frontal cortex operations, whereas engrained habits that rely on basal ganglia circuits were spared or enhanced.'[47] Essentially, people in stressful situations

---

45. Trial 2 p4904
46. e.g. Broadbent, D. *Decision and Stress*. 1971 London: Academic; Hockey GRJ. *Effect of loud noise on attentional selectivity*. 1970 Q. J. exp. Psychol 22:28–36.
47. Arnsten Amy F. T. *Stress signalling pathways that impair prefrontal cortex structure and function* Nat Rev Neurosci. 2009 10(6): 410–422.

cannot think clearly and resort to base instincts or go into 'auto pilot', following either instinct or learned behaviour.

What learned habitual behaviour would Robert Farquharson revert to in this highly stressful situation? Farquharson's paternal role was the stereotypical one of the breadwinner who had ceded parental responsibilities to the mother. His time with the boys revolved around taking them to sports or for fast food or the like. After the divorce, Cindy described the boys time spent with Farquharson as 'all fun and games, it wasn't real life'[48]. Issues regarding the children that required any degree of responsibility had always been handled by Cindy. It was Cindy who made decisions on where they could go and what they could do, who set the limits on their behaviour, who instilled discipline[49]. It was Cindy who was guiding them through childhood. Cindy was the one who could deal with important issues, with something as grave as life and death. So, when the ultimate tragedy occurred to those children, and Farquharson was running on instinct, is it so surprising that the only thing he could think of was Cindy? That he had to tell Cindy? That he needed her? Farquharson *instinctively* needed to go and see Cindy. Cindy was their mother, she was their true guardian. He was compelled to tell her, he needed her.

It is also not surprising that Farquharson was so obsessed with this single response to the crisis, repeating 'time after time'[50] that he needed to tell Cindy.[51] Focusing on a single response is typical in disaster situations,[52,53,54] and is referred to as 'perseveration'. People will attempt 'to solve a problem in a single way, again and again and again, regardless of the results'.[55]

We thus have two explanations for why Farquharson kept

---

48. Trial 2 p1182
49. See Morris, M *On Fathers Day* supra
50. Trial 2 p1798
51. Trial 2 p1799
52. Brindley, P. G. Tse, A. *Situational Awareness and Human Performance in Trauma* 2016 Trauma Team Dynamics pp 27-31
53. ibid
54. for a review see Munakata, Y, Morton, J. B., Merva Stedron J. *The role of prefrontal cortex in perseveration: Developmental and computational explorations*

asking, over and over, to be taken to tell Cindy of what had occurred. He either wanted to personally see her reaction to his unspeakable 'payback', that he gained some sense of satisfaction by telling her directly, or he followed a learned, ingrained, and instinctive reaction to the tragedy that had occurred to the boys. How do we distinguish between these two possible explanations? The thing about trying to interpret behaviour is that it is so often ambiguous, and this is why it is just so difficult, and dangerous, to interpret behaviour as proving guilt or innocence. The ambiguity is far too often interpreted in a manner that conforms to already held beliefs, readily lending itself to confirmation bias.

Let's look at another of Farquharson's 'strange behaviours', his request for cigarettes. Who would ask for a smoke if they had just had such a terrible and tragic accident? But then again, who would ask for a smoke if they had just murdered their three sons? Do murderers usually ask for smokes? Is that a sign of a murderer? But people in shock after a terrible accident do not ask for smokes? Studies for decades have shown that cigarette smokers desire a nicotine hit when they are in stressful situations.[56] The request for cigarettes may have made good theatre in the court room, painting Farquharson as uncaring, but it proves nothing either way regarding guilt or innocence.

What about Farquharson's 'refusal'[57] to use a phone to call emergency services? Doesn't that point to murder?

In his statement made two days after the events, Shane Atkinson said that he suggested that Farquharson call emergency services whilst driving towards Winchelsea, after recognising him as a local from Winchelsea. He never mentioned offering Farquharson his phone to make the call. Two years later at trial, Atkinson claimed that he had offered Farquharson the use of his phone at the scene, and suggested that he call emergency

---

55. Gorvett, Z *Survival is less about heroic actions than avoiding mindless mistakes* 2017 12 July BBC future
56. e.g. Silverstein, B. 1982. *Cigarette smoking, nicotine addiction, and relaxation.* Journal of Personality and Social Psychology, *42*(5), 946-950; Benowitz, N. L. *Nicotine Addiction* The New England journal of medicine 362.24 2010 2295–2303. PMC
57. E.g. Trial 2 p5147

services. Tony McClelland, who was with Atkinson the whole time, did not recall any offer being made of the use of a phone, neither at the scene nor in the car, nor did he recall any suggestion being made to call emergency services.

At no point did either of Atkinson or McClelland use the phone that Atkinson claimed he was carrying to call emergency services. They did not use the phone at the scene. After going to Cindy Gambino's house, and witnessing the upsetting scenes, they still did not use the phone to call emergency services but instead drove to the Winchelsea police station to raise the alarm. The police station was closed but Carolyn and Kirri Fausett, who lived next to the station, heard them causing a commotion and went out to the street to ask what was happening, and immediately called emergency services using their landline.[58]

At that stage, Atkinson and McClelland were 'quite frantic'[59] according to Carolyn Faucett and 'weren't making a lot of sense'.[60] Assuming that they had the phone with them the whole time it seems that, in their panic, they did not think to use it to call emergency services. 'I done the stupidest thing of me life and I took him back to Winchelsea because that's all he kept on saying' is how Atkinson describes their decision to leave the scene, rather than call emergency services when they were confronted in the middle of a highway with an incoherent man who was soaking wet and babbling about having 'killed his kids'. Like Farquharson, they were not thinking straight at the time. John Leach, a psychologist at the University of Portsmouth who studies human response during disasters, estimates that 80-90% of people respond inappropriately in a crisis.[61] Of course, there was no inference made that their 'stupid' decision implied that Atkinson and McClelland were co-conspirators in the crime. Such an inference is obviously ridiculous and was only reserved for Farquharson.

---

58. Trial 2 p1863
59. Trial 2 p1878
60. Trial 2 p1878
61. Gorvett, Z. *Survival is less about heroic actions than avoiding mindless mistakes* 12 July 2017 BBC Futures

Further, even if he *were* offered the use of the phone, there is no evidence that Farquharson *refused* it's use. There was contrasting testimony from McClelland and Atkinson about whether he was even *offered* the use of the phone, but no evidence that he *refused* the offer, because there was no evidence of him being cognitively aware of the offer. Atkinson and McClelland had tried to talk to him but 'we couldn't get no sense out of him'.[62] When Atkinson was asked how Farquharson reacted to his offer of the phone, he said that Farquharson had looked at him and said the same things that he had been saying throughout,[63] the repetitive comment 'I've got to go and tell Cindy'.[64] There was never any evidence of a rational verbal exchange between the men. To the contrary, the evidence indicated a man who was not making any sense, whose pre-frontal cortex had closed down.

Farquharson *was* able to direct them to Cindy's house, but such ingrained knowledge is *exactly* the type of function that his brain could deal with in a situation where stress had caused his brain's executive function to be severely impaired. He did not need to be thinking flexibly, nor use his 'working memory' to find his way to a house in which he had lived for several years. This was learned, repetitive behaviour.

According the prosecutor, Farquharson was 'calm, cool, clear, unemotional'[65] in front of the police officers who interviewed him, and that he must have 'put on an impressive show'[66] in front of the witnesses who testified to his anguish and grief that evening and in the subsequent days. If Farquharson was so good at faking hysteria, distress and anguish that he could convince his ex-wife,[67] wouldn't he also do it in front of the police? What if he appeared unemotional when interviewed by police because he had been raised to show respect to police and this was how he was brought up to speak to them? So it was his automatic,

---

62. Trial 1 p361
63. Trial 2 p1819
64. Trial 1 p381
65. Trial 2 p5083
66. Trial 2 p5133
67. Megan Norris *On Father's Day* Kindle Position 1326

learned behavioural response? What if he was trying to help by attempting to explain what had happened?

The prosecutor also portrayed Farquharson's behaviour in court as implying he was guilty, urging the jury to compare Robert Farquharson's demeanour to that of Greg King, claiming that it was 'obvious'[68] that King was in 'on going anguish'[69] and 'pain'[70] and that this contrasted to Farquharson's lack[71] of such anguish or pain, and that they should interpret

Farquharson's demeanour as 'a little bit cold hearted and a little bit calculating'.[72]

Other evidence about Farquharson's behaviour, like so many aspects of the case, mirrored the tactics used against Lindy Chamberlain, who was wrongly convicted for the murder of her daughter Azaria. Whilst being interviewed at Geelong hospital, Farquharson had not enquired about the children. When asked if he realised that the children had not made it out of the car, Farquharson responded 'I gathered that'.[73] Similarly, soon after Azaria had been taken by a dingo, Lindy Chamberlain's husband and alleged co-conspirator Michael had told a nearby camper that 'A dingo has taken our baby, and she is probably dead by now'. As the camper tried to comfort her, Lindy had said 'Whatever happens, it is God's will.' Apparently, innocent people should always hold out false hope rather than face grim reality, according to... well I have no idea, but that is what the prosecution in both cases seemed to imply.

There was evidence presented that Farquharson had failed to join the search,[74] that he should have dived back into the dam,[75] just as there was evidence that Lindy had not joined the search

---

68. Trial 2 p5074
69. Trial 2 p5074
70. Trial 2 p5074
71. Trial 2 p5074
72. Trial 2 p5075
73. Trial 2 4061
74. Trial 2 p5146 'his apparent lack of interest in the rescue efforts that occurred on his return'
75. Trial 2 p5146 'his failure to dive into the dam or make any approach to the dam on his return there'

for Azaria,[76] and that her husband Michael's initial search 'lacked urgency'.[77] Never mind the cases where guilty people *have* joined in searches, such as Cristian Rogel who joined the search for 15 year old school girl Carla Oyarzún, who he had raped and murdered in Osorno, Chile.[78] Or Sarthak Kapoor who helped the parents of Shreya Sharma, who he had murdered, search for her in the neighbourhood of her home in New Dehli, India.[79] Or Andrew Garforth who joined the search[80] for nine year old Ebony Simpson, who he had raped and murdered in Bargo, 100km from Sydney.

In the whole, evidence pertaining to Robert Farquharson's behaviour and demeanour can be incorporated into whatever narrative you want to weave. It is certainly possible that Farquharson repeatedly asked to see Cindy because he wanted to see her suffer. It is possible that he was faking hysteria, was faking shock, was faking anguish, and was faking grief, as is required to explain the testimony of multiple eyewitnesses, and it is possible that for all his skill at faking such emotions, he chose not to fake in front of police officers and not to fake anguish and grief whilst giving evidence during the trial. However, drawing such conclusions would require some other evidence of his guilt. Discarding the parts of the evidence that are consistent with innocence by concluding that he was faking requires that the remainder of the evidence in the case is sufficient to prove his guilt. Otherwise, discarding such evidence is simply confirmation bias.

An interpretation of Farquharson's behaviour and demeanour that is consistent with his innocence is relatively simple: he acted hysterically because he was hysterical; he appeared to be in shock because he was in shock; he appeared to be anguished and

76. Bryson, J. *Evil Angels* Kindle Location 8265
77. Bryson, J. *Evil Angels* Kindle Location 6184
78. González S., El Mercurio, *Atleta que violó y mató a menor fue sentenciado a presidio perpetuo*, 10 Dec 2009
79. Anand Mohan J, *Schoolgirl strangled in Delhi by 19-year-old who 'objected to her talking to other boys'* The India Express August 18, 2017
80. Tullis, A. *Ebony Simpson's murder remembered 25 years on*, Sydney Morning Herald, August 17, 2017

grieving because he was anguished and grieving; he acted instinctively, habitually, unable to think clearly or act appropriately, because he was in a highly stressful, crisis situation; he spoke to police in a respectful manner, trying to help; and his trial testimony was relatively unemotional because he is not comfortable expressing his emotions in such a public forum.

CHAPTER 17

PANTS ON FIRE

When Shane Atkinson and Tony McLellenad found Robert Farquharson 'mumbling'[1] and 'raving'[2] incoherently, he told them that 'I had a coughing fit and just passed out'[3] and ended in the water,[4] that 'I killed the kids, they drowned'[5] and repeatedly said that 'I tried to get the kids out but I couldn't.'[6]

During this time, Farquharson also said that 'it must have been the wheel bearing'.[7] According to the prosecution, this 'explanation was a straight out lie',[8] 'the accused told two conflicting stories about the cause of the tragedy; the wheel bearing story, the coughing fit blackout story. Two completely different stories.'[9]

Painting Farquharson as a liar who kept changing his account of the accident was a vital aspect of the prosecution case. In his final address to the jury, the prosecutor used the word lie or lies as applying to Farquharson on 23 occasions, as well as

1. Committal hearing p81
2. From Tony McClelland statement to police, see Committal hearing p80
3. Committal hearing p76
4. Shane Atkinson statement at 7.42pm 06/09/2005 to Det. Sgt. Brett Gallaughar at Winchelsea
5. From Tony McClelland statement to police, see Committal hearing p83
6. Committal hearing p76
7. Committal hearing p83, see also Trial 2 p1838
8. Trial 2 p4938
9. Trial 2 p4938

'dishonest nature',[10] 'strong reasons to be very sceptical about the truthfulness of anything he said',[11] 'deliberately deceiving',[12] 'You simply could not believe a word he would say',[13] 'misrepresentations',[14] 'dishonest',[15] 'brazenly deceive',[16] 'defied belief',[17] 'willingness to say anything',[18] 'deceitful',[19] 'entirely unworthy of belief',[20] 'simply not the truth',[21] 'prepared to say whatever he liked whenever he liked',[22] and 'manipulative'.[23]

Added to this, the prosecutor hammered the point over and over about Farquharson's alleged 'changing and evolving story',[24] 'changing and evolving story',[25] 'the changing and evolving story of the accused about the event',[26] 'changing his tune',[27] 'ever developing and changing account',[28] 'changing his mind like the weather',[29] 'ever changing account',[30] 'ever changing story',[31] 'It just changed all the time. It changed, it developed, as he went',[32] 'ever changing, ever expanding sort of account',[33] 'changing

10. Trial 2 p4995
11. Trial 2 p4996
12. Trial 2 p5134
13. Trial 2 p5134
14. Trial 2 p5135
15. Trial 2 p5135
16. Trial 2 p5136
17. Trial 2 p5136
18. Trial 2 p5137
19. Trial 2 p5063
20. Trial 2 p5138
21. Trial 2 p5139
22. Trial 2 p4953
23. Trial 2 p5140
24. Trial 2 p4935
25. Trial 2 p4936
26. Trial 2 p5160
27. Trial 2 p4936
28. Trial 2 p4944
29. Trial 2 p4950
30. Trial 2 p4950
31. Trial 2 p4952
32. Trial 2 p4953
33. Trial 2 p4952

inconsistent dishonest nature of things said by the accused',[34] 'changing accounts',[35] 'changing and evolving story'.[36]

In what sense was Robert Farquharson's purported comment about a wheel bearing a lie? In what sense had he told two different stories? If Farquharson's story is true, he had blacked out after coughing and woken up in the dam. When he awoke, he could not have known[37] how the car got from the road to the dam. So there were two things he needed to explain. Firstly, what had happened to *him* such that he had woken up in the dam? And secondly, how did the *car* get from the road to the dam?

Farquharson did not know much about cars 'I'm not a mechanic so – I don't know nothing about cars',[38] but he did know that 'doing a wheel bearing' affects the steering and can cause a car to veer off the road. When he proposed that 'it may have been a wheel bearing', this was his suggestion for how the car got from the road to the dam. When he said that he 'had a coughing fit, I woke up in the water and I couldn't get the kids out',[39] he was addressing the question of what had happened *to him*. The two statements are not in conflict at all, they do not *contradict* one another, they deal with two different aspects of what had occurred, one regarding what happened to *him* and the other regarding what happened to the *car*.

It turns out, of course, that Farquharson had not done a wheel bearing. But the speculation that had he 'may have[40] done a wheel bearing' could reasonably be made by a person who had blacked out after coughing and was trying to understand how his car ended up in a dam.

By contrast, if Farquharson is guilty, why would he say that he 'may have done a wheel bearing'? If he steered the car into the dam, he would have *known* that he had not done a wheel bearing,

---

34. Trial 2 p4995
35. Trial 2 p5122
36. Trial 2 p5160
37. People suffering cough syncope have amnesia: they don't recall what happened whilst unconscious.
38. Trial 2 p3773
39. Trial 1 p397
40. *or 'might have' or 'must have'*

so why would he suggest that he had? How does that help a guilty person? Hadn't he planned this cough syncope story by researching the condition and making up a previous episode and telling Darren Bushell about it? If he is guilty, why not go straight to the cough syncope story? The speculation about the wheel bearing makes sense if he is innocent, as something that a person in that situation could reasonably say, but it is an incongruous thing to say if he were guilty.

Painting the accused as a liar is an age old tactic of prosecutors. The prosecutor of Lindy Chamberlain told the jury that 'you are entitled to find that she invented the dingo lie... she lied about the animal; its appearance, what it did, where it went, what she did. She's lied about the blood in the car, the tracksuit pants, the dress, the giggle hats, the space blanket, and the baby's blankets... she's lied constantly and persistently and so has her husband.'[41]

If Farquharson is guilty then clearly he lied. But we are looking for evidence of whether or not he is guilty, so we cannot use the assumption of guilt as evidence that he lied. What were the other 'obvious',[42] 'clear'[43] and 'deliberate'[44] lies that the prosecutor referred to during his final address to the jury? As with the 'wheel bearing' comment, it is worth while exploring a few more of these 'lies' and 'changes of story' in detail.

The next alleged 'lie' of Farquharson regards the history and diagnosis of cough syncope. The doctor who examined Farquharson, Dr Christopher Steinfort, had concluded that he had 'classic cough syncope'. The prosecutor claimed that this diagnosis was based on the 'deliberate lies'[45] of Farquharson. According to the prosecutor, Farquharson 'told Dr Steinfort... that he had suffered two previous incidents of loss of consciousness as a result of coughing... One at work, and one at

---

41. Royal Commission of Inquiry into Chamberlain Convictions, Report, *Commonwealth Parliamentary Papers* (1987), volume 15, paper 192, Appendix A p53
42. Trial 2 p5135
43. Trial 2 p5089
44. Trial 2 p5018
45. Trial 2 p5018

the roadhouse',[46] and this was a lie he had made to bolster his history of cough syncope and affect the diagnosis.

What was the evidence for this alleged lie?

It stems from a consultation Farquharson had with Dr. Steinfort, during which Steinfort made his diagnosis of cough syncope. Dr Steinfort was in the habit of scribbling short-hand notes when conferring with his patients, for example if a patient described an incident where he/she 'came to', Steinfort would scribble *LOC*, indicating a loss of consciousness. In the shorthand notes that Steinfort took during the consultation with Farquharson, he had written each of these comments on different lines:

coughing plus, dizzy spell at workplace
lightly smoking at time of accident, LOC
at work, buckled over
went all dizzy – witnessed
remembers coughing fit, then LOC

During the first trial, the prosecutor asked Steinfort 'Did you understand him to say that he had a witness to the episode in which he lost consciousness at work and buckled over?', and Steinfort replied that 'I believe – well that is my interpretation of what I've written there, yes.' So Steinfort's reconstruction of a conversation from scribbled notes was the basis of Farquharson's purportedly claiming, falsely, to have lost consciousness in front of his boss.

After the first trial, however, Steinfort located a letter that he had written *on the day of the consultation with Farquharson*. The letter was to the referring doctor, a Dr. Kay. In this letter, Steinfort described Farquharson as having had an 'observed episode of near syncope' and another event where 'he remembers coughing and the next thing he remembers is regaining consciousness'. So on the actual day of the consultation, Dr. Steinfort did not recount that Farquharson had claimed two episodes of loss of consciousness. His descriptions of two

---

46. Trial 2 p5134

episodes fit with Farquharson's dizzy spell at work, witnessed by his boss, and with the story he told Darren Bushell about coming to in the service station. This letter contradicted the interpretation of the scribbled notes that Steinfort had made much later, during the trial.

Dr Kay himself, when referring Farquharson to Dr. Steinfort, described the two episodes Farquharson had related to him as 'two separate episodes of coughing and light headedness before the crash – one during a road home – second in front his boss at work prior to the accident'[47]. This is another second hand account of what Farquharson said that is different in detail but very similar in gist to the versions given by Susan Bateson and Darren Bushell.

All the versions, including the ambiguous shorthand notes of Steinfort, could have easily stemmed from the same episodes, without any deliberate lies from any of the witnesses including Farquharson. The prosecutor's assertion that Dr. Steinfort had been 'hoodwinked'[48] by Farquharson[49] does not hold up to scrutiny.

The next purported 'change of story' stems from the testimony of Leading Senior Constable Edward Harman, the first police officer to arrive at the scene. Harman spoke to Farquharson whilst the search for the car was still underway, and Farquharson told him that 'I've had a chest pain and I just blacked out over the bridge.'[50] The prosecutor called this his 'third story',[51] as he tried to make out that Farquharson kept changing his account.

Can't you have chest pain when you cough? There is undisputed medical evidence that Farquharson had a chest infection at the time.[52] Wasn't the chest infection related to the cough? How is the version relayed by Harman a different story, or contradictory to what Farquharson told the other people? Isn't

---

47. Trial 2 p4511
48. Trial 2 p5019
49. Trial 2 p5019
50. Trial 2 p1968
51. Trial 2 p4942
52. e.g. Farquharson v Queen VSCA 296 2012, p21, 22

it just a different detail of the same story? Do we require that Farquharson use the exact same sentences each time he recounts his story, that he just repeats his story verbatim? Is that what we expect of an innocent person, that they repeat the story as if reading from a script each time? If Farquharson had done that, would we conclude that he was innocent?

Farquharson was asked to recount what happened on many, many occasions. On that night alone, Farquharson recounted the story to Shane Atkinson and Tony McClelland, to Cindy, to Stephen Moules, to Carolyn Fausett, to Constable Edward Harman, to ambulance offices Lindsay Robinson and David Watson, to Dr. Bartley at Geelong hospital, and during a recorded police interview with Sergeant Smith and Constable Courtis. He told all of them that he had a coughing fit and blacked out, waking up in the dam. Most of these people gave evidence from memory, so it is actually notable how consistent their memories were of the gist of what he said. When one of the witnesses from the night reported a slight variation, that Farquharson made reference to 'chest pain' rather than a direct reference to 'coughing', is such a minor difference in detail of a second hand re-telling of the story really evidence of an 'ever changing story'?

There were a few more alleged Farquharson lies but they were all inconsequential. I will give one more illustrative example here and outline the rest in an appendix B, for completeness. This alleged lie is again regarding the coughing fit he had at work, where Farquharson had a dizzy spell witnessed by his boss, Sue Bateson. Whilst being secretly recorded, Farquharson 'told Greg King that Sue Bateson had sent him home from work after that coughing fit'.[53] This was 'a complete lie'[54] according to the prosecutor, because Bateson had testified that 'as far as she was aware'[55] Farquharson stayed at work for the rest of the day. An inconsistency in an inconsequential detail between two people's

---

53. Trial 2 p5059
54. Trial 2 p5059
55. Trial 2 p2852

memories of the same event ends up with Farquharson being brandished a liar.

The broader context here is that police had tapped Farquharson's phones and secretly taped many of his conversations, including several with Cindy and with Greg King. Adding to this were the numerous police interviews which were also taped. The police and prosecutors therefore had hours and hours of Farquharson's conversations to which they could listen, in order to pick up any inconsistencies in his stories and any differences between his versions of stories, and the versions of others. Given what is known about memory, one *expects* to find inconsistencies in such material, even when everyone tells the truth as they know it. Finding amongst all this material a minor discrepancy between Farquharson's memory of when he left work that day, and the memory of his boss, is not evidence of anything other than a confirmation of known flaws in our memories. What is notable is how few inconsistencies were found.

Further to these considerations, many of Farquharson's early statements and the first interview were made on the evening of the events. He was clearly in an extremely stressful situation, and this has implications for memory, with research[56] showing that 'the relationship between stress and memory is complicated. Veridical [true] memories may not always be accompanied by a high level of confidence and details. In particular, victims of violent or otherwise upsetting crimes may have vague and disjointed memories of the event, especially during a first interview soon after the crime, when stress levels are still high. It should not be surprising if a second interview, conducted when the stress hormones have returned closer to baseline levels, contains a more coherent story, with additional details that were not recalled on the first interview.' [57] These effects are physical, with studies showing that high stress levels result in the

---

56. Lacy. J. W. and Stark C. E. L. *The Neuroscience of Memory: Implications for the Courtroom* Nat Rev Neurosci. Author manuscript; available in PMC 2014 Oct 2
57. Lacy. J. W. and Stark C. E. L. *The Neuroscience of Memory: Implications for the Courtroom* Nat Rev Neurosci. Author manuscript; available in PMC 2014 Oct 2

prefrontal cortex essentially shutting down,[58] greatly inhibiting executive functions, i.e. processes including attention control and working memory.

Lawyers have long been aware of the vagaries of human memories, that they are not perfect, that they are flawed, that they are prone to manipulation, that they evolve. Lawyers were aware of memory flaws long before psychologists started studying them formally, and are very attuned to recognise, and then exploit to their advantage, any small inconsistency in memory and in the way a story is told, even if it is just a change in wording. They take advantage of these inconsistencies to cast doubt on the reliability of witnesses. They learn witness statements and 'exploit every teensy inconsistency between the minutiae of that document and the evidence you give the court from memory 18 months later',[59] according to award winning blogger *The Secret Barrister*.[60] This practice[61] is made significantly easier when hours and hours of taped recordings are available, as they were in the Farquharson case.

With Farquharson having two trials, many witnesses gave evidence twice, three years apart. It is interesting to read the witness statements in terms of inconsistencies. If each witness was branded a liar when they changed a small detail from one trial to the next, there would be no honest witnesses left in the case. Except Greg King, who memorized the third version of his statement and just regurgitated it verbatim in both trials. Does that make him the only credible witness? In fact, when King lost his way during the second trial,[62] he needed to have a break and return to the witness stand so that he could regurgitate his statement from the start, as he could not pick it up from part of

---

58. e.g. Arnsten, A. F., Raskind, M. A., Taylor, F. B., & Connor, D. F. *The effects of stress exposure on prefrontal cortex: Translating basic research into successful treatments for post-traumatic stress disorder* 2015 Neurobiology of StressV1, Pages 89–99
59. The Secret Barrister, 10 things you should know as a witness, Dec 8 2015
60. thesecretbarrister.com
61. see also Pozner & Dodd, 1993 Lexis Law Pub
62. Trial 2 p 3082

the way through. It was apparent that he was remembering his statement, not the events.

Similarly, if every time two witnesses to the same events and conversations were brandished liars when they gave inconsistent evidence, then the only evidence that would have been allowed would be the less reliable statements of single witnesses. Consider Shane Atkinson and Tony McClelland, who were together when they found Farquharson at the side of the road and drove him to Cindy's house. Shane claimed that he tried to offer his phone to Farquharson, while Tony does not recall Shane having had a phone at all. Shane claimed that Farquharson smoked between 3-5 cigarettes at the dam[63] whereas McClelland said that he did not smoke any.[64] Shane claimed that when they arrived at Cindy's house, he knocked on the back door and yelled out 'Cindy, Cindy, come outside',[65] and Cindy had responded 'What the fuck's going on?'[66] McClelland claimed that it was he who knocked on the back door, that a little boy had come out, and that McClelland asked him where Cindy was.[67] Do such inconsistencies between their testimony, and there were many, mean that they are both liars? Or that we should discard their evidence? No. We simply treat their memory evidence for what it is: flawed reconstructions of the events.

If inconsistencies are going to be brandished as lies, let us explore the inconsistencies of the prosecution star witnesses. Greg King gave three different versions of his statement, ending with a statement where he claimed that Farquharson had outlined precisely how and when he will kill his boys. Shane Atkinson did not mention a phone in his statement to police, he said that he had a mobile during the committal hearing, then by the trial he said that he offered Farquharson the use of the phone and he had refused to use it. Dawn Waite said nothing for four years and then changed her testimony in the two months

---

63. Trial 2 p1800, p1815-16
64. Trial 2 p1849
65. Trial 2 p1804
66. Trial 2 p1804
67. Trial 2 p1842

between the *voir dire* and the trial. Her evidence went from giving her high beams a 'quick flick' to driving along behind Farquharson with her high beams illuminating the insides of his car. Glen Urquhart changed his testimony regarding almost every aspect of the reconstruction evidence that was used to support the three steering inputs: a 220 degree turn changed to 15 degrees or less, a curved path through the long grass changed to a straight path, the camber of the road changed from sloping left to sloping right, the left wheels of Farquharson's cars passing through the left mark on the side of the road changed to the right wheels passing through the right mark. Yet it was only Farquharson who was brandished a liar in the case. Over and over he was called a liar. Over and over, the jury was told of his 'every changing story'.

Like with Lindy Chamberlain, none of Robert Farquharson's purported lies or changes of story stand up to scrutiny, and none amount to evidence of guilt. But the prosecutors' assertions of lies never really related to a rational evaluation of evidence. They were just ways to besmirch his character.

CHAPTER 18

THE GORILLA IN THE ROOM

'It was like watching some poor animal dying. You wanted to call out, "For God's sake, shoot him!"'[1]

Farquharson had not testified in the first trial but during the second trial 'Farquharson endured three days on the stand. The defence case never recovered.'[2] according to Helen Garner. Sergeant Jeffrey Smith called Farquharson's testimony 'unbelievably bad', explaining that 'every time things were put to him about "well how do you say this could happen?"' he responded "Oh, I don't know.. can't remember"…'I can't remember was like his biggest answer I think'[3].

The question is whether the testimony of Robert Farquharson provides any evidence that he is guilty. Because, just like branding inconsequential inconsistencies in a story as 'lies', lawyers discredit witnesses by eliciting responses of 'I don't know', or 'I can't remember'. This tactic was used extensively and devastatingly by the prosecutor on Robert Farquharson.

Let us look at an example. During his extensive police interview, when being questioned about what happened in the dam, Farquharson was asked 'Did you do anything with the ignition?' to which he responded 'I can't recall, honestly I could

1. Garner, Helen. This House of Grief: The Story of a Murder Trial (Kindle Locations 3316-3317). The Text Publishing Company. Kindle Edition.
2. Garner, Helen. This House of Grief: The Story of a Murder Trial (Kindle Locations 3333-3334). The Text Publishing Company. Kindle Edition
3. Crimes that Shook Australia

not recall...' When told that the ignition was turned off, Farquharson said 'Honestly I don't know.... I must have turned the car off or something'.

During his cross examination at trial, Crown Prosecutor Andrew Tinney refreshed Farquharson's memory of these answers, then proceeded:

Tinney: Why did the ignition of this car get turned off at all?

Farquharson: *Well, I don't know, I can't answer that.*

Tinney: Is there any other person who could have turned it off other than you?

Farquharson: *I can't answer that.*

Tinney: Oh, witness, is there any person in the car who could possibly have turned – or would have possibly turned off the ignition of that car other than you?

Farquharson: *Well, I mean Jai could have easily but I am not saying he did and I am not saying I didn't, I can't answer it.*

Tinney: Are you seriously suggesting that one of your children- - -?

Farquharson: *–I am not seriously suggesting – – –*

Tinney:- – – in the moments or however long it was before they died would have had any reason to turn off the ignition of that car?

Farquharson: *Well, I can't answer it. I am trying to answer it the best way I can.*

Tinney: Why did you turn off the ignition?

Farquharson: *I don't know if I did.*

Tinney: Why did you – sorry, you don't know if you did?

Farquharson: *Well obviously it's in the off so obviously that's happened but I don't know, I can't answer it.*

Tinney: You can't throw any light on why you would have done that?

Farquharson: *No*

Similarly, here is how the prosecutor asked about the lights, also found to be off:

Tinney: Why did you turn off the headlights?

Farquharson: *I don't recall having, having any headlights, I don't know.*

Tinney: Well, you had headlights, when you were driving along at just below 100, you had headlights, didn't you?

Farquharson: *Yep, they could have been bumped or anything, I don't know.*

Tinney: You think the headlight switch could have been bumped and they could have been bumped off?

Farquharson: *I can't answer it.*

Tinney: Is that your truthful answer to the members of the jury?

Farquharson: *Yes.*

Tinney: Did you have some reason for wanting it to be dark out there?

Farquharson: *No, I did not.*

Tinney: Was there any lights, light coming from the instrument panel?

Farquharson: *Look, I can't recall*

When the prosecutor gets such an 'I don't know' or 'I can't recall' response, he continues to ask the same question in a slightly different way.

Tinney: Was there any source of light at all in that motor car or around that motor car?

Farquharson: *No. Like I said, I can't recall*

Tinney: Are you saying there wasn't or you don't know whether there was or not?

Farquharson: *Well, I don't know.*

A highly experienced lawyer certainly made Farquharson look bad on the stand. That is to be expected. Do these responses of 'I cant recall' and 'I don't know' really point to guilt?

If Farquharson is to be believed, then there was around a minute between his 'coming to' and the car sinking. It was very dark. He was not sure where he was. He was trying to pull himself together and work out what to do. What needs to be considered in terms of what he recalls are not only flaws in memory, and the physical effects that stress has on memory, but also the nature of paying attention.

In a now famous experiment[4] dubbed the 'invisible gorilla test', cognitive psychologists Daniel Simons and Christopher Chabris asked participants to watch a video where two groups of people, three dressed in white, three in black, pass basketballs around. The volunteers were asked to count the passes among players dressed in white, ignoring the passes of those in black. During the video, a person in a gorilla suit walks in and out of the scene thumping its chest. Around half the participants failed to notice the gorilla, despite its prominence in the scene. The video has been viewed more than 16 million times on youtube[5] and lot of people were shocked to have missed the gorilla. 'It's hard to explain such a failure of awareness without confronting the possibility that we are aware of far less of our world than we think'[6] said Simons. Essentially, if we are not paying attention, or our attention in taken by something else, we do not see what is in our vision.

Magicians have long been aware of the disconnect between what people see with their eyes and what they focus on with their minds, allowing them to draw the attention of their audience away from those actions they don't want to be perceived. Researchers have been slow to catch up with magicians' knowledge about cognition, but the past decade has seen a rapid increase of formal knowledge in the field. Researchers have measured subjects' eye movements[7] as they watch magicians perform their tricks. 'What people actually saw was not related to where they were looking,' said Gustav Kuhn of Durham University 'Even though their eyes were focused on the objects, their attention was elsewhere'.[8]

The same thing is true about ears. How many times have you spoken to someone, well within their ear shot, but they have not

---

4. Simons, D. J., & Chabris, C. F. (1999). *Gorillas in Our Midst: Sustained Inattentional Blindness for Dynamic Events.* Perception, 28(9), 1059–1074
5. selective attention test
6. Choi C. Q. *Invisible Gorilla' Test Shows How Little We Notice* Live Science July 11, 2010
7. Kuhn G, Amlani A, Rensink R. *Towards a science of magic* 2008 Trends in Cognitive Sciences, 12: 349-354.
8. Bryner, J *Magicians Know More Than Scientists* Live Science July 23, 2008

heard what you said because they were not paying attention? They may know you said something, they just don't know what. In fact, we have two different words for auditory inputs, to hear and to listen. You may *hear* someone talking but you need to be paying attention, to be *listening* to them, in order to record in your mind what was said, and therefore to remember what was said. As with most aspects of the brain, things are quite complicated but in short, memories require attention.[9,10]

More generally, people are not good at multi-tasking.[11] People *can* multi-task by doing things sequentially, moving their attention back and forth between two tasks, and can also multi-task by, for example, breathing and reading at the same time, because there is no need to focus our minds on the act of breathing. There are some things that we can do without thinking, without focus, but those things will not necessarily imprint on our memories, although of course we will remember that we *must have been* breathing at the time. There are some behaviours[12] that we learn to do without consciously thinking about them, without paying attention, like walking or even driving.

If his story is true, what would Robert Farquharson have been paying attention to? He claims to have 'come to' and 'regained his senses' and not been sure where he was. It was dark. He was confused. What Farquharson did in this situation was to follow his normal routine. When disembarking the car with the boys, he had always followed a particular sequence, and Farquharson 'was a very routine person, didn't like anything out of routine'[13] according to his ex-wife Cindy Gambino. So we should not be

---

9. e.g. Chun, M & Turk-Browne, N. *Interactions between attention and memory* 2007, Curr Opin Neurobiol. 2007 Apr;17(2):177-84
10. see also Murphy G, Groeger J & Greene C, *Twenty Years of Load Theory – Where Are We Now and Where Should We Go Next?* 2016 Psychonomic Bulletin & Review
11. e.g. Pashler, H. (1984). Processing stages in overlapping tasks: Evidence for a central bottleneck. *Journal of Experimental Psychology: Human Perception and Performance, 10*(3), 358-377
12. e.g. Schacter, D. L. "Implicit memory: history and current status" 1987 Journal of Experimental Psychology: Learning, Memory, and Cognition. **13**: 501–518
13. Trial 2 p1170

particularly surprised that he followed his normal routine at that moment. In the confusion, he followed his routine. Turn off the ignition and lights, get out his door, go around and open the rear passenger side door and lift Bailey out, allowing Taylor to climb over the baby seat, while Jai got himself out the front passenger side.

When following his routine, Farquharson performed routine acts without paying much attention. His attention was presumably elsewhere, such as thinking 'Where are the fuck are we?', 'How did we get here?', 'What happened?', 'What is this water we seem to be in?', 'How should I get the kids out?' So in that timeframe of a minute or so, it is not surprising that he does not recall turning off the car engine, or turning off the lights. Those things he did routinely.

Consider the three SAS soldiers who drowned when they were trapped inside their sinking car, having veered off a bridge and into Port Phillip Bay. In that case, the handbrake of the submerged car was found to be on. Why would the driver put a hand-break on in the water? Can we interpret anything from that? Did it imply that the driver was guilty of driving into the bay deliberately in order to kill his companions? Of course not. The driver must have put the hand-break on instinctively, without thinking, his attention elsewhere.

Combined with the effects of stress on memory, it is not surprising that Farquharson could not recall turning off the engine and headlights, so his responses were perfectly reasonable in the circumstances. Yet the prosecutor makes Farquharson appear as though he is being deceptive. Once again, what makes this tactic so effective is the tendency for people to think that memory works like a video recorder, and to over-estimate their own memories. When hearing a witness respond 'I don't recall', it is natural for the juror to feel as though the witness should be able to remember. The witness must be hiding something!

Perhaps barristers are not aware of the tendency to over-estimate memories, but they are certainly aware that responses of 'I don't know' are often (mis)interpreted by juries as signalling deception... 'If you can't recall that detail, how can you I trust anything you say about what happened?!' The prosecutor knew that Farquharson had given those responses to certain question during his interviews, so he asked those questions over and over again during the trial.

What does research into deception tell us about responses of 'I don't know' and 'I don't recall'? I have noted earlier in the book that it is very difficult, perhaps impossible, to tell when people are lying.[14,15] Many people think they can spot liars, but research shows that they cannot. Fidgeting, blinking, looking away rather than looking someone in the eye, glancing upwards to the left; none of these activities are indicative of lying. The notion that deception shows up as 'micro-expressions', as depicted on the tv show *Lie to me*, is also unsupported by evidence.[16] One study that looked at various 'tells' did, however, find one tendency of liars: 'Liars are apparently less likely to say "I don't know" to unanticipated questions and to offer some answer, possibly because they are afraid that to do otherwise would look suspicious.'[17]

Answers of 'I don't know' are not indicative of deception and are normal responses of truth tellers. I am not suggesting that his responses can be taken as evidence that Robert Farquharson is telling the truth, but they do not prove that he was being deceptive, or that he was lying.

What about the substance of these questions? The fact that the ignition and lights were turned off has persistently been presented as evidence of Farquharson's guilt.[18,19,20,21] Isn't it

---

14. Bond, C. F., & DePaulo, B. M. (2006). Accuracy of deception judgments. Personality and Social Psychology Review, 10, 214– 234
15. Sporer, S. L., & Schwandt, B. (2006). Paraverbal indicators of deception: A meta-analytic synthesis. *Applied Cognitive Psychology*, 20, 421–446.
16. e.g. Porter, S & ten Brinke, L. *Reading Between the Lies* 2008 Psychological Science 19(5):508-14
17. Loftus, E. *Catching Liars* Psychological Science in thePublic Interest11(3) 87–88
18. see Crimes that Shook Australia (Norris?)
19. *Crimes that Shook Australia*, Series 2 Ep 1
20. Norris, Megan *On Father's Day: Cindy Gambino's Shattering Account of her Children's Revenge Murders* (Kindle Locations 1179-1180)
21. Farquharson v R [2012] VSCA 296

normal to turn off the ignition after an accident? Isn't that what you are supposed to do? Indeed, insurance companies advise that, after minor accidents, drivers should 'turn off your ignition to guard against fire'[22] while the NSW government website advises to 'Switch off the ignition of the immobilized vehicle to reduce the risk of fire'.[23] Consider that Farquharson consistently said that he initially thought they had driven into a ditch, it would make perfect sense for him to turn off the ignition.

As for the lights, the police diver testified[24] that her torch was useless in the blackened dam water, so there was no practical difference between lights on and lights off. It was pitch black either way. Why wouldn't Farquharson automatically, routinely turn the lights off along with the ignition? Without really thinking about it?

Similar to the questioning on the ignition and lights was the ongoing and persistent questioning about the children's seatbelts, which were all found to be undone, and whether Farquharson could remember undoing them. Once again, the barrister elicited a string of responses along the lines of 'I don't know' or 'I can't answer that'.

Yet Jai was 10 years old and Tyler 7. Both routinely fastened and undid their own seat belts. They did not need their father's help. It appears as though one of them, most likely Tyler, also undid two year old Bailey's belt. There is no dispute that Tyler had the ability to undo Bailey's belt: 'I reckon Tyler's undone Bailey'[25] said Cindy. It was not a difficult task for Tyler, although it was hugely heroic. So how does the evidence regarding the seatbelts point to Farquharson being guilty? It is certainly emotive to think of the children undoing their own seatbelts, and

22. Island Insurance, see also e.g. Kraft & Associates: "Turn off your ignition to guard against fire.", Liberty Insurance: "By turning off the ignition the drivers are reducing the risk of starting a fire", Geico Insurance: 'turn off the ignition. This will eliminate the risk of fire, especially since chances are good that the crash has caused an oil, fuel or coolant leak.'
23. NSW safe driving from NSW Transport Roads and Maritime Services
24. Trial 2 p2290
25. From transcript of secretly recorded phone call between Cindy Gambino and Farquharson ; Garner, H. *This House of Grief* Kindle Location 2717

that of their younger brother, and trying to get out of the car. However, the fact that the children's seatbelts were undone does not help distinguish between whether Farquharson had driven into the dam deliberately or by accident.

Another matter that received similar lines of questioning, but which again provides no evidence one way or the other in terms of guilt, concerned the locks. When the car was found, the rear driver's side door had a child lock on. However, that door was broken, it did not open from inside or outside, regardless of whether any locks were on or off. So it was inconsequential whether the child lock was turned on or off, it made absolutely no difference. Similarly, the rear passenger's side had the normal lock on. However, Bailey at age 2 was incapable of helping himself out of the car regardless of whether that nib was up or down, whilst Tyler at age 7 was perfectly capable of unlocking the door himself, as he climbed over the baby seat to exit the car. Whether it was up or down was inconsequential. The prosecution asked Farquharson over and over about these locks, but why would such inconsequential details have been on his mind as he drove home from Geelong to Winchelsea? Or during the brief time between 'coming to' and the car sinking?

None of these details of ignition, lights or locks provide evidence that helps to distinguish whether Farquharson drove into the dam deliberately, or accidentally, or whether he was guilty or innocent. But such small, irrelevant details provided opportunities for the prosecution to exploit a general misunderstanding about how memory works, and about the nature of paying attention, in order to portray Robert Farquharson as deceptive by eliciting repeated responses of 'I don't know', 'I don't recall', 'I can't answer that'.

Chapter 19

ANGRY, ANGRY, ANGRY

Meeting as teenagers, Robert Farquharson and Cindy Gambino were first acquaintances, then friends, then lovers, then husband and wife. By the time of the wedding they had two sons, Jai and Tyler. They then had another, Bailey. They were struggling along on Rob's meagre earnings as a cleaner. Cindy was thrifty, scrounging to pay for a new house. Cindy was also bored. She wanted more from her life, from her partner. She finally told Rob it was over, that she did not love him anymore, to pack his bags. The kids will stay with me, she told him, you can visit them whenever you want. Rob moved in with his father who lived nearby. Cindy Farquharson filed for divorce and reverted to calling herself Cindy Gambino. It was November, 2004.

Robert Farquharson was not happy when Cindy left him. He did not like her new man, Stephen Moules. Hated him. He was upset and, at times, angry with how things went down. Anger is 'a very prevalent emotion' in separation, according to Susan Pease Gadoua, a therapist and author of *Reflections for Healing and Rebuilding After Divorce*, so it was quite normal for Farquharson to display some signs of anger. If he did kill his own boys, however, he must have been extremely and abnormally angry. Not to mention violent.

When trying to determine whether Farquharson is guilty or not, it is important to ignore the *inferences* of anger that follow from the assumption of guilt, and instead look at the evidence pertaining to anger and violence that existed *prior* to the boys deaths. What evidence existed regarding Robert Farquharson's anger prior to Father's day, 4th September 2005? How angry was he at that time, according to the evidence?

Farquharson was not the only one upset at the breakdown of the marriage. Ten year old Jai was also having trouble adjusting to the new circumstances and was displaying behavioural difficulties and a degree of anger. Cindy suggested the family seek the help of a counsellor to cope with the changes their lives were going through. She found someone local, applied psychologist Peter Popko. Cindy and Jai had their first session with Popko in October 2004. In January 2005, Robert Farquharson went with Cindy and Jai to see Popko. Farquharson then saw Popko alone on multiple occasions in 2005, the last time in August 2005.[1] During the sessions, Popko gave Farquharson strategies to help him deal with the grief and loss of the relationship,[2] and to learn to live as a single person.[3] He encouraged Farquharson to express his feelings about the separation. These sessions provided a vital source of information about Robert Farquharson's state of mind in the period of time leading up to Father's day 2005.

At the trial, Popko said that Farquharson's level of anger was 'within the normal range. It didn't seem to be excessive.'[4] and that most of the anger that was present was directed at Stephen Moules.[5] Farquharson was angry about reports of Moules having yelled at Jai, and he was angry that Moules had lectured him on how he should discipline Jai.[6] Farquharson also complained about his children having to spend time with Moules' children, and that Jai in particular was not happy, did not like Moules[7] and did not get along with Moules' son Luke.[8]

1. Trial 2 p2827
2. Trial 2 p2827
3. Trial 2 p2832
4. Trial 2 p2828
5. Trial 2 p2828, also at p2832
6. Trial 2 p2829
7. Trial 1 p1489
8. Trial 1 p1489

Popko also testified that Farquharson had expressed gratitude for the manner that Cindy gave him open access to the children,[9] and praised her as a mother. Popko gained an impression of Farquharson as a protective and caring parent.[10] This impression was informed not only through his sessions with Farquharson himself, but also during his discussions with Cindy and with Jai.[11] At no time did Popko get any indication that Farquharson may hurt Cindy or the children.[12]

By June of 2005, seven months after the separation, Popko thought that Farquharson's mood had improved,[13] and that he 'seemed to be less preoccupied with going over what had happened in the past and more focused on future goals and future prospects.'[14]

The other important witness in regard to Farquharson's state of mind at the time is Cindy herself. Cindy had lived with Farquharson for more than ten years, and knew him and his moods, traits and emotions better than anyone.

Cindy's evidence regarding Farquharson's nature, and behaviour, came in two acts. Initially, she was adamant that Farquharson was innocent and during the first trial, she testified to try to help get him off. Later, she had changed her mind and thought he was guilty, so during the second trial she testified to try to help attain his conviction. I won't explore in detail the reasons for her changing her mind, partly because I would only be guessing. She said that Dawn Waite coming forward was 'the biggest clincher' as 'she had no reason to lie'.[15] However, the reasons may be more complex considering the pressure she had been put under, having received 'all sorts of disgusting hate mail'[16] for supporting Rob, having been told by a 60 minute

---

9. Trial 2 p2833
10. Trial 2 p2835
11. Trial 2 p2835
12. Trial 2 p2828
13. Trial 2 p2834
14. Trial 2 p2837
15. Norris, M. *On Father's Day* Kindle Location 6727
16. Norris, M. *On Father's Day* Kindle Location 5245

reporter to 'wake up, you're in denial',[17] and having been accused by the public prosecutor of not speaking up for her children.[18]

What is important regarding Cindy's change of mind is that, as with all witnesses, her evidence in each trial should be assessed and interpreted within the context of her different motivations. Assessing the substance of her evidence should not be influenced by the strong emotions that were evident in her testimony, first one way, then the other.

During the first trial, Cindy described Rob as 'gentle person' and a 'bit of a softie' with a 'heart of gold'. Cindy said that 'he was pretty much a softie and always gave in to what I wanted'.[19] Rob did not think having a third child was a good idea, but Cindy wanted one so they had Bailey. Rob did not think they could afford a new car but Cindy wanted one so they bought a new Commodore Berlina. Rob did not want to build a new house, preferring to buy an existing one but Cindy wanted a new house, so they brought a vacant lot and started building.

The reason Cindy left Farquharson was not due to violence, nor to anger issues, nor to rage.[20] There was never any police involvement, no restraining orders, no lawyers or courts required to arrange custody or access to the children. Cindy said she 'just found it hard to give myself to him'.[21] She loved him but was not 'in love' with him,[22] even though 'he was a very secure person, he was a very good provider'.[23]

During the second trial, Cindy confirmed her earlier evidence regarding Farquharson's nature during the marriage,[24] and why she left him.[25] When asked if he was 'a gentle person' she said that *at the time* she had 'thought he was'.[26] Cindy testified that there

---

17. Norris, M. *On Father's Day* Kindle Location 5245
18. Trial 2 p533
19. Trial 1 967
20. Trial 1 p970
21. Trial 1 p970
22. Trial 1 p970
23. Trial 1 p970
24. Trial 1 p970
25. e.g. Voire Dire Trial 2 p560
26. Trial 2 p522

was 'no violence towards me, no violence towards the children',[27] that 'there was arguing and stuff between Rob and I, but not violence'.[28] Referring to these arguments, she said that 'Rob would cop a lot from me, and he wouldn't fight back',[29] and that 'I was the one that would yell, he wouldn't yell back.'[30] She reiterated that she generally got her way in the relationship.[31]

Cindy added in the second trial that Farquharson 'always looked at his glass half empty, he always looked at what he didn't have and not what he did have'[32] and that he was 'always whinging and moaning and was never happy'[33].

When looking past the contrasting language that Cindy employed in the two trials, her testimony regarding the separation is also consistent. During the first trial, Cindy said that Farquharson had been 'pretty devastated'[34] but that the separation had been 'amicable'. During the second trial she said that at the time, *prior to* Father's day 2005, she was not 'aware of any ongoing situation of anger, towards her from the accused.'[35] She added that 'there was an underlying bitterness that *I didn't know about*'.[36] It was only *after* she believed he was guilty, that she concluded that he *must have been* angry and bitter.[37]

When asked to explain how Farquharson had displayed signs of being 'angry and bitter', Cindy said that 'he did not like our children anywhere near his [Moules] children'[38] and that this was evident 'in arguments that we would have… the same arguments about Stephen, the same arguments about the children being forced to be with Stephen's children…most of the arguments

27. Trial 2 p523
28. Trial 2 p1169
29. Trial 2 p523
30. Trial 2 p523
31. Trial 2 p523
32. Trial 2 1188
33. Trial 2 1169
34. Trial 1 p971
35. Trial 2 4896
36. Trial 2 p528
37. Trial 2 p529
38. Trial 2 p1176

were about the children being around Stephen'.[39] Farquharson's resentment of Stephen Moules was a recurrent theme. During the first trial, Cindy said that she did think he was having difficulty with the fact that she had taken up with another man[40] and that Farquharson had concerns over the influence that Moules may have over his children. He did not like his boys spending time with Moules and his children.

During both trials, Cindy described Farquharson as a loving,[41] devoted[42] and protective[43] father who was very close[44] to his kids. During the second trial, Cindy added that Farquharson had a 'love/hate' relationship with the boys. However, Cindy said that prior to Father's day 2005, she *believed* that he was a very good dad,[45] and that she had thought, *at the time*, that he only had a love relationship with them.[46] It was only after she believed he was guilty that she concluded that he *must have* had a 'love/hate' relationship with them. When pressed to explain how Farquharson had displayed any signs of hate, she said that 'I don't mean hate as in sheer hatred. It was – he didn't really want three children, but he accepted it. And, yes, he did love them. But then he would do things to torment them… it was like his way of play fighting, joking around, but taking things too far for a child to deal with and when I say that, on several, on so many occasions he would stir them up, thinking he was funny, and then when the children had had enough, they wanted to lash out at him.'[47]

The other new evidence that Cindy introduced in the second trial was that Farquharson had treated her and the children like 'possessions'. When asked what she meant by this, she said that 'I don't mean possessions as in things that you own, it was sort of like – I don't even know if there is another word for it… he

39. Trial 2 p1177
40. Trial 1 p973
41. E.g. Trial 2 p532
42. Committal Hearing, confirmed in Trial 2 p1237
43. Trial 2 p524
44. Trial 2 p1238
45. Trial p1254
46. Trial 2 p1255
47. Trial 2 p1368

always went in to defend us and if anything happened, he would defend us in whatever way needed to be defended. It was – there was a feeling from me of like, "Well, they're my children, you're my wife", it's, "You're mine, you're" – that sort of feeling. He was very protective. It was like the four of us were his, I guess the only way I can describe it is possessions as in he was protective of all of us... he never ever called them by their Christian names, he never called me by my Christian name'.[48]

In attempting to help get Farquharson convicted Cindy had presumably raised the most damning of Farquharson's character traits and behaviours. In this context, Cindy had charged that Farquharson took his joking play fights with his sons too far, not knowing when it went beyond being funny to being frustrating for them, that he was very protective of both Cindy and his boys and would always defend them, and that he had nicknames for each member of his family, preferring to use those over their Christian names.

Cindy's evidence certainly changed on the surface between the two trials, but in substance it remained consistent. Importantly, it was also consistent with the testimony of Peter Popko, the two agreeing that Farquharson was a caring, protective and loving father, agreeing that the boys were the main focus of his life, agreeing on the mild degree of anger that Farquharson displayed *at the time*, and agreeing that the focus of any anger or resentment was Stephen Moules and his relationship with the boys. Both agreed that, at the time, they did not perceive Farquharson to be any kind of threat to Cindy or the boys.

A number of other witnesses, including Farquharson's sisters Carmen Ross and Kerri Huntington, his brother in law Gary Huntington, his boss Susan Bateson, the local doctor Ian McDonald, Michael Hart, Wendy Kennedy, Kiri Fausett and Susan Hatty, also testified as to Farquharson's nature, his reaction to the separation, and his relationship with his children. Farquharson 'idolised his kids and loved his kids',[49] 'he was a

---

48. Trial 2 p1369
49. Kiri Fausett Trial 2 p1862

loving father...the boys and Rob had a really good relationship',[50] he was a protective father[51], being 'over cautious, I suppose you might say'.[52] He had 'loved his wife'[53] so was having trouble with the break up, especially in the first months. He 'had been hoping that the relationship could be reconciled but was told that it couldn't so he was upset but did not appear angry'.[54] He was 'not an angry person- he hasn't had an angry bone in his body.'[55] Farquharson thought Stephen Moules was a 'dickhead',[56] and complained about having the 'shit car' and about seeing Moules driving the good car that was now owned by Cindy. Farquharson did not like his children spending time with Moules and his boys, was concerned about the influence Stephen would have on his boys,[57] and about 'how his children were being treated',[58] especially after hearing a rumour around town about Moules having shouted and sworn at Jai out the front of the Post Office. Cindy's uncle Tillio Gambino made a statement on behalf of the Gambino family, telling the Herald Sun newspaper that 'He's a top bloke. He thought the world of those kids. He treasures them with all his heart.'[59].

Some of these witnesses were friends or family of Farquharson, so the tone of the evidence was often in his favour, but it is nevertheless notable that the substance of their testimony was very consistent, both with each other and with the evidence of Peter Popko and Cindy. Taken as whole, quite a clear picture has emerged, and there is a distinct lack of evidence for the existence of extreme anger, violence, or threats of violence prior to September 4 2005.

50. Michael Hart Trial 2 p4815
51. Wendy Kennedy Trial 2 p4717
52. Wendy Kennedy Trial 2 p4717
53. Michael Hart Trial 2 p4825
54. Dr. Ian McDonald Trial 2 p2785
55. Michael Hart Trial 2 p4829
56. Wendy Kennedy Trial 2 p4731
57. Trial 1 p973; see also Wendy Kennedy at Trial 2 p4783; Michael Hart at Trial 2 p4824
58. Trial 2 p1505
59. Norris, Megan *On Father's Day: Cindy Gambino's Shattering Account of her Children's Revenge Murders* (Kindle Locations 1349-1350). The Five Mile Press.

So why did the prosecution include anger as one of the key strands of evidence against Robert Farquharson? Why did the prosecuting barrister use the words *angry* or *anger* to describe Farquharson more than 50 times in his closing address to the jury? 'When sadness and anger and resentment arose they fell on very fertile ground in the heart and in the mind of Robert Donald William Farquharson',[60] 'far from letting go of the resentment, the anger, the sadness, the other negative feelings, he held on to them',[61] 'the refusal to let go, the growth of anger and resentment',[62] 'his own petty anger and resentment',[63] 'the apparent anger of the accused',[64] 'the considerable anger of the accused',[65] 'the accused was angry',[66] 'he was angry',[67] 'anger',[68] 'anger',[69] 'anger',[70] 'anger towards her',[71] 'the anger',[72] 'maintain his anger',[73] 'the accused was very angry, and very bitter',[74] 'resentment and anger',[75] 'anger and resentment',[76] 'murderous and obscene anger',[77] 'obvious anger',[78] 'the anger',[79] 'He was angry. He was bitter. He was resentful',[80] 'unhappiness and anger',[81] 'unhappiness and anger',[82] 'this anger, this

---

60. Trial 2 p4861
61. Trial 2 p4861
62. Trial 2 p4861
63. Trial 2 p4866
64. Trial 2 p4886
65. Trial 2 p4895
66. Trial 2 p4895
67. Trial 2 p4895
68. Trial 2 p4895
69. Trial 2 p4895
70. Trial 2 p4895
71. Trial 2 p4896
72. Trial 2 p4895
73. Trial 2 p4895
74. Trial 2 p4897
75. Trial 2 p4910
76. Trial 2 p5026
77. Trial 2 p5026
78. Trial 2 p5026
79. Trial 2 p5026
80. Trial 2 p5027
81. Trial 2 p5028

unhappiness',[83] 'overflowing with anger and resentment',[84] 'angry and resentful',[85] 'wronged, aggrieved, bitter, angry complaining man',[86] 'angry',[87] 'an angry, bitter, resentful man',[88] 'he was angry',[89] 'an angry man',[90] 'his anger',[91] 'that angry man',[92] 'hissy fit of anger',[93] 'anger and resentment',[94] 'angry at his wife',[95] 'angry and resentful and sad',[96] 'his anger',[97] 'that anger',[98] 'the anger',[99] 'angry',[100] 'pain and anger',[101] 'pain and anger',[102] 'pain and anger',[103] 'his anger',[104] 'the heart of the anger',[105] 'an angry and unhappy person',[106] 'the anger and aggression',[107] 'anger, resentment and selfishness',[108] 'his anger',[109] 'great anger',[110] 'anger and unhappiness',[111] 'angry, frustrated and unhappy.'[112]

82. Trial 2 p5028
83. Trial 2 p5028
84. Trial 2 p5029
85. Trial 2 p5029
86. Trial 2 p5029
87. Trial 2 p5030
88. Trial 2 p5030
89. Trial 2 p5031
90. Trial 2 p5038
91. Trial 2 p5038
92. Trial 2 p5038
93. Trial 2 p5040
94. Trial 2 p5040
95. Trial 2 p5051
96. Trial 2 p5154
97. Trial 2 p5054
98. Trial 2 p5054
99. Trial 2 p5065
100. Trial 2 p5066
101. Trial 2 p5066
102. Trial 2 p5066
103. Trial 2 p5066
104. Trial 2 p5067
105. Trial 2 p5068
106. Trial 2 p5069
107. Trial 2 p5070
108. Trial 2 p5070
109. Trial 2 p5071
110. Trial 2 p5158
111. Trial 2 p5158
112. Trial 2 p5158

Is that really the level of anger that can be adduced from the evidence? Who was the source of the information that led to this depiction of Farquharson as being so consumed by anger? You guessed it. Greg King. We are back to the conversation out the front of the fish 'n' chip shop. According to the prosecution, Farquharson was suppressing his anger when around all these other witnesses,[113] but to Greg King 'the accused showed himself to be overflowing with anger and resentment towards his former wife, to such an extent that he was unwilling or unable to hide that from his good friend Greg King and it bubbled over'[114].

Beyond that single conversation, King admitted that 'I haven't sort of seen a lot of him' and so 'I don't know' how Farquharson was dealing with the separation, 'I don't know' whether he had begun moving on with his life, as stated by Popko[115] and others.[116] When asked more generally about Farquharson's character, King said that 'he always had something to complain about, never happy'[117] but that he was a peaceful, non-violent and lovable bloke who loved his kids.[118]

Recall as well that when King confronted Farquharson with his version of what occurred in front of the fish and chip shop, and secretly recorded the conversation, Farquharson stated that it was Stephen Moules, and the way he interacted with the boys, that was the focus of any anger that he had. One can expect a murderer to make denials, but this explanation of Farquharson was consistent with the testimony coming from all other witnesses including Peter Popko and Cindy. It was Greg King's version that was inconsistent with the other witnesses.

Nearly all people get angry sometimes. There is, however, a large leap between anger and violence, another large leap between violence and murder, and a final large leap between murder and murdering your own children. So, even if the

---

113. Trial 2 p4904
114. Trial 2 p5029
115. Trial 2 p2837
116. Trial 2 p4832
117. Trial 2 p3070
118. Trial 2 p3118

prosecution did provide evidence that Farquharson was extremely angry about Cindy leaving him, it would need significant further evidence for him to be considered guilty. Yet the evidence suggests that Farquharson was *not* abnormally angry, was not generally an angry person, and was not a violent person. In the absence of an assumption of guilt, it was widely believed that he would not do anything to hurt his children and in fact would do anything to protect them. That is the evidence regarding anger in the case.

Farquharson's 'anger' is the last strand of evidence that was presented by the prosecutor in the circumstantial case against Robert Farquharson.

Chapter 20

INNOCENT OR GENIUS

Having now analysed all the evidence of the Farquharson case, it is time to assess it in totality and see what is the most likely conclusion to draw, regarding guilt and innocence. Recall, scientific knowledge is concerned with what is more or less likely, not what is possible or impossible, meaning that any conclusion will retain a degree of uncertainty.

I start with the presumption of innocence, and see if I can explain all the evidence within a coherent innocent story.

Cindy Gambino left Robert Farquharson and started seeing a new man, Steven Moules. Farquharson was hurt and resented Moules. This resentment ratcheted up a notch when rumours reached Farquharson that Moules was screaming at ten year old Jai in the street. Farquharson blamed Moules for Jai's recent behavioural troubles. Farquharson discussed taking custody with friends and family. Cindy, taking control of the situation as usual, took Jai and Rob to see a psychologist to help them cope with the transition to the new family arrangements.

During this time when Farquharson was 'pissed off' with Moules, he ran into an old friend Greg King one evening near the local fish 'n chip shop. He bad mouthed Moules, and to a lesser extent Cindy, puffing his chest out to act as though he was not someone to be trifled with, trying to regain some lost pride by declaring that he would prove himself. He may have even said that he was going to take the kids. The fact that his discussions with friends and family regarding custody had inevitably ended with the recognition that the children were best off with their mother, would not necessarily stop Farquharson from mouthing off about the possibility of taking them away from Moules. Farquharson was small, whilst King was a 'lad' from the footy club who had a penchant for brawls down the local pub, so it is not too surprising that Farquharson would mouth off to King. In fact, Farquharson was known for being mouthy, for liking to 'speak some bullshit' and this is how King had interpreted the conversation, explaining why he did not consider it important enough to tell Cindy or the police or anyone except maybe his wife, who did not recall being told.

Leading up to father's day, 2005, Farquharson had a cough, and went to the doctor and received medication. He had a coughing fit in front of his boss that caused him to go red in the face and get dizzy, also reporting to his friend Darren Bushell the same week that after having a coughing fit, he had 'come to' in a roadhouse carpark with the car having rolled.

On father's day, Cindy Gambino suggested that Farquharson have the boys for dinner, which he did not expect. He decided to take them to Kentucky Fried Chicken, and asked his friend Michael Hart if he and his son wanted to come, but Hart did not fancy the long drive to Geelong. Driving home from Geelong that night, Farquharson again began to cough, and then blacked out. His un-steered car followed the slope of the terrain, which was downward to the right, leading to a dam. There were no signs of breaking or sharp turns along the path of the car because he was unconscious, and his car crashed through the branch of a tree as it plunged into the unusually large and unusually deep dam.

When he came to, it was pitch black and he was not sure where he was. He started to follow his normal routine for getting his three children out of the car. When he got out his door, the car rapidly sank to the bottom of a dam that was more than seven metres deep. After realizing the futility of trying to dive down to the car, Farquharson swam ashore, scrambled to the road, and eventually managed to flag down a car. He was in a state of shock and was highly stressed so it was no surprise that the men in the car stated that he was incoherent. Farquharson knew his boys were lost and all he could think of was Cindy. He needed to tell Cindy. When asked how the car ended up in the dam, he guessed that he 'must have done a wheel bearing' but that all he remembers was coughing, and then waking up with the car in the dam. It was hard to get any other sense out of him, as he incessantly repeated that he needed to see Cindy, to tell the boy's mother.

The doctor who first saw Farquharson that night made a preliminary diagnosis of cough syncope. Another doctor who subsequently examined Farquharson on several occasions and ran a series of tests confirmed this diagnosis. Farquharson was subsequently witnessed blacking out after coughing on three different occasions by multiple witnesses.

This innocent scenario treats the bulk of the evidence at face value, and is straight forward. Farquharson was sick, he had cough syncope, and this caused him to have a car accident in which his three sons tragically died. He then went into shock and behaved like a person whose pre frontal cortex had shut down. Unfortunately, accidents happen on our roads, even rare ones.

Did I have to dismiss, ignore or explain away any evidence in that innocent scenario? The only evidence that really needed to be explained away, or dismissed, is Greg King's final statement according to which, Farquharson said that he would kill his children in a dam on a special day such as father's day, but that he would escape. One can readily dismiss the notion that Greg King recalled the exact words of that conversation. To assess the reliability of the gist of King's evidence, one must consider his nightmares and waking visions, the way the statement evolved and was added to, using known information, the fact that King believed that Farquharson was guilty, King's interaction with police who encouraged him to remember more, and the vast change from King being highly uncertain as he tried to recall details of the conversation, to being 100% sure by the time of the trial. Such 'false confidence' is a big red flag that is often involved in miscarriages of justice. Considering all these factors, it is plausible that the conversation at the fish 'n' chip shop involved Farquharson blowing off some steam and puffing out his chest, trying to regain some lost pride, and that King had re-interpreted it and increasingly embellished it after the children drowned. It is possible that King had mixed his dreams and visions in with reality.

According to memory research, this explanation for King's evolving statement actually seems *more plausible* than believing King's final statement. It is significantly *unlikely* that King had gradually recalled accurate details of the conversation over a three month period in the manner described.

Let us now try to fit all the evidence into a guilty scenario. The prosecution never presented such a scenario during either trial. Rather than weaving a narrative of what occurred and how it explained all the evidence, they just presented the various 'strands' of evidence and left it with the jury. Sure, not all details in every crime are known, but in this case the prosecution never even took a position on whether the murder was planned or not: 'Whether it was a spur of the moment killing or one planned for months does not need to be proved'.[1]

So we are left with two options, a narrative of a planned murder, or of an unplanned murder. I first consider an unplanned murder scenario.

If there was no plan, you have to concede that there is strong evidence that Farquharson has cough syncope because without the plan, how do you explain Darren Bushell's evidence of cough syncope from before the events? Without the plan, you are also conceding that Farquharson had not told King of a plan to kill his children. So you are conceding that Greg King's evidence is wrong, that it is unreliable. So the same conclusions regarding Greg King's evidence need to be inferred in both the innocent and unplanned murder scenarios, both invoking memory flaws.

What evidence are you left with if you concede that Farquharson had cough syncope and admit that you don't believe Greg King? There was just the anger evidence that again came from King, but was contrary to all the other witness testimony

---

1. Trial 2 p5161

on Farquharson's predisposition. And you have the evidence of Farquharson's behavior after the events. Are we going to convict him because one witness, whom you have conceded is unreliable in this scenario, said he was angry and because of some strange behaviour after losing his three sons in the most horrific way imaginable?

Further, the path of the car is difficult to explain in a scenario that lacked a plan. Why did Farquharson veer the car in a manner that left no sharp turns or braking? Why didn't he just drive straight into the dam instead of crashing through a tree branch? Driving in a manner that made it look like an accident would take planning.

Having dismissed the unplanned narrative as being remotely possible but severely lacking supporting evidence, I tried to put together a guilty narrative that includes a plan and that can explain the evidence.

Farquharson is a nonviolent man who has never shown signs of anger, but has reached his breaking point. He is so angry at being left by his wife, that he decides to kill his three sons as an act of revenge against her. He successfully hides this anger from his wife, from the psychologist that he is seeing to help him deal with the break-up, and from most of his friends and family who consider him very protective of his children and consider that he is trying to move on with his life. He is seething quietly, privately. He starts planning how to make the murder look like an accident. One evening, by chance, he runs into Greg King at the fish n chip shop and it all spills out. He tells King that he hates his children, that he plans to kill them, that he will make it look like an accident by drowning them in a dam, and that he will do it on a special day such as father's day. King recalls telling his wife about this very important information, but his wife does not remember it. Perhaps she was distracted by her own children. King does not tell anyone else that Farquharson was planning to murder his own children. The details of the plan only get repeated by King *after* the events.

Meanwhile Farquharson, somewhere, hears about a condition called cough syncope in which one blacks out after coughing.

He researches the condition, either on a computer or perhaps in a library. He learns that cough syncope causes a blackout for a short period of time, and that he fits the profile of a sub-set of people who may be susceptible to cough syncope according to case studies. Or maybe he just got lucky with these details, but he definitely finds out that cough syncope is only diagnosed by history.

Note the fact that Farquharson must have done research into cough syncope does not follow directly from any evidence; it is something we had to *infer* when constructing the planned murder scenario. He needed that information to make the plan. Following this inference, we need to assume that Farquharson hid the fact that he knew how to search the internet, hid the internet search he did into cough syncope and hid all trace of his ever having searched the internet for anything, let alone cough syncope. As for the alternate idea that he did the research in a library, there is no evidence of him ever entering a library and nor is there any evidence that the information he needed regarding cough syncope was found in any material at any public library. In fact, the information he needed would almost certainly not be found in any public library, it was only found in specialised medical journals.

Anyway, Farquharson somehow finds out that he needs to create a history of cough syncope as part of his plan. So one day he is driving and by chance he sees his mate, Darren Bushell, and invents a story about coughing and then 'coming to' in his car at the service station. Farquharson either has a cough during this time, or has faked having a cough and fooled his doctor into diagnosing a respiratory tract infection. Either way, he then fakes a coughing and dizzy spell in front of his boss, although he does not fake blacking out on this occasion. Perhaps he decided to be subtle in creating this history of cough syncope?

A few days later is father's day. There are no plans for Farquharson to take the children, so his plan for killing them on father's day in a dam is given a lucky break when Cindy suggests that he take them for dinner. Another lucky break for the plan comes when Michael Hart declines to join Farquharson and the boys for dinner. Perhaps he would have waited for some other special day like Christmas if these fortuitous co-incidences did not occur, although one wonders why he picked out Father's day specifically when speaking to King a few months earlier, and it seems he had been preparing the coughing part of the plan for the past couple of weeks.

On the way home from Geelong, Farquharson stops past his sister's house and sees his brother-in-law and niece. Claiming he wanted to retrieve Tyler's football that he had left there a week earlier, Farquharson is really just creating a facade of normality. Back on the highway, just five minutes from Winchelsea and coming down the overpass, Farquharson steers off the road toward the dam. He has chosen a place where the road slopes to the right so he can claim he blacked out. He makes sure not to turn or break sharply, lest he leaves signs of being conscious, and even smashes through a tree branch to make it appear as though he were not in control of the vehicle, having subtly veered enough to miss the trunk. He then quickly opens his car door and gets out. Farquharson must have been somewhat knowledgeable about the difficulty of escaping cars or he would not have thought of this particular plan, but it was not really possible to plan on getting himself out. Anyway, things somehow work out and he gets out.

Farquharson then swims to shore, walks to the road, and flags down a car. Two young men stop to help, and Farquharson puts on an act of being in shock, talking in an incoherent manner. When the men ask what happened, he momentarily forgets his planned cough syncope story and suggests he might have done a wheel bearing, even though he was conscious so he knows that he did not do a wheel bearing, and knows that he will get found out on this. When asked again, he remembers his plan and says that he had blacked out after coughing.

He insists on being taken to see Cindy so he can see her suffering, but hides the pleasure he gains when telling her, instead acting like he is still in shock. He fakes being upset and cries to friends and family, and appears distraught in the hospital, but does not fake being upset in front of police who describe him as calm. Over the next days he puts on a show of being upset and in shock, except when being questioned by police. During secretly taped phone calls with Cindy over the next month he pretends that he is upset and does not taunt her or appear to gain any satisfaction from her suffering. Maybe he has regretted his actions?

After losing his first trial, he realizes that he needs to establish a more extensive history of cough syncope. He admonishes himself for not having faked more episodes prior to the murder, which seems an obvious thing to do when planning to create a history of cough syncope. And he kicks himself for not instead saying he had fallen asleep at the wheel. Anyway, he decides he needs to fake further episodes of cough syncope. So, sitting in a crowded workshop at prison, he starts coughing and then collapses off his chair and hits the ground and fakes being unconscious. Even though he breaks his leg he remains unresponsive. During the second trial he decides that another episode is required, so he coughs and then collapses at his sister's house, wedging himself between a chair and a cabinet and remains unresponsive as his sister and her husband lay him on his side.

Again, there is no direct evidence that Farquharson is faking in this narrative, the witnesses all stated that he had blacked out. We have to *infer* that he is faking from the other evidence that points to guilt.

There are other guilty narratives that could be woven to try to fit the evidence, but those that I can come up with are all convoluted and spend more time dismissing evidence, and inferring interpretations of events for which there is no evidence, than simply following the evidence. I suspect that if there were a straight forward guilty narrative that fit all the evidence, the prosecution would have presented it. Two prosecutors in two trials neglected to put the pieces of the puzzle into place to provide a picture of what occurred because putting the pieces together makes a convoluted and strained story compared to the straight forward interpretation of evidence that is afforded by assuming that it was a horrible accident.

The telling part is that it is very difficult to conceive of someone coming up with such an unlikely, crazy sounding story, and then getting all the details correct. Details about how cars sink, details about who gets cough syncope, how it is diagnosed, how long unconsciousness lasts, details about how people behave when they are in shock or are highly stressed. Many of these details are very obscure: the details of sinking cars that Farquharson got correct were not known by the police experts, whist the details of cough syncope that he got correct were not initially known by Professor Naughton, the expert medical witness. The story of Farquharson sounds so much like bullshit at first glance, but when you scrutinize the details of every aspect of his story, they hold up. Details that would be very difficult to get correct. The innocent story stands up to scrutiny.

Along with Luke McMahon, I went to see Farquharson's barrister, Peter Morrissey, to get his impressions of the case. Like Sergeant Urquhart on the other side, this case had a strong impact on Morrissey, who fought and lost two trials for someone he truly believes is innocent. In Morrissey's view the only alternative to Farquharson being innocent is that he is some sort of unrecognized, gifted genius, given his ability to get so many obscure details of such an incredible story correct.

By contrast, every piece of evidence of the prosecution case falls apart when you look at it in detail. It just does not stand up to scrutiny. The reconstruction evidence was simply wrong. The prosecution medical expert was biased by misleading and irrelevant material, was working beyond his area of expertise, and did scant research into cough syncope prior to making his determination. A determination that was, at best, misleading in the certainty with which it was presented. Greg King's statement evolved in lock-step with the evolution of his certainty in Farquharson's guilt. And on and on. The details just do not hold up to scrutiny.

I have no doubt that the prosecution of Robert Farquharson was done in good faith when compiling the evidence against him. So where did things go so wrong?

Chapter 21

INTO THE TUNNEL

Jeffrey Smith was in charge of the police response on the night of the accident, and interviewed Farquharson in hospital that night. Within the first two days of the investigation, Smith had written two lists, titled 'he did it' and 'he didn't do it';[1] Smith was consciously formulating his opinion of guilt at the very beginning of the investigative process.

In the 'he did it' column Smith had 10 items, including 'the crash couldn't have happened the way he said it happened'[2] and 'the car was still under acceleration as it went into the dam'.[3] How did Smith know these things prior to a reconstruction being performed? Shouldn't the placing of these items have waited until this aspect of the case had actually been investigated? Another item in the 'he did it' column was the 'ignition was off'. Yet this is a neutral observation: when a person runs their car off the road in an accident, they are *supposed to* turn off their ignition, and besides, when leaving a car one may routinely switch off the ignition automatically, without a thought.

Smith could not think of anything to write in the 'he did not do it' column, besides 'no one could be that evil'. Hardly a sign of having an open mind on the case and waiting for all evidence to be gathered.

It seems Smith had already made up his mind based on the

---

1. Crimes that Shook Australia Season 2 Ep 1
2. Crimes that Shook Australia Season 2 Ep 1
3. Crimes that Shook Australia Season 2 Ep 1

interview with Farquharson at the hospital when he believed that Farquharson was lying,[4] 'I don't think after you listen to Farquharson that you can come to too many conclusions other than he killed his kids'[5] and the preliminary assessment of the scene made by Sergeant Exton.

Once they get a suspect in mind, often based on a person's demeanour or a perception that the suspect is not acting like a person should in the circumstances, investigators can fall into the trap of assessing evidence through the lens of guilt, finding excuses to dismiss evidence that points to innocence. Tunnel vision. Whilst it is often hard to point to direct evidence of tunnel vision, there are indicators, or red flags. One red flag is the time that belief in guilt was formed and the origin of that initial belief. Research[6] shows that there is increased chance of tunnel vision when officers begin to weigh guilt and innocence prior to evidence being gathered.

In many cases the evidence is clear from the beginning and an initial belief is a correct one, and this makes it easy to slip into the routine of following that first instinct. It is the cases where first impressions are wrong that cause troubles, and this is why investigators need to remain open minded whist evidence is still being gathered. First impressions are lasting because humans are so susceptible to confirmation bias, the main ingredient of tunnel vision.

Another, less direct indictor relates to an *effect* of tunnel vision, whereby evidence itself changes in response to the investigator's certainty in guilt. In the words of Sherlock Holmes 'It is a capital mistake to theorize before one has data. Insensibly one begins to twist facts to suit theories, instead of theories to suit facts.'[7] Authority figures are particularly influential on memories.[8]

4. Megan Norris, *On Fathers Day*, Kindle position 1293
5. Crimes that shook Australia Season 2 Ep 1
6. O'Brien, B. (2009). *Prime suspect: An examination of factors that aggravate and counteract confirmation bias in criminal investigations*. Psychology, Public Policy, and Law. 15. 315-334
7. Sir Aurther Conan Doyle: *A Scandal in Bohemia* 25 June 1891 The Strand Magazine
8. Leding, T *False Memories and Persuasion Strategies*, Review of General Psychology 2012, Vol. 16, No. 3, 256–268

When police who are convinced of guilt interact with witnesses, it is natural for the witnesses to recall things through a prism where the accused is guilty and they are helping the police 'do the right thing'. When multiple pieces of witness evidence systematically change to become increasingly incriminatory, and these changes coincide with interactions between the investigators and the witnesses, then red flags are raised.

Detective Clanchy listened to the recording Farquharson's interview at Geelong hospital and agreed with Smith. Farquharson was lying. Clanchy also believed Farquharson was lying during his interview in Melbourne a couple of days later. By this stage Clanchy had formed a 'reasonably strong suspicion'.[9] These suspicions were confirmed by the reconstruction report of Glen Urquhart, at which time he thought yep, he's guilty.[10] Unfortunately it was a deeply flawed reconstruction report. Was the poor nature of the report influenced by the fact that Urquhart's bosses, Clanchy and Smith, already had their suspicions and in fact, his direct boss Smith had already concluded that 'the crash couldn't have happened the way he said it happened'? A vicious circle. This cross pollution of suspicion and evidence is how tunnel vision can spread through an investigation.

Let us look further at the cross pollution of evidence that occurred in the case; passing evidence that purports to prove guilt to witnesses, who thereby become biased. When lead investigator Clanchy handed Professor Naughton a case brief, and asked for an opinion on a medical condition, the brief included Greg King's final statement. No mention of Greg King's previous two statements or how his final statement was arrived at. The brief also included the reconstruction report of police expert Glen Urquhart, stating that the car was deliberately steered. There was even a statement made by Stephen Moules, Farquharson's arch enemy.

Did Clanchy also influence other witnesses, by informing them

---

9. As stated in interview between Clanchy and Luke McMahon
10. As stated in interview between Clanchy and Luke McMahon

of prosecution evidence? We do know from the court records that Clanchy told Cindy Gambino about evidence given by Susan Hatty[11] and also told her that there was a new witness in the case, Dawn Waite[12]. Did Clanchy indicate that Wait's evidence was incriminatory? Cindy did declare that the evidence of Waite was 'the biggest clincher'[13] in her decision to change her mind regarding Farquharson's guilt,[14] and testify against him. If Cindy was going to be a witness in the case, why was she told of the nature other evidence that was purported to be incriminatory?

Dawn Waite's evidence initially cut both ways and arguably even supported the defence. In particular, the evidence that the car 'veered' off the road contradicted the reconstruction evidence given by Glen Urquhart, who testified with dramatic emphasis in the first trial that a 220o turn of the steering wheel was required to explain the 'sharp' turn of the car off the road. Waite's evidence supported the defence reconstruction expert, whose model showed the car veering off the road. Considering that the reconstruction evidence was the most important evidence in the case, why wasn't Waite's testimony interpreted as supporting the defence? Didn't the evidence she gave of the car 'veering' off the road make the lead investigator question the reconstruction evidence? Indeed, didn't it make the reconstruction expert Glen Urquhart question his evidence?

Let us look at what happened after Dawn Waite came forward with her evidence.

On 16 April 2010, Glen Urquhart submitted a supplement to his 2005 statement pertaining to his reconstruction evidence. Urquhart had revisited the computer simulations he had made of the car's path from the road to the dam. This was said to be done 'as a result of material put to him at the previous trial'[15] when he had testified that the car had turned sharply off the

---

11. Trial 2 p564
12. Trial 2 p525
13. Norris, Megan. On Father's Day (Kindle Location 6727). The Five Mile Press. Kindle Edition
14. Trial 2 p527
15. Trial 2 p614

road. Urquhart now presented a scenario where the initial turn was far more gentle. Is it a coincidence that Urquhart revisited this aspect of his evidence after Dawn Waite gave her statement that she saw the car 'veer' off the road, emphasising that there was no sharp turn? As it stood, Waite's evidence would have contradicted Urquhart's evidence and supported the defence expert's scenario. By adding supplementary simulations, Urquhart was able to 'find another course consistent with what he observed at the scene... with a less severe or sharp angle of departure from the road, the initial steering input'[16]. Of course, Urquhart still stuck to his mantra that three steering inputs were required.

It is true that Urquhart had been criticized about this aspect of his evidence, i.e. the starting point and size of the initial turn. Yet he had also been heavily criticized for using a flat surface in the simulations. Why did he only revisit the aspect of the evidence that was inconsistent with the evidence of Waite? Why didn't Urquhart also revisit the flat surface of the terrain used in the simulations? Why didn't he create a three dimensional model? Was it because a simulated car would naturally roll down the slope toward the dam, if such a slope were included in his model? Would that have been an inconvenient truth?

It could just be a coincidence that the crown could now present a case where two key witnesses, Waite and Urquhart, gave consistent and indeed self-reinforcing evidence.

Except that this alignment of prosecution evidence with Dawn Waite's testimony does not end here. On 19 April 2010, the pathologist Dr. Byron Collins, working on a brief for the defence, met with the pathologist working for the prosecution, Dr. Michael Burke. After this meeting, Collins stated in a report that he was 'of the robust opinion that the most likely position for Jai to have been in the vehicle in order to sustain the constellation of injuries, particularly the left sided head injury, would be the front passenger seat and it is my understanding that Dr Burke shares this view.'[17] And indeed, Burke did share that

---

16. Trial 2 p614

view.[18] This evidence would have contradicted the testimony of Dawn Waite, who stated that she saw the three boys all 'squashed up' in the back seat. The report of Collins, with the agreement of Burke, would have rendered Wait's evidence essentially useless to the prosecution.

Prior to writing his own report, however, Dr. Burke changed his opinion and reported that it was 'possible' that Jai was seated in the back seat. As with Urquhart, it is safe to assume that Burke had a discursive relationship with the lead investigator Clanchy, as pathologists work closely and interactively with homicide detectives, it is the nature of their relationship[19]. I do not know precisely what it is that prompted Burke to revisit this part of his evidence, just as I do not know precisely what prompted Urquhart to revisit the starting position of his simulations but not the flatness of the terrain. All I know is that these two expert witnesses for the prosecution both changed their evidence at a very similar time, April-May 2010, that the evidence changed in such a way that it became consistent with the evidence of the new prosecution witness Dawn Waite, and that both the experts were in a discursive relationship with the lead investigator.

In the end, neither Dr. Burke nor Dr. Collins' evidence regarding where Jai was seated in the car was put to the jury. Without consensus, it was no longer strong evidence and the defence was concerned about the prejudicial effects of autopsy photos being shown to the jury, which would have followed from this line of questioning. The two sides thus agreed not to raise this issue with the pathologists during the trial.

The result was that the prosecution's three witnesses could present evidence that was consistent: the path suggested by Dawn Waite was supported by their reconstruction expert, and her claim regarding the seating positions of the children were not contradicted by the pathologist. That is how a circumstantial case is built, with each strand of a cable strengthening the other, rather than pulling in different directions. Indeed it is telling that

17. Trial 2 p2698
18. Trial 2 p2698
19. According to two senior Victorian pathologists that I contacted via email.

the prosecutor described evidence in a circumstantial case as 'like the strands in a cable which may all support one another', and then laid out the various strands rather than employing the other oft used metaphor for a circumstantial case, which is the jigsaw puzzle, where all the pieces fit together to reveal what occurred. The choice of metaphor is not surprising, because in this case the pieces did not fit together, and the prosecution never put them together. It was thus imperative that all the strands of the police's evidentiary cable pulled in the same direction.

The 'updated' reconstruction and pathology reports were not the only evidence that changed to become more incriminating toward Farquharson, as has been outlined in this book. There was Greg King's evidence that changed to become increasingly incriminatory, as well as increasingly certain, as he became increasingly convinced of Farquharson's guilt. The regular interactions between King and lead investigator Clanchy are a matter of court record.[20] Cindy Gambino did not change the substance of her evidence, but the change in the tone of her evidence could not be more stark in terms of its incriminatory nature. Her interactions with Clanchy are also a matter of court record. When Cindy Gambino told Clanchy that she would testify for the prosecution, Clanchy replied that 'you've just made my year'.[21]

Dawn Waite changed her evidence between the voir dire and the trial, particularly pertaining to the use of high beams and hence her ability to see inside Farquharson's car when approaching from behind, but also with respect to her level of certainty. It is a matter of court record that between her voir dire testimony and the trial, Waite met with Clanchy,[22] to review the transcripts of her voir dire testimony. In our legal system, the prosecution is allowed to prepare witnesses for the trial, although there are rules[23] against 'coaching the witness'. Yet it is

20. Trial 2 p237, p248
21. Norris, M. *On Father's Day: Cindy Gambino's Shattering Account of her Children's Revenge Murders*, Kindle Locations 5122-5123 The Five Mile Press. Kindle Edition.
22. Trial 2 p1667
23. see e.g. *Re Equiticorp Finance Ltd* (1992) 27 NSWLR 391 for what is permitted

well established that police officers can influence witnesses subconsciously. If a witness needs help preparing to give evidence, which is understandable considering the intimidating nature of the adversarial system and of cross-examination, why can't a neutral, court appointed officer provide such support? Why should a person who has an interest in ensuring that the evidence is as incriminating as possible, be given that task?

We have also seen that Shane Atkinson's evidence pertaining to having offered Farquharson a phone changed from his first statement, to the committal hearing, to the trial, becoming increasingly incriminatory.

That is a who's who of the most important prosecution witnesses. In every single instance, the evidence of the witnesses became increasingly incriminatory. The only significant witness who did not dramatically change his evidence was Professor Naughton, although he did change the basis on which his evidence relied after having read almost nothing on cough syncope when making his original statement. But we already *know* that Professor Naughton was given incriminating evidence by Clanchy *prior* to reaching his *initial* conclusions. We also know that Naughton used the prosecution friendly term 'extremely unlikely', despite the significant uncertainty that surrounds the causes of cough syncope, and the lack of extensive scientific evidence pertaining to these causes.

It is not possible to isolate any single example of changed evidence as being influenced or manipulated, and there is no implication that there was a conscious, organized effort by police investigators toward influence or manipulation. Yet the pattern is very clear and without these changes in witness evidence, the prosecution case falls apart. When investigators become convinced of guilt, not only does confirmation bias affect them and the way they assess new evidence, the resultant tunnel vision has broader implications with witnesses becoming biased, even if unconsciously so.

A final indicator of tunnel vision is when police and/or prosecutors become overzealous, pushing the boundaries of the rules to secure convictions that they believe are warranted. An example is to not fully disclose information that may be helpful to the defence.

In the Farquharson case, the lead investigator Clanchy failed to disclose that Greg King was under investigation for assault. The police had received a subpoena from the defence requesting any information regarding prior convictions, court appearances, intervention orders or police briefs compiled against Greg King, which was returned on 27 April 2007. In May 2007, Clanchy was informed by another police officer, Sergeant Baker, that Greg King had admitted to an assault that occurred on 24 December 2006. Clanchy did not inform anyone regarding these pending charges against King, deciding that 'it was an ongoing police investigation'[24] and 'he hadn't been charged'.[25] This was despite Clanchy being aware at the time that 'the lawyers for the accused were interested in Mr King and his background'.[26] King was eventually charged on 5 October 2007, the day that the guilty verdict was handed down against Farquharson. Just a coincidence.

The court of Appeal ordered a re-trial based on this failure to disclose, and the defence were able to highlight the charges against King in second trial. That may seem like a fair outcome, undoing this error. However, the Court of Appeal could not undo the tunnel vision that, along with the other indictors we have seen, is revealed by the failure to disclose.

Once convinced of guilt, police move from investigating to 'selling' mode, such that their job is to gather enough evidence to ensure conviction. In the Farquharson case, the police did this part of their job very well. When a guilty verdict was reached, they celebrated. It really was a job well done. They had determined that Farquharson was guilty and they gathered and organized their evidence in a manner that was able to convince a jury to return a guilty verdict. If Farquharson was actually guilty, we could even call this good police work. The shame is that the thorough and systematic way that the police set about securing

24. Trial 2 p250
25. Trial 2 p250
26. Trial 2 p258

a conviction was not matched by a thorough and systematic investigation into determining whether Farquharson was guilty in the first place.

Tunnel vision is more than a single person losing perspective. It is a systematic contamination of the investigative process. It leaves its mark on the analysis and evolution of evidence and witness statements. Best practice requires detailed record of early witness statements, and the recording of all police enquiries and interactions with witnesses, rather than just exploring final statements that are made during trials. Just like with eyewitness line-ups, where police (should) follow protocols that reduce the likelihood of signalling toward a particular photo, so should interactions with witnesses follow protocols aimed at reducing the influence that authoritative figures such as police can have on a witness's other types of memory evidence.

Of course, the defence can challenge evidence and point out changes in witness accounts and opinions. And if the defence can extract an about face by a witness, or expose a deliberate lie, that will have a detrimental effect. But such dramatic exposés are not the norm. More often than not the witness believes their contaminated memories. They do not know they have been contaminated, they seem just like any other memory, because they are just like any other memory: malleable, changing, fitting with current world views. Incremental changes in a story, increased details being recalled, incremental increases in confidence in memories, are very hard for a defence to challenge. The defence just looks desperate as they attempt to challenge seemingly small details of every single prosecution witness.

Through single minded determination for achieving a conviction, police can, intentionally or not, organize witness evidence such that it looks increasingly incriminating, self-consistent and self-reinforcing, and that becomes very persuasive in the hands of a skilled prosecutor.

Chapter 22

TRICKS OF THE TRADE

'What does it matter, you might ask, that the accused had this tendency to be a bit of a complainer? Never happy, to be a bit negative, what's that got to do with anything, if he had a tendency to whinge and moan? Is that just led as some sort of attack on his character by the Crown for no reason? Well, of course it's not. [That] aspect of the accused's personality ... may be an important thing to your minds, an important aspect of the case. Because of course it's the Crown case that out of anger and resentment and out of an unwillingness and inability to move on and get on with his life... and the harbouring of those negative feelings, that the accused...made a decision to kill his children to get back at his former wife. Whom he thought had wronged him and ruined his life. And so, if he is a person who had a negative personality, a negative mindset, may not that have been an important part of the circumstances in which such murderous and obscene anger could grow? Could fester?'

This diatribe from prosecutor Andrew Tinney was character assassination in its worst form. Not simply attacking Farquharson's character, but openly inviting the jury to infer Farquharson guilty of murder because he is a moaner and a whinger. What evidence or study links these character traits of whinging and moaning, to an increased likelihood of violence and in particular, to murder?

The reason the prosecutor linked these character flaws of Farquharson to anger and murder was because the evidence showed Farquharson to have neither an angry nor violent personality. If Farquharson had a violent past, the prosecutor would have played that up to whatever degree trial rules allowed. Indeed, a history of family violence[1] and controlling behaviour[2] has been linked to a greater likelihood of filicide and I have no objection if that had have been raised in court, although the presentation of 'tendency' evidence is a tricky area of law that tries to balance the probative value of predisposition evidence against its prejudicial effects. But there was no history of family violence of controlling behaviour presented in this case. So instead, the prosecution just attacked Farquharson's character based on whatever character flaws were available, then linked them to murder. No one likes a moaner.

When it comes to determining guilt and innocence, the adversarial system involves more than simply analysing evidence; each side employs sophisticated methods of persuasion. Barristers are judged by their ability to persuade juries and win cases. It is not simply the weight of evidence that decides outcomes, but the skill of the barrister, 'the power of persuasion'.[3] Barristers are charged with persuading juries, and have developed methods of persuasion as a central part of their profession. Character asassination is one of the various methods of persuasion that have been practiced and honed by barristers over years and generations, and modern science can provide insights into many of them. I will not attempt an exhaustive exploration of the methods employed in the case of Robert Farquharson, but I do want to highlight a couple of other examples from the case.

The central rhetorical technique used in the Farquharson case has already been mentioned: repetition. The prosecutor repetitively used of the words 'angry' and 'liar', or associated words, with such words repeated in the final address 53 and 36 times respectively. This appeals to the tendency for people to believe something simply because they have heard it many

---

1. E.g. Brown, T., Tyson, D., Fernandez Arias, P. Monash University Filicide Project *Submission To Roy Al Commission On F Amil Y Violence (Victoria)*
2. E.g. Ferguson, L (2009), Dispatches Child Homicide Study: Main Findings ; Sidebotham, P. & Retzer, A. Arch Womens Ment Health (2019) 22: 139
3. Levine, D. as quoted in the Oral History Project, NSW bar association

times, a tendency that is now referred to as the *illusory truth effect*. The *illusory truth effect* was first formally identified and studied scientifically in 1977.[4] Researchers found that participants' confidence in repeated statements increased over time, and 'simply repeating false information makes it seem more true.'[5]

Of course, the value of repetition has been known long before it was formally studied. It has been reported that Napoleon believed repetition to be the only 'figure in rhetoric of serious importance'.[6]

Repetition is not limited to influencing obscure facts about which we have no real knowledge; it can even bolster belief in statements that contradict our prior knowledge. In one study, when participants were told that a 'sari is the skirt that Scottish men wear', even those who knew that Scottish men wear kilts increased their truth ratings that Scottish men wear saris, and decreased their confidence that the statement was false. A further study indicates that people tend to remember repeated information, even if they were told it was false. Participants were given various statements labelled 'reliable' and 'unreliable' and were asked to rate the truth of those statements two weeks later. In the interim, some of the statements were repeated. The participants tended to rate the repeated statements as more true, even if they were labelled unreliable. Repeated information feels true, even if it goes against what we already know. Little wonder barristers have long found repetition a powerful rhetorical tool in their efforts to persuade juries.

Another skill of a barrister is their ability to cross examine, to discredit witnesses in the eyes of the jury. Ian Barker, who successfully prosecuted Lindy Chamberlain despite the fact that she was innocent,[7] was considered 'the best cross examiner in

---

4. Hasher L., Goldstein D., Toppino, T. *Frequency and the conference of referential validity*, Journal of Verbal Learning and Verbal Behavior. 1977. 16. 1
5. Fazio, L. *Unbelievable news? Read it again and you might think it's true* in The Conversation, December 6, 2016
6. Hertwig, R., Gigerenzer, G., Hoffrage, U. *"The Reiteration Effect in Hindsight Bias"* Psychological Review, 104, 1 (1997), 194-202 who quote from Le Bon, G. *Psychologie des foules* Alcan, 1895
7. I am not implying that Barker was aware that Chamberlain was innocent, I just state

the land'.[8] Some tactics used in the cross examination of Robert Farquharson such as painting him as a liar, and repeatedly leading him to say 'I don't know' or 'I don't remember', mirrored those used by Barker when cross examining Lindy Chamberlain.

Of course, the defence also cross examines witnesses. Does that mean the two somehow cancel each other out? What if one barrister is more skilled, or just more ruthless, than the other? What if one witness is better able to withstand cross examination than another? Is that a sign of a reliable witness, or just a mentally strong one? Or perhaps a sign of an experienced witness, like expert witnesses? Do we end up at the truth because both sides are able to twist evidence to be biased in competing ways? At the end of a witness's evidence, it can be particularly difficult to pick up the pertinent evidence, with barristers so often focusing on irrelevant but emotive aspects of the witness's testimony.

Is this the best way to distinguish guilt and innocence? Richard Feynman described science as a method for separating ideas. Take two competing theories and see which one best matches the observed data. The criminal justice system also seeks to separate ideas or theories. There are two theories presented, one pertaining to guilt and the other to innocence. Like science, the aim is to determine which theory is most likely to be correct.

In medieval England, several methods were available for settling such questions, when people make competing claims as to what has occurred. One method was trial by battle, which was decided when one side yielded, or in some of most serious criminal cases, was slain.[9] The battle was overseen by judicial officers after each combatant swore that their cause was just, invoked the judgement of God and committed to not use sorcery.[10] God would ensure that the person with the just cause

---

the facts that she was innocent and that he successfully prosecuted her. It is widely acknowledged that Barker showed himself to be a highly skilled prosecutor during the Chamberlain trial.

8. Marsden, J
9. W. Blackstone, Com Mentari E3s38-41; 4 W. Blackstone, Commentaries *341, 342, *reprinted in* I W. Holdsworth, A History Of English Law 678-79 (7th ed. 1956)
10. ibid

was victorious. An alternative method was a wager of law, which was essentially a test of a claimant's standing in the community.[11] The litigant would swear an oath to his claims, and would win the case so long as his oath was supported by several other 'compurgators', who swore supporting oaths.[12]

The other option available to settle disputes was trial by ordeal, popular through medieval Europe.[13] Again the premise was that God would intervene if the person undergoing the ordeal was in the right. Two common ordeals in England involved burns, either by carrying a red-hot iron bar, or placing an arm in boiling water. The outcome was determined by whether or not the litigant's burns continued to fester after a set period of time.[14] The third common ordeal was being immersed in deep water, which required that the litigant sink briefly, rather than float, to win a case.[15]

It takes a conscious effort to recall that the goal of these processes was to determine which litigant has the legitimate claim, or in a criminal trial, to determine whether the accused is guilty or innocent. I think we can safely assume that these are not the most accurate methods of separating the two theories, guilt and innocence.

When placed in this context, our current adversarial criminal justice system, which developed and evolved gradually from these roots, is indeed a significant improvement. The idea of the adversarial system, and indeed one of its strengths, is that it encourages the adversaries to find and present their most persuasive evidence and arguments.[16] No-one is more motivated than the interested parties themselves. The system also allows the decision makers (judges and juries) to assess and compare the most consequential proof proposed by each litigant.[17]

11. T. Plucknett *A Concise History Of the Common Law* 116-17 (5th ed. 1956); 1 W. Holdsworth note 25 at 115
12. yes, it was a men's world
13. Landsman, S *A Brief Survey of the Development of the Adversary System* Ohio State Law Journal, vol. 44, no. 3 (1983), 713-739.
14. ibid.
15. ibid
16. ibid

There is an assumption that each side will be competent and resourced enough to research and compile the most consequential proof. A serious problem for accused such as Farquharson is the mismatch in resources, with the state able to call upon significant institutional capabilities and knowledge,[18] giving them a distinct advantage. Not all defendants are O.J. Simpson.

Then there is the danger of such a highly competitive, winner takes all system, which is the promotion of a win-at-all costs attitude. A set of rules have therefore been established such that tactics 'intended to mislead or prejudice the trier of fact, are forbidden'.[19] However, it is a blurry line that separates a legitimate argument based on the evidence, and an argument that will mislead the jury. In celebrating the career of a fellow barrister, Ian Barker said of Paul Byrne that 'his powers of persuasion were a positive menace to the administration of justice'.[20] High praise indeed.

It is not all that surprising then that errors are made. Our justice system is ok when put in a historical context, but is hardly infallible.

---

17. ibid
18. See e.g. Edmond, G. *(Ad)Ministering Justice: Expert Evidence and the Professional Responsibilities of Prosecutors*" [2013] UNSWLawJl 35; (2013) 36(3) University of New South Wales Law Journal 921
19. See e.g. Landsman, S *A Brief Survey of the Development of the Adversary System* Ohio State Law Journal, vol. 44, no. 3 (1983), 713-739.
20. ibid

CHAPTER 23

UNINDICTED CO-EJACULATOR THEORY

Even within a fallible system, the conclusions I drew from the evidence in the case against Robert Farquharson almost seem too easy, too one sided. Could our legal system really get it so wrong? Not to mention all those reporters who followed the case?

Most miscarriages of justice are a little like visual puzzles. They can appear very complex and you can stare at them for minutes on end until someone points out the badger hiding among zebras, for example. Each time you look at it from then on, the badger jumps out at you, it is easy to see. The fact that the person is innocent was usually right in front of you the whole time, staring you in the face.

The clarification process involves following the evidence in the most straight forward manner, ignoring media hype, ignoring myths about demeanour and behaviour, looking at evidence rather than the prosecutor's description of evidence, understanding the qualities that determine the reliability of witness evidence, looking at evidence as it was first attained, and following how that evidence evolves rather than just looking at the final product that is presented in court.

Prosecutions of innocent people are generally based on convoluted explanations of evidence, elaborate stories, exaggerated reliance on unreliable evidence, and making excuses as to why important evidence that points to innocence can be ignored. Police and prosecutorial misconduct also occur in some cases, with exculpatory evidence withheld or incriminating evidence invented. Barring these cases, it is no surprise that evidence against innocent people is circumstantial, highly convoluted, and that no single piece of evidence is strong, unambiguous and holds up to scrutiny.

Let us look at a couple of illustrative infamous miscarriages of justice.

Meredith Kercher, a 21 year old British exchange student, was brutally murdered in her own bedroom in Perugia, Italy in 2007. Her American roommate, Amanda Knox, and Knox's Italian boyfriend of a month, Raffaele Sollecito, were accused of killing Meredith Kercher soon after the horrific crime was discovered. The accusations were initially based on Knox's 'odd behaviour': she did not immediately call police when she had returned home and found the front door open and small drops of blood in the bathroom, and later allegedly did a cartwheel at the police station. The police subjected Knox to a gruelling and extended interview, which they did not record as per regulations, during which she admitted to being at the scene, an admission she subsequently retracted. Knox's admission to being at the house on the night of the murder was certainly evidence, but the way it was garnered, her rapid retraction, and the contradictions between details she provided and subsequently uncovered evidence, put it at the weakest end of 'confession' evidence. Regardless, it certainly provided motivation for the police to follow these leads.

When police started to actually gather physical evidence, however, it pointed not to Knox and Sollecito, but to a man named Rudy Guede. Guede's DNA was all over the murder scene, as were his bloody handprints, his unflushed faeces was in Kirchner's toilet, the method used to break-in to the house was identical to the way Guede had broken into the law office of Paolo Brocchi just two weeks earlier, and Guede had fled for Germany. A more straight forward case could not be found. DNA, fingerprints, blood, faeces, suspect specific modus operandi (MO), and a suspect on the run. It does not take Sherlock Holmes to solve this case.

But the investigators already had their suspects firmly in their sights. Instead of simply following the very clear evidence, they invoked elaborate stories to fit the evidence to their theory of Knox and Sollecito being the killers. It was now indisputable that Guede was involved, so there must have been three killers, Guede, Knox and Sollecito! This particular form of tunnel vision is common enough to have its own moniker, 'the unindicted ejaculator theory' whereby prosecutors, when they discover that the DNA from a rape scene does not match their suspect, change their story to include multiple rapists, rather than move their focus to the person who's DNA is at the crime scene. The Norfolk Four, the Central Park Five, Daryl Hunt and Jeffrey Deskovic are some infamous U.S. examples, or better said victims, of 'the unindicted co-ejaculator theory'.

In the Knox and Sollecito case the ejaculator, Rudy Guede, was eventually indicted and convicted but bizarre interpretations of evidence were required to keep Knox and Sollecito in the frame. Knox and Sollecito must have engaged Guede, who they barely knew, to join them in a masochistic sex game, orchestrated by Knox. Evidence of a break-in must have been staged. The similarities between the method of the 'staged' break-in and Guede's previous break-in two weeks earlier, was taken as further evidence of the guilt of Knox and Sollecito, because no-one would be so stupid to re-use the same methods from a crime for which they had been so recently caught. Of course, there is a far simpler explanation for why the two break-ins were done in the same way. Meanwhile, the lack of Knox's DNA in Kirchner's bedroom was attributed to a clean up, as though she were able to remove her own DNA but not Guede's.

The investigators put too much weight on their ability to assess people's demeanour, and ignored studies[1] regarding interview techniques and the reliability of information obtained

---

1. Kassin S, Drizin S, Grisso T, Gudjonsson G, Leo R, Redlich A, *Police-induced confessions, risk factors, and recommendations: looking ahead* Law Hum Behav. 2010 Feb;34(1):49-52

under stressful situations and under intense police pressure. They settled on their suspects and stopped following the evidence, instead working to find ways to match each piece of the incoming evidence to their suspects.

Lindy Chamberlain was wrongly convicted of murdering her 9 week old daughter, Azaria, at Uluru, Australia in 1981. Simply following the evidence readily leads to the conclusion of innocence: Dingo's had been attacking children in the area; dingo tracks were found near the tent where Azaria went missing, with indications that the dingo was dragging something; dingo hairs were found inside the tent; blood was also found in the tent, whilst the police alleged Lindy had murdered Azaria in the car; a camper heard a dog's growl just prior to the time Lindy saw the dingo leaving the tent carrying something in its mouth; no blood was found on Lindy or her clothes; witnesses heard Azaria crying after the time the police allege that the murder occurred; and there was never any indication of a motive, nor of Lindy having any history of violence or of giving any hints of being capable of harming her children.

But the police had already determined that Lindy was guilty, based on her strange behaviour. To fit the evidence to the suspect, the prosecution presented a theory whereby, within five- to ten-minutes, Chamberlain went to her tent, changed into track suit pants; took Azaria to her car and cut her throat with some scissors; waited for Azaria to die; hid the body in a camera case in the car; cleaned up all the blood in the dark including blood on the outside of the camera case; removed the tracksuit pants, grabbed some baked beans for her son from the car; returned to the tent to leave some blood splashes in preparation for her dingo story; then brought her son Aidan back to the campfire. She later returned to the tent, and cried out that she saw a dingo taking her baby from the tent. The evidence of dingo tracks near the tent were dismissed as being coincidental, as were the tracks that indicated that the dingo was dragging something, as was the evidence of a camper who heard a dog's growl around that time. Just coincidences. The fact that no one noticed blood on Mrs Chamberlain's clothes in the hours after the disappearance was explained as being fortunate. The fact that Chamberlain opened the car, where the body was allegedly hidden, to give a dog the scent of Azaria from the clothes in the car was interpreted as a daring act, and pure luck that the dog did not find the dead Azaria stuffed in the camera case. The witnesses who heard Azaria cry after the time of the alleged murder, and prior to the time that Chamberlain called out about the dingo, were dismissed as being mistaken or covering for Chamberlain.

The police were certain of guilt and were determined. They scoured the planet to find experts who were willing to help 'prove' their case with what turned out to be biased, junk science; they painted her as a liar because of some inconsequential inconsistencies in her story, which she had told multiple times; and they fed the media beast that painted her as cold, a bad mother, a liar, and as a murderer. The prosecutor did the rest.

Of course, such analysis is much easier with hindsight, and things are less clear in the moment when the investigators are working at the coalface. But that is, at least in part, the point. Confirmation bias is more prevalent when investigators are asked to form a hypothesis of guilt early in the evaluation of evidence, compared to when they are not asked for a hypothesis until after reviewing all the evidence.[2] Further, police officers rate disconfirming or exonerating evidence as less reliable or credible than guilt-confirming evidence that supports their initial hypotheses.[3]

Once police have settled on a suspect, they can actually influence the nature of the evidence itself by, for example, leading witnesses, coercing false confessions, and biasing experts. This can occur even when the investigators are acting

---

2. O'Brien, B. (2009). *Prime suspect: An examination of factors that aggravate and counteract confirmation bias in criminal investigations*. Psychology, Public Policy, and Law. 15. 315-334
3. Ask, K. and Granhag, P. A. (2007), *Motivational Bias in Criminal Investigators' Judgments of Witness Reliability*. Journal of Applied Social Psychology, 37: 561-591; Ask, K., Rebelius, A. and Granhag, P. A. (2008), *The 'elasticity' of criminal evidence: a moderator of investigator bias*. Appl. Cognit. Psychol., 22: 1245-1259

in good faith. The lesson is to continue to collect evidence in a neutral manner, and to assess the totality of evidence once it is collected. Colleagues from outside the investigation should be brought in to independently assess the conclusions, to play devil's advocate, to challenge the narrative and to test alternative theories and whether they can explain the evidence.

Not all witness evidence is equal, not all confessions are equal, not all alibi evidence is equal, not all forensic science is equal. The various forms of evidence all need to be understood and weighed in each individual case. How long elapsed between an event and a witness statement? How confident was the witness at the time of the statement? Did they become more confident at trial? Why? How were interviews of witnesses and the accused conducted? Was the confessor fed information by police? Has the expert been given material that purports to show the guilt of the suspect but is irrelevant to their analysis? There has been an explosion of research that employs scientific methods to answer these types of questions.[4] This research can help to understand how to obtain, preserve and weigh evidence. The results of these such studies need to be filtered into the policing and legal systems. All evidence should be treated in the most scientific manner possible.

---

4. See e.g. John Wixted, Laura Mickes *Eyewitness Memory Is a Lot More Reliable Than You Think*, Scientific American, June 13, 2017

Chapter 24

THE AGE OF INNOCENTS

Deoxyribonucleic acid, or DNA, is a molecule that stores biological information, holding the genetic characteristics of each living organism and providing a blueprint for their growth, development and function. DNA was first isolated in 1869 by Friedrich Miescher at the University of Tübingen, in Germany. He raised the idea that DNA may be related to heredity. In 1953 James Watson and Francis Crick deduced[1] the double helix structure of DNA, publishing their study in the journal *Nature*.[2]

Methods were subsequently developed to extract small, variable parts of human DNA that are unique to each individual.[3] DNA profiling had been born, and was first used in the investigation of the murder of 15 year old Dawn Ashworth in the U.K. town of Enderby in 1986, using techniques developed by Professor Alec Jeffreys. The results were stunning. Not only did the DNA analysis lead to the capture of the culprit, Colin Pitchfork, it was able to link Pitchfork to the murder of Lynda Mann that had occurred three years earlier in a nearby town, and to exonerate 17 year old Richard Buckland who had been wrongfully charged with killing Ashworth. This new crime fighting tool could convict the guilty, resolve cold cases and

---

1. Using X-ray diffraction data taken by Rosalind Franklin and Maurice Wilkins
2. Watson, J. D., & Crick, F. H. C. *A structure for deoxyribose nucleic acid*. Nature 171, 737–738 (1953)
3. Family members can have very similar, sometimes indistinguishable, DNA profiles.

exonerate the innocent. And it worked retrospectively: cases where evidence had been preserved and DNA samples were available could be reviewed, and the guilt, or otherwise, could be determined for those who had proclaimed their innocence.

The process of using DNA to exonerate innocent prisoners was taken up systematically in the USA, in a large part by the Innocence Project,[4] based in New York and officially founded in 1992. By the beginning of 2020, 367 miscarriages in the U.S. had been uncovered using DNA, 192 with the involvement of the Innocence Project, with an average time in jail for the wrongfully convicted of 14 years.

Once innocence was emphatically proven by DNA, the cases could be reviewed, and the *causes* of the miscarriages could be identified. The main causes of miscarriages of justice[5] in cases uncovered by DNA evidence are eyewitness mis-identification, which occurs in 69% of cases, invalid or improper forensic science which occurs in 44% of cases, false confessions occur in 28% of cases, while informants/snitches are involved in 17% of cases. The mathematically inclined will realise that this adds to well over 100%, even though these factors are not the only causes of wrongful conviction. This is because a combination of two or more causes is usually present in each case.

DNA exonerations are just the tip of the iceberg of wrongful convictions, because it can only be used in a minority of cases, those revolving around identity, and where traces of DNA from the scene are available for re-testing. But with the newly found definitive evidence that miscarriages of justice occur far more frequently than was previously assumed, and armed with new knowledge of their causes, exoneration by methods other than DNA have become increasingly common in the U.S. The University of Michigan keeps a data base[6] that has documented 2614 exonerations between 1989 and 2020, with an average of 8.8 years spent in jail.

The number of exonerations has been increasing markedly,

---

4. http://www.innocenceproject.org/
5. The innocence project
6. http://www.law.umich.edu/special/exoneration/Pages/about.aspx

from 22 in 1989 to 75 in 2000 to over 180 in 2016. This increase is attributed[7] to the U.S. judicial system having recognized the existence of miscarriages of justice, and becoming better at handling such cases, including an increase in the number of people working on miscarriage cases and structural changes to the justice system itself. In other words, the number of miscarriages is not increasing, just the rate of detection. A case in point[8] is Dallas County in Texas, which has a far larger number of exonerations than other similar counties in its region due to the creation of a Conviction Integrity Unit in 2006, and a policy of keeping all biological samples indefinitely which allows for retrospective DNA testing. Unfortunately, such responses by the legal system to the reality of wrongful convictions have remained relatively isolated, and un-coordinated.

The overall *rate* of wrongful convictions remains difficult to calculate, largely because they require significant resources and effort to uncover, resources that are not available to the vast majority of prisoners. There is an exception to this, however, that allows an estimate of the rate of wrongful convictions for a particular class of convict in the U.S., those on death row. Far more attention and resources, both before and after conviction, are devoted to people facing the death penalty than to other criminal prosecutions, allowing a thorough review of each conviction and the evidence that was used to attain it. Research shows that *at least* 4.1%, one in every 25 death row inmates in the USA were wrongfully convicted.[9] This does not automatically equate to one in 25 of those executed having been innocent, as cases where evidence is not clear cut have a higher chance of having the executions stayed, reviewed, or commuted to life sentences. On the other hand, the notion that no innocent person has been executed is fanciful, given these findings.

Research showing that one in 25 convicted of capital murder

---

7. Ed Pilkington, *Record number of people exonerated of crimes in US in 2013* the Guardian, 4 Feb 2014
8. ibid
9. Gross, S. R., O'Brien, B., Hu, C. & Kennedy, E. H., *Rate of false conviction of criminal defendants who are sentenced to death* Proc. 2014, Natl Acad. Sci. USA

was innocent undersells how poorly the U.S. criminal justice system does. Consider that there was likely overwhelming evidence in many of the death row cases and many were not even contested in terms of who was culpable. The rates of wrong decisions in contested cases must be higher than one in 25, perhaps significantly higher.[10]

Meanwhile, across the Atlantic, the UK was also entering the age of innocents, but this was driven less by DNA and more by investigative journalism. *Rough Justice* was a BBC television series that ran from 1982 to 2007 that uncovered the wrongful convictions of 18 people. Legendary U.K. campaigner Thomas Sargant, a key researcher for *Rough Justice*, was instrumental in the release of 25 innocent people from prison. In 1990, the team behind *Rough Justice* moved to channel 4 and set up a similar program, *Trial and Error*, which broadcast along-side a revamped *Rough Justice* until 1999. *Trial and Error* also exposed a spate of judicial errors, including the cases of Peter Fell, Mary Druhan, Sheila Bowler and Danny McNamee, all of whom had been wrongfully convicted of murder.

These tv shows brought the ire of the UK legal establishment, who did not think that the justice system should be subjected to the scrutiny of journalists. Chief Justice Lord Lane condemned the 'outrageous methods' used by Peter Hill and Martin Young of *Rough Justice* in uncovering the wrongful conviction of Anthony Mycock in 1985. During Mycock's appeal, Lane interrogated, and castigated, both Young and Hill. In the end, Mycock's appeal was upheld 'reluctantly',[11] with Lane later accusing the Rough Justice journalistic team of 'a deliberate attack on the integrity and reliability of the criminal justice system'.[12] Lord Denning, Lord Justice of Appeal, was even more explicit, stating that 'After a decision has been given by Judge and Jury, the Media must not go around trying to get what they call 'fresh evidence' so

---

10. see Gross, S & O'Brien, B. *Frequency and Predictors of False Conviction: Why We Know So Little, and New Data on Capital Cases*, 2008 Journal of Empirical Legal Studies Volume 5, Issue 4, pp. 953-55
11. Young, M. *Opposable Truths* 2015 Publisher: Matador
12. Obituary of *Lord Lane* 24 Aug 2005 Telegraph

as to show, if they can, that the decision was wrong. That is undermining our system of Justice altogether.'[13]

Real head in the sand stuff.

The resistance of the legal establishment was finally broken by the unravelling of the wrongful convictions of the Birmingham six by Chris Mullen for the tv series *World in Action,* and in his book *Error of Judgment: The Truth About the Birmingham Pub Bombings.* The Birmingham Six had been wrongly convicted of planting bombs that killed 21 people in two Birmingham pubs in 1974. Lord Lane was widely considered to be biased when dismissing the first appeal brought by the Birmingham six in 1988, infamously stating that 'the longer this hearing has gone on the more convinced this court has become that the verdict of the jury was correct.' But by 1991 the case against the Birmingham six had collapsed, with the forensic analysis shown to be demonstrably wrong, confessions shown to be forcibly attained and police shown to have fabricated and suppressed crucial evidence. West Midlands Chief Constable Dave Thompson called it 'the most serious failing in this force's history.'[14]

The cases exposed on tv were certainly not the first cases of wrongful conviction in the U.K.'s history. In 1950, Timothy Evans was wrongfully convicted and hanged for murdering his wife and daughter, while the real killer John Christie remained free to kill four more women. The hanging of Evans was a significant factor in the abolition of capital punishment in the U.K. The public nature of the exposure of miscarriages broadcast on television and flashed on the front pages of newspapers during the 1980's also forced a response from the U.K. legal system. A Royal Commission of Justice was convened in 1991, leading to the creation of the Criminal Cases Review Commission (CCRC). An extra layer of review had finally been added to the criminal justice system, in recognition of its high

13. *Re-Trial by Television: The Rise and Fall of 'Rough Justice'* 2011, producers: The Open University, BBC Bristol
14. Martin Robinson, *They ran away like cowards: Birmingham pub bombing victim's sister calls on the 'gutless culprits' to surrender as coroner orders inquest into claims police missed TWO warnings before the 1974 massacre,* Daily Mail, 1 June 2016

rate of failings and the impotence of the appeals system in terms of righting wrongs. After the CCRC was established, the number of convictions that were overturned in the U.K. jumped from four or five per year to 20 or 30.[15] As with the U.S., the wrongfully convicted, sitting in jail for crimes they did not commit, were finally being found because the CCRC had the resources and powers to investigate. Since its inception, the CCRC has referred around 50 cases per year back to the appeals system and around two thirds of such appeals have been successful.[16]

Even with the CCRC, miscarriages continue to be missed in the U.K. For example, Victor Nealon was wrongfully convicted in 1997, yet the CCRC twice refused to investigate the case. Nealon was finally released in 2013 due to new DNA testing. After spending 17 years in jail for a crime that he did not commit, Nealon was given £46 and spent his first night of freedom on the streets. He was not entitled to any compensation. Criticisms of the CCRC persist,[17] along with calls for reform, but even in its current form there is no doubt that there are fewer innocent people in U.K. prisons as result of the establishment of the CCRC.

No country is immune to miscarriages of justice, including infamous cases such as David Milgaard in Canada, David Dougherty in New Zealand, Dolores Vázquez in Spain, Hermine Rupp in Germany, Keiko Aoki in Japan, Huugjilt in China, Sture Bergwall in Sweden, Patrick Dils in France and Amanda Knox and Raffaello Sallecito in Italy. The universal nature of miscarriages of justice stems from the fact that many of the problems transcend cultural boundaries and differences in legal systems. The vagaries of human memory that can result in unreliable witness testimony, the associated lack of protocols for preserving such memory evidence, poor forensic analysis

---

15. Hamer, D. & Edmond G. *Truth or lies: overturning wrongful convictions* The Conversation November 27, 2013
16. Criminal Cases Review Commission Annual Report and Accounts 2016/17
17. e.g. Heaton, S. *The CCRC—is it fit for purpose?* 2015, Archibold Review, Issue 5 **2015 Thomson Reuters (Professional) UK Ltd**

that lack scientific standards, false confessions resulting from poor interviewing techniques, over-zealous policing with tunnel vision and the associated noble cause corruption, and prosecutorial over-reach all transcend national and cultural boundaries.

Australia has had its fair share of miscarriages of justice, including Colin Ross who was hanged in 1922 for a crime he did not commit, Lindy Chamberlain, Andrew Mallard, John Button, Darryl Beamish, Gordon Wood, Kelvin Condren, Edward Splatt, Henry Keogh, Derek Bromley, Ray, Brian and Peter Mickelberg, Graham Stafford, Roseanne Beckett, Fred McDermott, Raymond Geesing, Ziggy Pohl, and Alexander McLeod-Lindsay. This is not an exhaustive list and miscarriages are certainly not a thing of the past: in 2017 Gene Gibson was released after spending five years in prison for a manslaughter that he did not commit, whilst Sue Neil-Fraser and Kevin Henry are both currently serving life sentences for crimes that evidence strongly suggests they did not commit. Not to mention Robert Farquharson.

Despite this, most Australian states refuse to acknowledge that a problem exists, and have not provided any additional review body for correcting wrongful convictions. There has been a tendency in Australia to consider wrongful convictions a U.S. problem and draw distinctions between our justice system and the U.S. justice system.[18] The South Australian Attorney-General John Rau dismissed the need for a Criminal Conviction Review Commission in his state, declaring that 'South Australia is not Texas. This State is not awash with wrongful convictions and the falsely imprisoned.'

Why didn't Rau compare South Australia to the U.K.? The similarities of the legal systems in Australia and the U.K. make it highly unlikely that their rates of miscarriage differ significantly. So why should criminal conviction review be deemed necessary in the U.K. but not in Australia? What is there to lose? If there really is no problem, then the review panel will confirm this and will not need many resources because of the lack of cases.

---

18. for a balanced discussion, see ibid at p278

History in the U.K. and the U.S. suggest that this is wishful thinking, with increased review invariably resulting in increased numbers of miscarriages being identified and corrected. Is this what the Australian legal system fears, that they will be unmasked as being fallible? Do they remain stuck in the arrogant mentality of the U.K. legal system of forty years ago?

South Australia did make some changes to its laws in 2013, allowing a further appeal when there is 'fresh and compelling' evidence that was not available at the time of the original trial. Whilst Henry Keogh was exonerated under this new legislation after spending 19 years in prison, Derek Bromley remains in prison where he has been for more than 35 years, despite overwhelming evidence that the original case against him was hopelessly flawed. Bromley has been eligible for parole for more than a decade but remains behind bars purely because he maintains his innocence. Admission of guilt is a requirement of the parole board, making innocence an insurmountable burden to freedom. Tasmania made similar amendments, which allowed a new appeal for Sue Neill-Fraser whose clear wrongful conviction would have been overturned years ago if there was a working system.

In Victoria, where Farquharson languishes in jail, this legal right to revisit a conviction after you have had an appeal rejected was finally approved in 2019. Prior to that, he only procedure for further review was to submit a petition to the Governor, who then refers the petition to the Attorney-General.[19] Attorneys-General could then refer the case back to the appeals court, which would hear the case in the form of a new appeal. By including the Attorney-General, the process was political, and the power is not a legal right but is discretionary. An example of how politics then enters the process is the case of Jason John

---

19. NSW and the ACT also have powers for post-conviction reviews by judicial inquiry by application to the executive or the Supreme Court. See Crimes (Appeals and Review) Act 2001 (NSW) pt 7; Crimes Act 1900 (ACT) pt 20. For detailed discussion of these provisions see Bibi Sangha and Robert Moles, Miscarriages of Justice: Criminal Appeals and the Rule of Law in Australia (LexisNexis, Butterworths, 2015) 3.5.

Roberts, convicted along with Bandali Dabs of killing police officers Gary Silk and Rodney Miller. Huge political pressures, from family, the police association, and ultimately the public who were rightly appalled at this crime, make ordering a review extremely difficult for the government. It was therefore little surprise that the petition for a new trial for Roberts was denied, despite an extensive report authored by Victoria's most respected homicide detective, Ray Iddles, that raised questions about his conviction, and despite the Attorney-General receiving independent advice from a Queens Council barrister that recommended that the case be returned to court for review. Very few cases were ever referred to the appeal court in via petition to Attorney's General.[20]

What about the appeals court itself? Don't the convicted get the chance to appeal? Won't the appeals courts catch the miscarriages? Farquharson lost his appeal. Surely that confirms that he is guilty! Why are more reviews even needed?

Appeals courts are constrained by a preference for finality, for treating the original verdict as final,[21] and have a strong deference to the jury, making them loath to question any fact-finding conclusions made by the jury, including the guilty verdict. These 'constraints upon review undermine any suggestion that appeals provide a reliable and comprehensive mechanism for correcting factual error'.[22] Appeals courts are more concerned with errors of law, generally accepting decisions of juries regarding facts and regarding the verdict. It is not the role of the appeals court to assess the evidence and decide for themselves whether they agree with the jury's verdict. In fact, appeals courts will support the jury's verdict even if they disagree with it,[23] so long as a guilty verdict was 'open to the jury' based on the evidence.

---

20. Sangha, Bibi *The statutory right to second or subsequent criminal appeals in South Australia and Tasmania* Flinders Law Journal, Volume 17 Issue 2 (Dec 2015)
21. ibid
22. see e.g. Hamer, D. *Wrongful convictions, appeals, and the finality principle: The need for a criminal cases review commission* 2014 University of New South Wales Law Journal, The, v.37, no.1, 2014, p.270-311

Once convicted, the appellant is presumed to be guilty rather than innocent.[24] As an illustration of the importance of that shift from the presumption of innocence to a presumption of guilt, consider the case of Ryan Ferguson who was convicted of a murder he did not commit, based on the false testimony of two witnesses who were pressured by the prosecutor. When the witnesses recanted their testimony, saying that they had lied at his trial, the appeals court found that their recantations were not reliable as they had changed their story. Ferguson lost his appeal and stayed in prison. Never mind that the original conviction was entirely based on the testimony of these same, unreliable witnesses. Now it was Ferguson who had the burden to prove innocence, and the witnesses were considered too unreliable to meet that burden. A higher appeals court eventually freed Ferguson after he spent ten years in prison, based on a failure of the prosecutor to disclose certain information and not due to the recantations of the key witnesses.

This is hardly a U.S. problem. When serial killer Eric Edgar Cooke confessed to killing both Rosemary Anderson and Jillian MacPherson Brewer, along with another six murders in and around Perth, he was not believed by the Appeals courts. How could they believe the word of a murderer? Darryl Beamish and John Button, who had been wrongfully convicted for the deaths of Anderson and MacPherson Brewer, remained in jail and served out their sentences.

Professor Brandon Garrett from the University of Virginia studied 250 miscarriages in the U.S. that were later uncovered by DNA evidence, and found that more than 90% had lost their appeals[25] and the 10% who had won their appeal were usually prosecuted again. Once again, DNA had shone a torch on our legal system: not only are miscarriages of justice more common than previously thought, appeals processes are 'incapable of

---

23. Ratten (1974) 131 CLR 510, 519 (Barwick CJ). See also M (1994) 181 CLR 487 as cited in ibid.
24. ibid
25. Garrett, B. L. *Convicting the innocent: Where criminal prosecutions go wrong* 2011 Cambridge, MA: Harvard University Press

detecting innocence in these (now indisputable) innocence cases'.[26]

There is no systematic study of the (lack of) success of Australian Appeals Courts success in overturning wrongful convictions, but the major constraints on appellate courts, finality and deference to jury decisions, are shared by Australia,[27] the U.S. as well as the U.K.. Lindy Chamberlain had two appeals dismissed, for example, and we have already seen the manner in which Lord Lane dismissed the appeals of the Birmingham six in the U.K. 'The Court of Appeal remains at the heart of the problem of wrongful convictions in this country [the U.K]'[28] according to solicitor Glyn Maddocks who represented Anthony Stock who was jailed for ten years for a robbery he did not commit. There is no reason to believe[29] that Australian appeals courts are any better than those in the U.K., or indeed those in the U.S., at correcting wrongful convictions.

As for the High court of Australia, it has largely shunned opportunities to act as the last bastion of justice in this country, relieving itself of responsibility to correct injustices even when new evidence proves a person innocent. In the words of Justice Kirby, 'By the authority of this Court [the High Court of Australia] ... fresh evidence, even if it were to show a grave factual error, indeed even punishment of an innocent person, cannot be received by this Court exercising its appellate jurisdiction ...[the prisoner] would be compelled to seek relief from the Executive.'

The overturning of the George Pell decision by the High Court, which found that the evidence could not support a guilty verdict, was unusual. Is this case a pointer to the future? Will the Court become more willing to consider the evidence base of potential miscarriages? Or is the Pell case going to be a one-off?

26. Aronson, J. D. & Cole, S. A. . *Science and the death penalty: DNA, innocence, and the debate over capital punishment in the United States.* 2009 Law & Social Inquiry, 34, 603–624.
27. Op cit Hamer, D. 2014
28. Maddock, G. *What does it take to overturn a miscarriage of justice in the UK?* Oct. 2014 Shine a Light
29. again, see Op cit Hamer, D. 2014

There is nothing stopping appeals courts from assuming a more active role in detecting and correcting miscarriages of justice. In Victoria, the grounds for appeal set out in the crimes act includes the phrase 'any other ground',[30] meaning that they are essentially unbound in what they consider during an appeal. The limited boundaries within which they assess appeals stem from precedents from their own court, precedents that were created when there was an assumption that trial courts were essentially infallible. The recent conclusive proof of significant rates of wrongful convictions should be enough to unbind those shackles of precedent, increasing the possibilities for review. The appeals courts have ignored these recent developments, resulting in a forfeiting of their role in administering justice. 'The problem with miscarriage of justice cases... is the Court of Appeal's lack of willingness to engage with (or even recognise) the problem and its often intransigent, often arrogant and dare I say obdurate view that it knows best and is constrained by its own previous decisions, however wrong they may have been' states Guy Maddocks, a view that is not fringe or extreme, having been endorsed by academics from 18 U.K. Universities, by lawyers and by innocence campaigners.[31]

Along with finality, jury deference is steeped in the history of our court system. One justification is that juries are thought to have an advantage over appeals judges due to their ability to assess witnesses during the trial. Yet studies show that people are extremely bad at interpreting demeanour and using it to gauge witness reliability. Appeals courts prefer to cling to disproven lore handed down from their precursors, than to reconsider the balance between seeking justice and merely seeking procedural fidelity.

Appeals courts in Australia have largely hidden behind

---

30. Victoria Crimes Act 1958, section 567(c).
31. the statement that forms part of a submission to the U.K. House of Commons justice select committee review of the Criminal Cases Review Commission, written by Dr Dennis Eady and Professor Julie Price of Cardiff University's innocence project and co-signed by academics at 18 universities, and various lawyers, quotes and endorses the following rem

precedent and tradition to absolve themselves of responsibility for faults in the system. If they truly want to honour the courts proud traditions and great responsibilities as being guardians of justice in our community, the Courts of Appeal would be using up to date knowledge to widen the scope of their appeals to reflect recently revealed realities. Miscarriages of justice occur and they need to be recognized and rectified. The most important lesson that the legal system can learn from the scientific method in this regard is the need for review. Scientific results are constantly being reviewed. The U.K. brought in a body with powers to review criminal cases. Australia's refusal to follow suit is driven by little more than hubris.

Chapter 25

THE SUPERMARKET CARPARK

'He'll have a long time to think about what he's done and all the lives he's ruined' said Cindy Gambino's dad Bob, when Robert Farquharson was sentenced to spend 33 years in prison.

The first time I saw Farquharson he had already spent eight years in prison. He told me his brain shuts down for large stretches of time, 'it just sort of switched off'. Atif Rafay, who has spent more than half his 40 years in a Seattle prison after being wrongfully convicted of murdering his parents and sister, refers to prisons as 'disgustingly efficient contraptions for turning men into ghosts'. Anne Irwin and Farquharson's sisters Kerri and Carmen do their best at trying to stop Farquharson turning into a ghost. They visit, they tell him about their lives, their families. They have always believed in his innocence. He has always maintained it. 'When I wake up, I can look at myself in the mirror. That is what keeps me going.' Another prisoner in Farquhrason's unit, a murderer, has grown his hair long, and it falls over his face. Can't look at himself in the mirror, according to Farquharson.

These women, Anne, Carmen, Kerri, also share Farquharson's dream that one day he will be freed. Vindicated.

What is he going to tell Greg King when he gets out? 'Jesus fucking Christ Kingy, what the fuck were you even on about? How could you fucking say that bullshit?' It is clear that a confrontation with Greg King has been swirling around and around his head as he kills 33 years of dead time. He has rehearsed the lines a thousand times or more. He works on his theories of how and why King came to tell these stories, how he got himself in too deep with the cops and could not back out. How he probably organized testimony with his wife, hoping that their contradictions would soften the evidence. Hours pondering a narrative of what went wrong with fucking Kingy, of trying to work out how it all came to this.

And then there is what he would like to tell Cindy. How could she lose faith, and believe he did it? How could she? 'I would never, ever…' he said 'I would never ever do that to her, that's what I want to tell her, I would never ever…' She knew him. That is what wants to tell her. She knew him. All the other bullshit and all the bull-shitters. They didn't know him. She knew him.

These are the things that occupy the mind of Robert Farquharson as his hair goes white and as lines multiply on his skin, waiting while the preponderance of his life expires. 'There are no colder comforts than knowing precisely all that one has missed and that is forever irrecoverable' says Rafay.

The last time I visited Farquharson, his right index finger was stuck to his palm. Trigger finger. He had the problem when I first visited two years earlier but it had progressively worsened. He is in constant pain, a pain that demands most of his waking attention. Despite a long standing medical opinion that he needs surgery, his repeated requests to schedule an operation have been ignored for more than five years; it is easy to dismiss the protests of a man who killed his three children. I am sure that many would consider justice is well served by adding the denial of medical care to his 33 year jail sentence. Let him suffer. If he did kill the three boys in that way, I would be tempted to think it myself. I just wonder where such a system of inflicting additional, pain related punishment starts and ends, and who is authorized to impose it.

Farquharson did get surgery for his eyes after developing a pre-glaucoma condition related to the diabetes he developed whilst eating the prison food. So at least he can still see. I guess it is troublesome and costly to house blind prisoners, so the authorities were not going to let his eyes go.

Anne, Kerri and Carmen have been pilloried by the community for supporting Farquharson. They have been called many things, the nicest of which are 'naïve' and 'in denial'. The same things Cindy was called when she stuck by Farquharson. The abuse has come not just from the public, but from members of their own family. From cousins. From nephews. Why wouldn't they believe the police? Why wouldn't they believe the newspapers? The documentaries? Famed author Helen Garner? The podcasts? Their classmates? People in their office? Anne says that 'the incredibly harsh and angry reaction I have got from people who think I sympathise with a person who murdered three children has been shattering'. Anne, Kerri and Carmen remain undaunted, unbowed, as they continue to fight for Rob, to put hope in a system in which they long ago lost all hope, because it is the only system there is.

In late 2018, Kerri saw Greg King enter a supermarket in Geelong, just minutes from the KFC where Robert Farquharson had taken his boys for dinner some 13 years earlier. Overwhelmed by emotions, her instincts were telling her to flee, but Robert Farquharson was not the only one who had been rehearsing a confrontation with Greg King. Kerri was not going to let this opportunity pass. She waited in the carpark, and confronted him when he came out. 'What was said during that conversation? What did Rob say?' Kerri demanded. 'Look me in the eye and tell me the truth'. 'Ask Rob' said King, 'I did, now I am asking you.' 'You have to move on from this' replied King, avoiding direct engagement with Kerri's demands.

But so many have not moved on. Cannot. Not accident reconstruction expert Glen Urquhart. Not defence barrister Peter Morrissey. It has changed the trajectory of their lives. Not Anne, Kerri or Carmen. Nor their children who grew up within the turmoil of this drawn out family trauma, as the ripples of the tragedy of losing three children gained momentum, and the number of victims multiplied. Robert Farquharson cannot move on. Cindy has not moved on, how could she?

Was Cindy naive when she said 'I believe with all my heart that this was just an accident and that he would not have hurt a hair on their heads'? The aftermath of this tragedy was not characterized by naivety, but by ignorance. Ignorance of the wealth of research that has been done using the scientific method that can inform the analysis of all types of evidence, and every step of the investigative and judicial processes. Ignorance is thinking you can spot a liar. Ignorance is thinking memory works like a video recorder. Ignorance is thinking four year old memories are reliable. Ignorance is thinking police who believe in guilt can interact with witnesses without influencing them. Ignorance is thinking that expert witnesses are not influenced by biased, irrelevant material, or by interacting with police. Ignorance is thinking that forensic evidence can be the same thing as science, without needing to use the same processes or methodologies. Ignorance is thinking that prosecutors do not exploit well researched memory flaws and cognitive biases to persuade jurors. Ignorance is believing that the criminal justice system always gets it right when the science of DNA has proven that it does not.

Anne, Kerri and Carmen are not naïve. They know what they know. Kerri says that 'there is no way I would ever stand by him if I ever thought that he could have done this. They were our boys too. I would be one of the first to make sure that he paid for what he did!' Anne agrees, 'If any of us had any inkling that he had done this intentionally there is no way we would sympathise with him…There would be absolutely no way you could forsake honouring the memory of three little boys to support a murderer. But we know he isn't one.'

APPENDIX A: THE RECONSTRUCTION

Figure A.1.1: An overview of the dam and Princes Highway looking back toward Geelong. Farquharson had been travelling in the same direction as the red car but had run the road somewhat further back toward Geelong.

The reconstruction evidence can be clarified by organizing it into stages, and taking it step by step. What we know: the car driven by Robert Farquharson went from the Princes Highway, traveling on the left side of the road toward Winchelsea, into the dam which is off the right side of the road. You can see in Figure A.1.1 an overhead shot of this stretch of road, which comes down from an overpass and is bending rightward as the road passes the dam.

I proceed by looking at the path from the road to the dam in stages. The first thing we want to know is how the car got from driving along the left side of the road, to leave the road on the right hand side. I will call this stage 1. The prosecution expert claims that a steering input was required during this stage, to get the car from the left side of the road, to leaving the road on the right.

Between the road and the dam there was a right-handed bank sloping towards the dam, and sections of short and long grass. There were tracks in the long grass, showing the path of the car through that region. Between the road and the long grass, however, there was a section of short grass. There were no clear marks[1] on this short grass to delineate the route between the road and the long grass. I call the path through the short grass stage 2. The prosecution expert claims that a steering input was required during stage 2, to prevent the car from veering rightward down the slope toward the dam.

The path of the car through the long grass, as already mentioned, is the only region where the trajectory of the car is relatively easy to ascertain, and we call this stage 3. It is well established that the long grass was flattened by Farquharson's car, so the trajectory of the car through this region is relatively clear.

Finally, there is more short grass through which the car travelled, leading to the dam. I call the path through the final section of short grass stage 4. Toward the end of stage 4, the car side-swiped a tree prior to entering the dam, providing a good idea of one point through which the car passed. Besides this point, there were no clear marks in the short grass to help us determine the precise path of the car though stage 4, similar to the lack of marks in the short grass of stage 2. The prosecution expert claims that a steering input was required in stage 4, turning the car rightward to prevent it from crashing into the trunk of the tree.

The Physical Evidence

The physical evidence left by Farquharson's car, which can be used in the reconstruction:

– At the edge of the road, two marks were identified as possible tyre marks resulting from vehicles leaving the road. Neither of them could be linked to Farquharson's car by their physical characteristics: no tread analysis was possible. The two marks were too close together to match the width of Farquharson's car, so one or the other may have come from Farquharson's car. Not both. Several other vehicles also crossed over the edge of the road that evening, including ambulances and fire-trucks. Yet only these two marks were found, so vehicles were crossing this road edge without leaving a mark. Therefore, it is entirely possible Farquharson's car crossed the edge without leaving a mark.

-The marks through the long grass. There was never any dispute that

---

1. The defence claim that aerial police photos show marks in the short grass which corroborate their proposed car path, but these marks have a degree of uncertainty and we will deal here with the physical evidence that is accepted by both sides, i.e. we will be generous to the prosecution.

Farquharson's car travelled through the long grass along the path indicated by these marks.
   -The broken fence through which the car travelled as it left the long grass.
   -The debris of broken car lights and broken branch from the car crashing through a tree at the edge of the dam.

THE RECONSTRUCTION

STAGE 1: On the road

i) Physical Evidence on the road: no marks of any type, including skid marks or tyre marks, were found on the road.

Significance: Marks on the road may have helped indicate where the car turned, how sharp the turn was, given an indication of any braking, and may have helped determine the speed at which the car was traveling.

ii) Road Camber: Roads are not entirely flat: most have a small slope toward the edges, helping to drain water. A detailed study was made of the road camber. In some regions the camber of the left lane sloped left, with the crown (highest point) in the centre of the road, between the lanes. This is the most common position for the crown. However, there are also regions on this road, coming down the overpass, where the crown is in the left lane, and the camber slopes to the right, even from the left lane.

Significance: Unsteered cars tend to follow the slope of the road. If the road slopes left, the car will tend to pull to the left. If the road slopes right, the car will tend to pull right.

Re-enactment Evidence

The prosecution presented re-enactments of driving down this section road. The reconstruction expert took his hands off the steering wheel at one specific part of the road, and showed that the car veers left when travelling at 64km/hr. The defence made some similar drive-through re-enactments, with drivers taking their hands off the steering wheel, and found that the cars veered right. In these defence experiments, the drivers took their hands off the wheel at a different part of the road to where the reconstruction expert took his hands off the wheel in the earlier experiments.

Witness Evidence

There was evidence given by Robert Graham, a retired tow-truck operator who was called to an incident where a truck driver had fallen asleep when driving down the same overpass and heading in the same direction as Farquharson. The truck went off the road to the right, and was heading toward the dam when it came to a stop. The owner of the property containing the dam, Cam Everett, testified that eight vehicles had gone off the road in that area over the past ten years, four of which (including the Farquharson case) had been travelling in the direction toward Winchelsea.

Analysis

There is no physical evidence marking the path of the car on the bitumen road, so the car may have drifted slowly from the left to the right lane then off the road, which would be consistent with Farquharson's claim of losing consciousness, or it could have taken a sharp turn rightward as claimed by the prosecution in the first trial. The physical evidence to distinguish these scenarios, in terms of marks on the bitumen, does not exist.

The different results of the experimental drive-throughs done by the prosecution and defence are reconciled by the measurements of the road camber that showed that the slope of the road varied: on some parts of the road, an unsteered car will veer left, whilst on other parts of the road it will veer right. As there are no physical marks on the road, it is impossible to say where Farquharson's car started turning toward the right, so neither option can be ruled out.

Conclusion

Coming down the overpass, there are regions of the road that slope downward to the right, so it is possible for an unsteered car to veer rightward. There was no *requirement* for the first steering input that was asserted by the prosecution. The evidence is therefore consistent with Farquharson's claim of lost consciousness.

One other factor can be considered here, and that is the tendency of Farquharson's car to 'pull right', supported by the testimony[2] of mechanic James Jacobs who test drove the car earlier in 2005. Subsequent to Jacobs assessing the car, Farquharson took it to for a wheel alignment. The prosecution relied on this wheel alignment as evidence that the car did not pull right at the time of the accident.

However, there was further evidence that the wheels on Farquharson's front tyres did not match, with the left one around 10 mm higher than the right one. According to reconstruction engineer Dr. Shane Richardson, this difference 'would cause the vehicle to drift to the right'[3] even on a flat surface.

---

2. Trial 2 p2740
3. Private communication.

STAGE 2: across the short grass to the long grass

Physical Evidence: no marks that could definitively be associated with Farquharson's car were found in the short grass.

Slope

There was a slope downward toward the dam in this region. The downward slope would cause the car to veer rightwards. The degree to which the car would veer right would depend on a number of factors, including the size of the slope, the speed of the car, the angle of the car across the slope, i.e. the precise direction of the car as it left the road, the amount of friction between the tyres and the ground, and details of the particular car's dimensions and car mechanics.

Analysis

The path of the car through the short grass needs to be inferred from knowledge of where the car the car left the road and from where it enters the long grass. We know where the path through the short grass ends, because of the clear marks in the long grass, but as noted above, we do not have perfect information of where the car left the road, nor at what angle. We therefore need to consider a number of different possibilities.

Firstly, I assume that one of the marks on the edge of the road is indeed from Farquharson's car. This simplifying assumption is supported by an argument put forward by the police expert witness: it is *unlikely* that more than one car crossed the edge of the road in this region, which is somewhat aligned with the path of the car through the long grass. Such an argument does not rule out the possibility that *neither* mark comes from Farquharson's car, which we will consider at the end of the analysis.

Also, the terrain is not smooth, so there is a possibility of 'bump steer' where the car wheels bump into a tuft of grass, for example, and has its direction altered. In our initial analysis we ignore this possibility, as it simplifies things.

Note that when making these simplifying assumptions, a degree of uncertainty enters our analysis, and in the conclusion. The implications of such simplifications need to be considered and commented upon.

These simplifying assumptions allow four different possibilities: **a.** the right wheel of Farquharson's car passes through the left mark; **b.** the right wheel of Farquharson's car passed through the right mark; **c.** the left wheel of Farquharson's car passed through the left mark; **d.** the left wheel of Farquharson's car passed through the right mark. These possibilities are shown in **Figure A.2**, where the path through the long grass and the marks on the edge of the road are shown.

Let us look at the rules that we need to apply. As there is a downward slope in the direction of the dam, we expect an unsteered car to veer rightward. No experiments were done on this particular slope to place constraints on the magnitude of this rightward tendency. No evidence was presented from other experiments on similar slopes to give a range of possibilities for the magnitude of the rightward turn for different speeds, grass lengths, hardness of surface, angles between the car direction and slope, and car mechanics. We therefore need to consider a full range of possible rightward turns, from almost straight to clear right turns, although turns approaching 90 degrees would be unlikely.

Importantly, the rightward veer can only increase, it cannot decrease. So the rightward veer can initially be small, and can then continue to veer rightward at the same rate, i.e. with the same arc, or it can increase its turning rate. The rate of turn cannot decrease, i.e. the car cannot 'straighten'. We do not expect an un-steered car on this sloped terrain to veer left, nor to straighten (under our assumption of no bump steer).

So, we take the four allowed starting points for the car, and only allow the car to veer rightward, either steadily rightward or increasingly rightward. Using these rules, I ask whether the car is able to traverse a path that is *consistent with the physical evidence*, without the need for a left hand turn or a straightening.

Starting with the **case a**: the right wheel of Farquharson's car passed through the left hand mark. Regardless of the angle the car left road, and regardless of how slight the right hand veer is at the beginning, the car cannot join the path made through the long grass unless there is a left hand turn. So, if the right wheel passed through the left hand mark, we can *infer* that the car was steered left. Someone was in control of the car.

Similar conclusions are drawn for **case b**. If the right wheel of Farquharson's car passed through the right hand mark, then a left turn is required for the car to join the path through the long grass. This case is shown in **Figure A.2.b**. This is the case that is pushed by the police expert, who claims that the right wheel of Farquharson's car passed through the right hand mark, and that this implies that a steering input to the left was *necessary*. This is the basis of the second steering input asserted by the prosecution.

In **Figure A.1.2 case a** we show this situation. The black lines show the path through the long grass. The grey lines show a possible path through the short grass, where we have made the degree (arc) of the right turn the same as that through the long grass. In our rules, this grey line can be straighter at the beginning but needs to bend rightwards. No manipulation of this grey line that follows our rules is able to match the path through the long grass. A left hand turn is required, or a straightening, which would violate our rules and indicate that the car was being steered (or bump steered). **Case b** is similar to case a, but requires a very small straightening (if any at all).

For **case c**, where the left wheel of Farquharson's car passed through the left hand mark, it is possible for the car to veer rightward after leaving the road, and to smoothly join the path through the long grass. This case is shown in **Figure A.1.2 c**. There is no requirement for a steering input in this

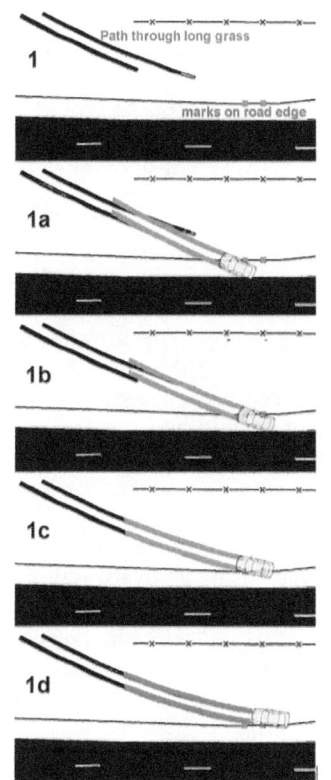

A scaled schematic of possible paths between the road and the long grass.

Black lines show the path through the long grass which was relatively well marked as the car pushed down the grass. These black lines come from the measuring markers put along the edges of the path at the scene. These measurements are not exact but do give reasonable approximation to the path of the car in this region.

Grey dots show the marks identified on the side of the road, where one side of the car may have passed. The marks cannot both be from Farquharson's car as they are too far apart. So there are four possible cases, depicted as grey lines in 1a-1d. The depicted grey lines have the exact same rightward arc as the green lines.

a: the right wheels cross at the left mark. A steer leftward is required in this case.

b: the right wheels cross at the right mark. A smaller leftward steer is required in this case than in case 1a.

c: the left wheels cross at the left mark. A smooth arc joins the grey line to the black path, veering rightward at a similar rate the whole way. No steering input is required.

d: the left wheels cross at the right mark. The car eaves the road at a smaller angle in this case than in 1c. The car is initially veering only slightly rightward but the arc increases until the grey path meets the black path. Again no steering input is required.

Figure A1.2 The various available paths that are consistent with the physical evidence at the scene.

case. The car veers continuously rightward down the slope. This is the case that is pushed by the defence expert in the case.

For the fourth case, where the left wheel of Farquharson's car passed through the right hand mark, we would need the car to leave the road at a small angle and travel reasonably straight when it first leaves the road, veering only slightly right, and to increasingly veer right in order to join the path through the long grass. This option is possible within our rules, and is shown in **Figure A.1.2 d** as a grey line, where the arc of this line is different to that of the previous and grey lines. This grey line starts relatively straight with a small rightward veer, and the right turn increases as it gets closer to the long grass. As for case c, there is no requirement for a steering input. One may argue that the car would not travel this straight across such a slope, but some experiments would need to be done to support such an argument. No such experimental evidence is available.

Finally, we need to consider the case that neither of the marks was made by Farquharson's car. This was not ruled out by any physical evidence and remains a distinct possibility. We are no longer restricted to the four options explored so far, and a large range of paths through the short grass in stage 2 are now possible. But we can use the above 4 cases to understand these possibilities. If the car leaves the road anywhere to the *left of case c*, the situation is similar to *cases a and b* and a left turn, or straightening would be *necessary*. If the car leaves the road anywhere to the *right of case c*, then a left turn is *not necessary*: the car can leave the road and veer rightward, and still join the path through the long grass.

Conclusion

The lack of direct physical evidence in stage 2 allows for a range of possibilities to match up with the evidence that exists at the scene. As was the case for stage 1, some of the possibilities do require a steering input, but some do not. The scenario pushed by the prosecution and the scenario pushed by the defence are both consistent with the physical evidence at the scene, as are a range of other possibilities. It remains possible for a car to pass through the short grass of stage 2 without being steered. Again, Farquharson's claim to have lost consciousness cannot be disproved. Uncertainties from bump steering, that we ignored in the analysis, will not discredit these conclusions. Rather, bump steering would add more possible ways that the path of an unsteered car could be consistent with the physical evidence.

STAGE 3: path through the long grass

Physical evidence

The long grass was pushed down by Farquharson's car as it travelled toward the dam. The slope was rightwards toward the dam in this region.

Analysis

The car's path through the long grass is relatively well defined. However, there does remain a degree of uncertainty, and it is crucial to analyse the uncertainties in all forensic evidence. A number of witnesses described the path, and I won't go through each individually, but most agree that the path curved toward the right, including police officers Exton and Peters. Peters in particular spent a lot of time photographing this path in the daylight, and concluded that the marks through the long grass are `curving to the right'[4]. However, the police expert witness Urquhart changed his view, initially agreeing that the path curved rightward, but later stating a belief that there is straight section in this path.

The left and right sides of the path through the long grass were marked out

---

4. Trial 2 p. 2478

by police officer Courtis. The marker points were not parallel, with the left side showing a continuous rightward curve, while the right markers showed a possible straight section. Of course, the markers should be parallel if they are marking tracks of the two sets of wheels. The markers also varied in their distance apart. Apparently, there is some inherent uncertainty with this type of evidence. The nature of this uncertainty was explained by the police expert witness Urquhart, who remarked that `the tyres were rolling across grass so the grass was being displaced. It's more difficult under that condition to actually define clearly an edge of a tyre mark'.[5] He also said in the first trial that `it is not simply the case that you can look at the photographs and say there's a clearly defined edge and it's safe to use that as an edge from which you can take those measurements.'[6]

Conclusions

With the uncertainties in the path through the long grass, a straight section through the long grass is possible. However, a path veering rightward through the long grass is also clearly possible, and is consistent with the physical evidence, and with most witness accounts. Such a rightward veering path does not require any steering inputs from the driver, and would be consistent with Farquharson being unconscious.

STAGE 4: final path through short grass to the dam

Physical Evidence

At the start of stage 4 where the short grass began, the car crashed through a wire fence. There were no marks through the short grass, but there was debris and broken branches where the car crashed through the tree on the edge of the dam. The terrain continued to slope rightward toward the dam, although the slope was not as steep as that through the long grass.

Analysis

A right turn, or veer to the right, was required in this final stage for the car to travel from the path in the long grass to the point where it crashed through the tree. The slope was again downward toward the dam, meaning that the car can be expected to veer right even without any input from the driver. Remember that the degree that a car will turn right may be affected by the size of the slope but also the speed of the car and the friction between the tyres and the ground. It is possible that the car slowed down through the long grass, or was slowed down by crashing through the fence, and the friction may be different in this short grass near the dam due to different soil and different grass coverage. A small bump steer is also possible. So it is hard

---

5. Trial 2 p3438
6. Trial 1 p2022

to constrain exactly how much we expect the car to veer right in this section, and no experiments were performed or referred to.

Again, the uncertainty in the path through the long grass needs to be considered when analysing the subsequent path through the short grass. If one assumes that the car follows the same rightward arc as allowed by the marks in the long grass, then the car will crash through the tree branches in the manner consistent with the evidence. This is the position pushed by the defence. If one assumes that the car straightened at the end of the path through the long grass and was heading directly toward the tree trunk, then the car would need to veer right to crash through the branch rather than the trunk of the tree. This is the position pushed by the prosecution, who also assert that any slope in this region is insufficient to account for such a veer to the right. No experiment was performed to support this assertion, so there is no evidentiary basis for ruling out the possibility of a rightward veer caused by the slope of the terrain in this section.

Conclusion

Both the defence and prosecution scenarios are consistent with the physical evidence at the scene, given the uncertainties in the path through the long grass and the uncertainties in the degree we expect the car to veer right due to the slope. These uncertainties in the path mean that there is no *necessity* for a steering input in this stage. The car may have simply veered rightward down the slope and into the dam.

The Fence

At the start of stage 4 through the short grass, the car crashed through a wire fence. Significant damage was done the right side of the car, indicating that side reached the fence first. This is consistent with the direction of the car through the long grass. The wire fence tore through the metal sheeting of the car in the front right corner, indicating that the wire became considerably taut before the car broke through.

In my analysis of stage 4 I ignored the possible impact of the fence, which the defence expert claims could have resulted in a right turn, a claim disputed by the prosecution expert. No evidence was provided either way, so it is difficult to see how either possibility can be excluded, providing another possibility for a rightward turn of an unsteered car in this final stage. Another possibility is bump steer which tends to increase the rate of turn, so a car veering right will start to veer more sharply.

Summary

In summary, the car could have simply followed the slope of the road, which was downwards towards the dam. In each stage, there are possible paths that did not require steering inputs from a conscious driver, and that were consistent with the physical evidence. None of the three steering inputs asserted by the prosecution are *necessary* according to the physical evidence at the scene. It was possible for an un-steered car to veer rightward due to the slopes on the road and the terrain between the road and the dam. There is nothing that shows that Farquharson had to be in control of the car. Of course, this does not prove his innocence, but the physical evidence of the path of the car is consistent with his story and does not provide any evidence of guilt.

Each of the 3 steering inputs asserted by the prosecution occurred in regions where no physical evidence was left by the car. No marks were found on the road, where the first steering input was claimed to occur. No marks were found in the short grass just off the road (stage 2), or in the short grass leading to the dam (stage 4), where the second and third steering inputs were claimed to occur. Each of the asserted steering inputs needed to be *inferred* from the surrounding evidence. The paucity of direct physical indicators left by the car meant that a range of possible paths are consistent with the evidence. This full range of paths was not fully explored by the prosecution expert witness.

Some Comments

I comment here on a couple of less technical arguments that were made in court. Firstly, the car only slightly missed the tree trunk, which may have prevented it from reaching the dam. The prosecution asserts this is evidence that the car was steered, with Farquharson turning rightward to avoid slamming into the tree trunk. If he were steering the car, why did he crash through the tree at all? Why head in the direction of the tree? Wouldn't a steered car aim for the dam in the clear region between the trees? Or did he plan to hit the tree so that it looked more like an accident? But wouldn't that imply that hitting a tree is actually what we expect if it were an accident? Why wasn't the fact that he hit the tree simply interpreted as evidence that he was not steering the car?

Similarly, for the second alleged steering input, the left turn or straightening after the car left the road. Why would a person steering the car toward the dam turn left, veering in a direction *away from* the dam? Why not just drive toward the dam?

Nothing can be proven either way by these types of speculations: we could go around and around in circles for hours. Either side can just cherry pick parts of these arguments to bolster their beliefs. Confirmation bias. Best to stick to the physical evidence.

THE EVIDENCE PRESENTED IN COURT

To understand the failures of the prosecution reconstruction evidence, it is crucial to understand that the task of the prosecution and defence reconstruction experts were different. The defence needed to provide a single path that an unsteered car could take that was consistent with the physical evidence. This would show that Farquharson could indeed have been unconscious as the car went from the road to the dam. By contrast, the prosecution had to consider all possible paths from the road to the dam, and use the physical evidence to exclude[7] *every* path that an unsteered vehicle may take. Or at least show that an unsteered path was very unlikely. Merely presenting a single path that is consistent with the evidence, and that did require steering, is not enough for the prosecution. Otherwise, the defence could point to a path that is not excluded and say 'it remains absolutely possible that the car took this path which did not require steering input from a driver'. In such a case, there would be no physical evidence of Farquharson's guilt.

The computer simulations

In the first trial, the prosecution expert, Sergeant Urquhart, presented simulations he had made using accident reconstruction software called PC Crash.[8] This is world leading computer software that is used by law enforcement agencies in the U.S. as well as Australia. Urquhart used PC-Crash to model the path of the car from the road to the dam on a computer. On the basis of these simulations, Urquhart told the court that in order to steer off the road, the wheels of Farquharson's car turned 16.5o to the right, and that this required a 220° turn of the steering wheel. Here is how this was presented to the jury (Jeremy Rapke is the prosecuting barrister in the first trial):

Urquhart: …16.5 degrees is the angle at the tyre to road interface that was required to get that car to steer off the road to the right.

Rapke: So the tyres had to turn 16 and a half degrees to get it to turn off at the angle that you've calculated the car left the road?

Urquhart: Yes

Rapke: In order to get the wheels to turn 16 and a half degrees, is it possible to calculate how much steering input is required? In other words how much the steering wheel has to be moved to move the wheel 16 and a half degrees?

Urquhart: Yes.'

Rapke: How much is that?

Urquhart: A 220 degree turn of the steering wheel.

At this point, Rapke produced a steering wheel prop and asked Urquhart to demonstrate a 220° turn of the wheel. The steering wheel had been taped so that the jury could follow the rotation of the wheel. Notably, Urquhart's arms where crossing to produce the required turn, highlighting the effort

---

7. Technically, it needs to be shown the they are highly unlikely, rather than "excluded". Discussion of liklihoods in science comes later in the book.
8. http://www.pc-crash.com/

required. Animations of the computer simulations were also shown, depicting the path followed from the left side of the road to the dam.

Dramatic. Definitive. Compelling. Simple to follow and grasp. Backed up by computer modelling, using state of the art, internationally recognized computer software. Persuasive stuff.

Oh, and total junk.

Where do I start in explaining all the ways that this evidence is wrong? And how did I know it was junk science as soon as I read a brief description of the evidence in Helen Garner's book about the trial? And why did this compel me to look closely at the evidence in the Farquharson case, uncovering an astonishing gap between the standards of scientific and judicial inquiry, and between scientific and forensic analysis?

I use computer software that models the Universe in my job as an astrophysicist. Using such software is my field of expertise. The software incorporates physical laws, including gravity, gas cooling due to emission of photons, and star formation, in a similar way that accident reconstruction software incorporates laws of physics to model processes such as momentum, friction at the road surface, and gravity on slopes. So, my job is to use computer software programs that code the laws of physics in order to reconstruct a dynamic object's history, given a set of observational evidence. Similar to what Urquhart was doing when he used PC-Crash for accident reconstruction. Weather predictions use similar computational techniques.

I have refereed a large number of studies for important journals in the field, including Nature, the Astrophysical Journal (where the Cosmic Microwave Background studies were published) and the Monthly Notices of the Royal Astronomical Society. So I have learned what to look for in submitted articles, and what mistakes are commonly made. For any article that involves computer simulations, there are a couple of basic things to look at first: initial conditions and applicability.

Firstly, what are the initial conditions that the study employed, and did the author correctly account for uncertainties in the initial? Did the results get affected by using incorrect initial conditions? In particular, if the observed evidence allows for uncertainty in initial conditions, then it is necessary to do the simulations with a range of possible initial conditions and determine whether this affects the conclusions of the study. So, for example, twenty years ago the Cosmic Microwave Background was not as accurately measured as it is today and there remained significant uncertainty in the constituents of the Universe. Therefore it was common for researchers to model the Universe with a range of initial conditions, such as with and without a cosmological constant.[9]

Another example is in simulations of two galaxies colliding into each other. One such case is the collision between our own Milky Way galaxy, and a small galaxy known as the Sagittarius dwarf galaxy. We know what this ongoing collision looks like now,[10] because we can observe it. But to simulate the collision, we need to consider a range of possibilities for how the two

---

9. e.g. Kravtsov, Klypin & Khokhlov, 1997 ApJS 111 73K

galaxies looked in the past. So we need to model a range of different initial values for the mass of Sagittarius, and different values of the initial orbit.[11] We then analyse which of the models is best at reproducing all the observed physical evidence.

Weather predictions use similar computational techniques, and the initial conditions used in these simulations are also extremely important.[12] The weather bureau takes observations of current weather conditions as initial conditions for computer programs that then predict the weather tomorrow, and indeed for the next 3-5 days. One of the biggest problems with the predictions is the imperfect observations of current weather conditions, meaning that the initial conditions of the simulations have a significant degree of uncertainty. A range of initial conditions are all compatible with current observations. To deal with this, an ensemble of different simulations is run with a range of initial conditions.[13] This results in an ensemble of different predictions for the weather in 1-5 days' time, and the forecaster is trained at understanding which is the most likely outcome. The models result in a range of possibilities, each with different probabilities of occurring. The best weather websites therefore provide such probabilities, rather than simply making a definitive prediction. Such sites may state that there is a 75% chance of rain tomorrow, rather than 'tomorrow there will be rain'. Note that these models are currently not able to predict weather beyond the next 5 days, largely because of the uncertainty in the initial conditions: any 10 day forecast is just using historic data, and providing the typical conditions for that day of the year.

So what initial conditions were used in the reconstruction simulations of Sergeant Urquhart, which led him to conclude that a 220° steering turn was required for the car to leave the road? Urquhart assumed that the car turned right from a single, particular position on the road, as can be seen in figure 2. Why was this initial condition chosen for his simulation? Recall, there was no physical mark on the road that identified where the car started to turn rightward. Why couldn't the car have started veering right earlier, closer to the top of the overpass? In such a case, a far smaller steering input was required to get the car to leave the road. *With no physical evidence ruling this out, it was essential that the reconstruction simulations consider this possibility.* There is no physical evidence that ruled out the scenario where Farquharson's car veers slowly rightward from much further up the overpass. Without testing the full range of initial conditions that were allowed by the physical evidence, the results of the simulations were essentially meaningless.

Yet the jury in the first trial were presented with this definitive and damning result that a 220° turn of the wheel was required to get the car

---

10. technically we also have important uncertainties on how the system looks now, such as uncertainty in the mass of yet Milky Ways Dark matter halo. These uncertainties also need to be considered.
11. e.g. Law & Majewski 2010 ApJ 714 229L
12. e.g. Palmer 2000 'Predicting uncertainty in forecasts of weather and climate' in Reports on Progress in Physics, Volume 63, Number 2
13. as well as range of different parameters for modelling the physics

off the road. Were the jury to know that this result was junk science? Why would they? They have been told of Sergeant Urquhart's credentials and experience, and were shown convincing looking simulations and demonstrations. Yet for someone with experience in computer simulations of physical processes, the fundamental flaw in the forensic evidence was glaring and easy to see. Having a meteorologist on the jury would have been very helpful to the defence!

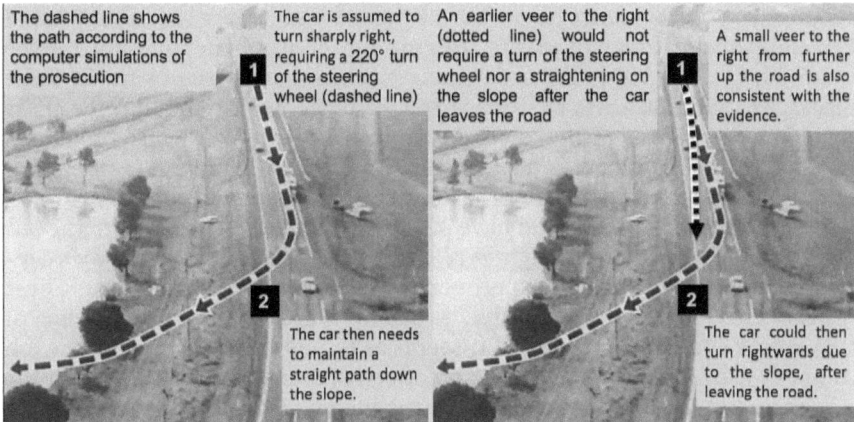

Figure A.1.3: different assumptions about where the car started veering rightward allow different paths on the road. The police reconstruction in the first trial only considered one possibility, which required a sharp turn rightward, shown on the left. A gentle veering to the right is also possible, if the car started the veer further up the road, as shown on the right. No physical evidence was found on the road that can distinguish these two possibilities.

The initial condition problem relating to the first alleged steering input was propagated to the second alleged steering input that arises in Urquhart's simulations. By making an initial 220° turn the car leaves the road at a sharp angle, and then finds itself on a bank that slopes rightward. To then reach the path through the long grass, the car would need to either turn left, or at least straighten. But an unsteered car would not straighten, when the slope is to the right. This straightening is the second steering input, allegedly required to prevent the car veering further to the right. But if the car veered off the road at a much gentler angle, then there is no need for this left turn or straightening. The car could leave the road at a gentle angle and then veer to the right as it traversed the bank. As expected.

To be precise, the marks through the long grass were at a 30° angle to the road, and Urquhart's model assumed that the car left the road at 30°. If the car left the road at a gentler angle, say 5°, the car could then veer rightward, reaching the long grass at 30°. Such a rightward veer is precisely what is expected on such a downsloping bank.

The initial condition problem also applies to the three drive through reconstructions that were performed. Urquhart drove down the highway and let go of the steering wheel, to determine how an unsteered car would react. He let go of the wheel at the same place on the road but at three different speeds, 64km/hr 80km/hr and 100km/hr. For the lowest speed the car veered left, while the higher speeds the car went straight. This was supposed to be evidence that the car would not veer right. But what if Farquharson lost control of the steering wheel at a different spot on the road? Measurements of the road camber, which sloped rightward in some places, as well as a series of drive throughs presented by the defence show that there are areas of the road where cars do in fact veer right. It was incumbent on Urquhart to perform his experiment using a large range of initial conditions, i.e. letting go of the wheel at a range of different places. Not to mention that he should have performed the experiments with the left tyre 10 mm larger than the right tyre, as was the case for Farquharson's car.

As it is, the drive through experiment of Urquhart was meaningless. These experiments highlight a central problem which runs through all of Urquhart's evidence in the case. It seems as though he considered it his job to propose a single path that the car followed, that was consistent with the evidence. But, as stated previously, it was incumbent upon him to consider the full range of paths that are compatible with the physical evidence, and show that none of these possible paths could have been followed by an unsteered car. No analysis or experiments were performed that even attempt to achieve this, meaning that the prosecution fell well short of demonstrating that the car was *necessarily* being steered.

Knocking down a straw man

Having shown the simulations of a proposed path that required steering inputs, Urquhart then purported to show simulations of what an unsteered car would do. He made three simulations that show the path the car would take if it made the initial 16.5° turn (220° of the steering wheel) and then remained unsteered after that. The three simulations differed only in car speed. The simulations showed that, in such circumstances, the car would continue turning in an arc and would not follow the known path through the long grass, and showed that the car following such an arc would not end up in the dam. The first problem, of course, is that there is no reason to believe the initial 16.5o turn. This is a classic `straw man' argument: Urquhart ruled out a path which was obviously wrong in the first place, and was not anything like the path suggested by the defence. Again, it was necessary to simulate cases where the car veered gently off the road. We stated above that it was incumbent for the prosecution to rule out *each and every* possible unsteered path, showing that each is inconsistent with the evidence. Yet all they did was show a single, meaningless path and show that it was not possible.

But there is an even more fatal problem with these simulations, the second issue I alluded to when modelling events using software that encodes the laws of physics. It is very important that the result of simulation experiments is not affected by using the software beyond its scope. Urquhart had done his simulations using a flat surface, without any slopes included. Yet the road and bank off the road were measured to slope rightward, which tends to make the car veer rightward, as stated by Urquhart himself. So, of course an unsteered car in a model where the road is flat will not veer rightward! The question that needed to be answered was whether an unsteered car would veer rightward *because of the slopes*. Urquhart has failed to even address this central question with these meaningless simulations. He did successfully knock down a straw man though.

Training

As we will see when reviewing a couple more of the central pieces of reconstruction evidence, Urquhart's testimony changed dramatically from the first trial to the second. Part of the change in testimony came from the fact that Urquhart was barred from showing his simulations in the second trial. The Court of Appeal expressed concern regarding the flat nature of the simulations, and the presiding judge in the second trial, Lex Lasry, could also see that a model using a flat surface was useless. It is a concern that an expert in the field needed to have this pointed out by a judge, who has no experience of accident reconstruction and has never used this type of software.

Urquhart was a very experienced and well credentialed police officer, with an honours degree in engineering at the University of Melbourne. So what went wrong? How could his simulation evidence be so poor, so far below standards that would be expected in science? It comes down to the gulf in training that exists between scientists, and many forensic analysts. Let us compare the training that Urquhart received in using software to simulate car accidents, to the training that I received in using software to simulate the Universe. Urquhart took a one week course on the use of the software PC-crash. I undertook a three year apprenticeship, in the form of PhD, under the supervision of Dr. Daisuke Kawata, an expert on galaxy formation software, who had actually built the software himself. During that training, I was given increasing responsibility for planning of studies, and increasing responsibility in writing scientific articles for submission to journals. The level of analysis and rational thinking required to publish a scientific article is non-negotiable, and my prospective career relied on the development of such skills. Urquhart never had to present his results for peer review, meaning that the high standards required for publication in peer review journals, the standards demanded of me and my collaborators, were never imposed on the simulation work of Urquhart. On top of all this, I write papers along with collaborators, other people with years of experience working in this specialized field. Each of these collaborators critically assesses the work before it is even sent to a journal. It was only in my fifteenth year as a researcher that I wrote a single author paper. Even then I asked some close friends for feedback prior to submitting to a journal. Critical comments from collaborators is another important part of the scientific process that is missing from the simulation evidence and from forensic evidence in general.

I have no doubt that software such as PC-Crash can be a valuable tool in accident reconstruction, if used correctly. But the users need to be properly trained. It may be good business for PC-crash to train a large number of police officers in the basics of the program, by charging for week long courses. But it is not helpful for the police force to have a lot of people spending a fraction of their time misusing this type of software because they don't have the extensive training that is required to achieve meaningful results. It would be far better to have a small number of highly trained experts, who can specialize in using the accident reconstruction software. Separation could be created between the investigating officers and the modellers, with expert modellers working in an independent environment, reducing the types of biases that we have discussed at length in this book.

Tunnel Vision

It is important to emphasize the role that the simulations played in the conviction of Robert Farquharson. It is wrong to point to the second trial, where this particular piece of junk science was excluded, and conclude that this analysis was not significant to the case. Recall, the police officers suspected Farquharson from early in the investigation. Suspicion is one thing. Police can have hunches. The question is, when did this investigation change from being an investigation into whether the deaths were an accident, into an exercise in gathering enough evidence to secure a conviction? When did the police and prosecutors move from 'investigation' mode to 'selling' mode? Lead Investigator Clanchy identified the original report from Urquhart as the time he was convinced of Farquharson's guilt. You can imagine the reaction when the report reached his superior officers: here was proof, physical evidence, showing that they were right all along. He is guilty, just as their gut reactions had told them. Now it was just a matter of building their case, gathering enough evidence to ensure a conviction. A move from inspection to selling. Their focus narrowed: their vision was becoming tunnelled in one direction.

Wrongful conviction does not only occur in the courtroom. It is a process in which errors compound, and begins at the investigation level. Researcher Jon Gould finds that most cases of wrongful conviction involved more than one error, sometimes as many as four or five, and that "errors are often sequential and build upon each other"[14]. Once in selling mode, all evidence

---

14. Gould, J et al. *Predicting Erroneous Convictions: A Social Science Approach to Miscarriages of Justice* (March 1, 2013. Univ. of San Francisco Law Research Paper No. 2013-20

and information is assessed purely for its value in adding to the case for conviction. This is the essence of tunnel vision, a manifestation of confirmation bias. Once in selling mode, there is an increased capacity for error, for misinterpreting evidence in a manner that suits your case, that confirms your bias.

What would have happened if Urquhart's original report stated that the relative paucity of evidence at the scene made it impossible to rule out an unconscious driver? Would the investigation have proceeded with such vigour? Without any other physical evidence, it is highly likely that charges would never have been laid.

A further continuing consequence of the misuse of PC-Crash software also needs mentioning. The original simulations played a central role in arriving at the conclusion that 'three steering inputs' were required for the car to enter the dam. This was a crucial theme throughout the prosecution case, in both trials. As the nature of the reconstruction evidence changed dramatically through the course of the hearing and the trials, this mantra of 'three steering inputs' remained all the way until the very final remarks of Urquhart at the end of the cross examination, even though these conclusions had become increasingly disconnected from the evidence presented. This disconnect between the physical evidence, and the need for a conscious driver to make 'three steering inputs' becomes increasingly clear when I look further at the reconstruction evidence presented by the prosecution.

More Detail on the Marks

The issue was whether two marks at the side of the road were made by Farquharson's car. The two marks were first identified by officers Exton and Kok, who believed they showed where the car had left the road, and marked them with yellow paint. This initial assumption that the marks showed the left and right wheels of Farquharson's car was wrong, because they were too close together to match the distance between the wheels of his car. The question remained as to whether one or other of the marks was made by Farquharson's car. If either of the marks could be specifically matched to Farquharson's car, then that could be used in the reconstruction of the path of the car. If the marks could not be matched to Farquharson's car, then the reconstruction would have to consider a range of possibilities as to where the car left the road.

As stated in the book no castings were made of the marks. No photographs depicted the treads. No analysis was made to match the marks to Farquharson's treads. Yet a definitive match was asserted, leaving no room for doubt and no need for any indication of uncertainty to be relayed to the jury.

So how was this 'evidence' justified? Firstly, the very existence of the right mark needs to be established. The photographs taken on the night do not show any evidence of the mark. Throughout the trial, various officers, including Urquhart and Exton, claimed that the photos did not depict what they saw with their own eyes. When Sergeant Peters returned the following day, in daylight, to photograph the scene, he did not take any close up shots of the marks at the edge of the road. When he returned another day later to take more photos, the marks had been disturbed. This is quite extraordinary, considering how crucial those marks are to the reconstruction evidence presented by the prosecution. The police had an obligation to close off the area and return in better light with a photographer and capture the marks that they claimed to have seen. Without photographs, there is no forensic evidence that either of the marks even exist.

So, we need to rely on eyewitness testimony for the very existence of the crucial right side mark. In his testimony, Sergeant Exton was reluctant to describe the two marks in any way other than 'where the car left the road', without actually describing any of the features that he witnessed. Recall that he was wrong from the outset when he testified that 'on the gravel verge there was two rolling tyre prints left by the vehicle',[15] because the marks he identified cannot have both been made by the same car, at least not Farquharson's car. Exton had also painted the marks at an angle that he later testified was incorrect. If the marks were clearly visible rolling prints as he claimed, then presumably he would have been able to mark the angle correctly.

Constable Kok, who was actually looking at the marks and directing Exton where to apply the yellow paint, described the right mark as 'Just a mark, I don't know whether it was from a tyre'[16] and said that it had no well-defined shape.

Sergeant Courtis, who also inspected the scene that night, said that in order to see the marks 'I had to get up really close'[17] and that he could 'see some raised tread pattern'[18] in each of the marks and that it was clear that they were rolling tire prints[19] that came from Farquharson's car. Yet, when recording his observations on the night, Courtis registered the marks using code 572, the code for scuff marks, and explicitly wrote 'scuff', whilst he had registered the path through the long grass using the code 583, which is the code for rolling tyre prints, and had written in the description 'rolling print, near side' and 'rolling print, offside'.[20] If he saw rolling tyre prints, why didn't he mark that down on the night? Presumably he was aware by the trial that Urquhart was using at least one of the marks as a rolling tyre print depicting where Farquharson's car left the road.

Sergeant Urquhart made his own assessment of the marks. In the second trial, he said of the right mark that 'there was something that I observed within the yellow paint marks that led me to believe that a tyre had travelled over that.'[21] Yet previously, in a voir dire, when asked this question about

15. Trial 2 p 2346
16. Trial 2 p 2051
17. Trial 2 p 2199
18. Trial 2 p 2200
19. Trial 2 p 2195
20. Trial 2 p 2254
21. Trial 2 p 3576

that same mark 'Between the two yellow stripes were you able to discern, using your own eyes, any particular disturbance to or impression upon the aggregate surface?' Urquhart had answered 'Of that particular mark, no' and he stated that between those right hand yellow paint marks 'doesn't show an area of disturbed earth'.[22] Regarding what he saw between the left hand yellow paint lines, Urquhart contradicted Courtis and Exton, saying that 'I didn't believe... that there was anything on the surface that led me to think that a tire had crossed at that particular point'.[23] This also contradicted the evidence he himself had given previously, when he said there was 'some disturbance to the aggregate that I could see, and you can see it in the photograph as well'.[24]

Urquhart explained the inconsistencies in his own evidence by the fact that he was not 'prepared for this line of questioning' in the previous voir dire. The concern is that the contradictory opinions of Urquhart were given with the same degree of confidence, without elucidating any uncertainty, and both were sustained under extended questioning by the defence council. In the first trial, Urquhart gave different evidence again regarding what he observed, evidence that contradicted both these already contradictory statements about the marks. He stated that, on the night at the scene, he had 'concurred with the two markings, the two sets of paint marks'[25] and determined 'that was the position where the car had left the road'. It was only later when he put them on the scale plan and realized that they could not both be correct, that he formed the opinion that the left mark was incorrect.

All of this illustrates why eyewitness evidence is just no substitute for careful forensic tyre matching and for actually getting photographic evidence of these marks. The inconsistent accounts mean that the evidence for just the existence of either of the marks, and in particular the right hand mark that was used in Urquhart's reconstructions, is weak, particularly as it does not show up in the photographs that were taken.

Regardless, let us accept the eyewitness evidence for the right hand mark, and let us even accept that it is indeed a rolling print made by a vehicle, rather than a scuff mark that could be made in a range of other ways. Of course, we are accepting the evidence with the requisite degree of uncertainty attached, an uncertainty that would compel a scientist to also explore the consequences of this evidence being wrong. With this caveat, we then proceed to ask how it was established that it was Farquharson's car that made the right mark. Evidence was given at trial that a significant number of vehicles had crossed over the road's edge that evening, although no one was monitoring exactly how many. Yet only two (or one, depending on which witness you believe) marks were found at the edge of the road, meaning most vehicles crossed that edge without leaving a mark. Why couldn't that mark have been made by the car of Shane Atkinson and Tony McClelland when

22. Trial 1 p186
23. Trial 2 p 3576
24. Trial 1 p186
25. Trial 1 p1830

they were stopped by a hysterical Farquharson waving them down? What about the ambulance, firetruck, SES trucks, or the various cars of others who had rushed to the scene prior to the arrival of the police form the Major Collisions Unit? What evidence was presented to link that right mark to Farquharson's car in particular?

Urquhart asserted that the differentiating feature was speed. '*At a higher speed you're more likely to get a disturbance of gravel even for a car travelling straight than you are at lower speeds. That's not to say that at lower speeds it can't happen. My view is that it's just simply more likely at a higher speed*'.[26] Note that he says 'more likely': so how could he have stated so definitely that the mark was made by Farquharson's car? Secondly, is speed really the most important factor in determining whether a car will leave such a mark? Is it even a factor at all? No studies were cited, and no experiments were done in order to *verify* this assertion. The assertion was thus not scientific in nature, and may not even be true. Why would a fast moving car be more likely to leave a mark on the side of that particular road than a slow moving car? Even if we accept that leaving a mark depends on speed, what about weight? Wouldn't a fire-tuck, or SES vehicle, be more likely to leave a mark than a car? What about braking? Tony McClelland and Shane Atkinson braked heavily in that region when they were flagged down by a frantic Farquharson. What about turning the wheel at that point? What if someone who rushed to the scene had turned their wheels to navigate down the embankment? Would that be more likely to leave a mark than a car travelling straight? What about differences in the soil in different areas; some soil may be looser than other soil? Even if speed is a factor, it will not be the only factor. All this makes the assertion that the mark was made by Farquharson's car uncertain. Highly uncertain. Meaning that the reconstruction expert was *obliged* to fully explore the consequences of the alternative possibilities. Remember, his task was not to propose a single path, it was to explore every possible path that was consistent with the physical evidence.

Extraordinarily, Urquhart went further. Not only did he assert that the right mark was made by Farquharson's car: he asserted that it was made by the *right wheels* of Farquharson's car. So, even if we accept the weak argument, based on speed, that the right mark was made by Farquharson's car, what evidence was presented that it was made by the *right* wheels rather than the *left* wheels? How could one differentiate? No rationale was ever proffered for this assertion, despite the question being raised multiple times over the various hearings and trials. Urquhart simply states 'that's my opinion that I believe the vehicle was travelling over that mark',[27] and 'it's always been my position that the driver's side tyres have crossed that right side mark'.[28] When again pressed for the reasoning, he says 'That's always been my position'[29] and when asked 'is there more to it?' Urquhart responds 'No, no, and I think we went through it in quite a lot of detail in the last

---

26. Trial 2 p3442
27. Trial 2 p628
28. Trial 2 p625
29. Trial 2 p629

trial, and my position hasn't changed.'[30] Indeed, his position did not change: he makes the same unsubstantiated assertion in both trials. An assertion that is not supported by any physical evidence at the scene, and is unscientific in nature. An assertion that helped form the basis for Urquhart's reconstruction, the most important piece of evidence in the case.

The Camber

Initially, after looking at the highway down which Farquharson was driving, Urquhart formed the opinion that the camber of the road sloped to the left. 'The lie of the road was such that the constructive cross fall when travelling in a westerly direction was a downward slope from the centre of the road to the bitumen edge. The consequence of this is that a vehicle travelling in a westerly direction would tend to drift to the left, or downhill.'[31] This is the most common road design, with a high point, or `crown', in the centre of the road between the lanes. Urquhart explains that the slope, or `camber' of the road will determine which way that an unsteered car will veer.

This opinion of Urquhart about the camber was wrong. The defence expert, David Axup, measured the camber and determined that the crown was in the left lane, and that the camber was toward the right, even for cars travelling in the left lane. So, the road sloped right and the car could have veered right, toward the dam, due to the camber. This is a very important piece of evidence. So why didn't Urquhart measure the camber himself? Why did he form the opinion that it sloped left, when in fact it sloped right? Why not measure it to make sure? Urquhart explained this oversight by saying that `if you…can conduct real world on-site testing, that will always beat a theoretical… examination of data'[32], referring to the drive-through tests he made to assess how an unsteered car would travel along the road. This is a valid point: calculating the path of the car along a road with varying slopes is not something that can be done easily in the head, nor with pen and paper. One should do experiments. In fact, this is where correct use of software such as PC-crash could have actually helped. Putting the cross falls into the program and testing how an un-steered car veered on that sloped section of road is something within the realm of what PC Crash could do, so long as it was coupled with real world drive-throughs that could help to constrain the input parameters such as the coefficient of friction.

Urquhart argues that experiments are more important than cross fall measurements in these cases. Of course, in a murder case one would expect both the taking of cross fall measurements and performance of experiments. But let us forgive Urquhart for favouring experiments. If we are to choose one over the other, then experiments are probably the more important. The problem is that when he performed experiments, he released the steering wheel at one single point of the road, a point where the camber of the road

30. Trial 2 p629
31. Glen Urquhardt's 2005 Report
32. Trial 1 p2011

sloped left. Now that he had data showing that there was a region of the road where the camber tilted right, toward the dam, he needed to also test what happened to an unsteered vehicle on that part of the road, where the slope was to the right.

When confronted with the data showing the cross fall was actually toward the dam, Urquhart first stated that 'there was nothing in that data that was provided to me that would explain a veer to the right.'[33] Despite earlier stating that a slope to the left would cause the car to veer left, he is now saying that a slope to the right would not cause a car to veer right. When shown experiments during the second trial that demonstrated that cars veer to the right on that part of the road, he finally conceded that an un-steered car may veer right on that section of road, but stated that 'I do not believe that the camber alone is sufficient to have caused the vehicle to run off the road at the angle that it did'.[34] How does he reach that conclusion? Consider that there is no evidence regarding the path of the car on the road, and no evidence of the angle that the car left the road. We only know that the path through the long grass makes an angle of 30° to the road. Urquhart had given evidence that, in terms of road camber, real world testing is more important than theoretical examination of the data. He had also stated that 'where the tyres of the car are situated within the lane can have more or less effect on, from the camber, on the path the vehicle might travel'[35] and that the degree of veer will depend on speed 'At a higher speed it will take longer to simply change direction'. But now he is stating that, merely through examination of the data, he can determine that the camber of the road cannot explain the path of the car off the road. Once again, no basis for the conclusion exists: no experiments were done, no computer modelling was made that used the camber data. His stated belief is totally unscientific in nature, is contrary to his own general statements on whether the evidence allows such a conclusion to be drawn and it defies the simple statement he made that a car will follow the camber of the road. Yet, in the second trial, his unsubstantiated conclusion is the basis of the alleged first steering input of Farquharson.

Recall Richard Feynman's warning that there is a tendency to stop an experiment when we get the answer we expect or desire, while looking much more closely at results that are against our expectations. Did Urquhart stop doing drive-throughs on different parts of the road, and not bother to actually measure the road camber, because the first drive-through gave him the answer he wanted, that his colleagues and superiors expected?

Related to this is the speed that Urquhart estimates Farquharson was driving. The drive throughs were done at three speeds, and it was only at the lowest speed of 64km/s that the car actually veered left, which was the strongest result in terms of hinting at guilt. At 80 and 100km/s, the car had gone straight. So, is it a co-incidence that Urquhart formed an opinion that

---

33. Trial 1 p2013
34. Trial 2 p2624
35. Trial 2 p3478

the car had been travelling at around 60km/s? Here is how he explained his process of forming that belief 'When it comes to calculating a vehicle's speed there is certain ways that we can do that. If a car is skidding we can measure how far the skids are and we can calculate a speed. If a car is yawing, as I have described earlier, we have a technique that we can use to calculate the speed of the vehicle when it starts yawing. Clearly those two weren't present here and weren't able to be used. A third method you can look at is what's called the speed from fall. That is whereby a vehicle or an object for that matter jumps. So, what we have here is a car leaving the edge of the dam, I measured the height of the water being 400 millimetres. What you need to know though is where the vehicle has landed. There is no physical evidence because it's water, as soon as it's landed it's changed, it's like a stone in a pond, it's gone, so there is no physical evidence that you can determine how far the vehicle has travelled before it's struck the water. Without that distance, you can't quantify a speed. So the three aspects that – that I certainly was looking for in terms of calculating a speed weren't available to me. So that brought me back to the first five tests that I did at 60, 70, 80, 90 and 100 and driving that vehicle to gauge a feel, and I guess part of that is my experience with these matters. At the end of the day what I've always maintained is that I believed that the vehicle was travelling at a speed of between 60 and 80 kilometres per hour but that I tended to the low side of that with the likely speed around 60 kilometres per hour.'

Urquhart outlines the various procedures that may, if carefully applied, help determine the speed of a vehicle. He then explains why each of these methods was not possible in this case, due to a lack of available physical evidence. So, instead of stating this and declaring that he could not determine the speed, he makes up an answer and invokes 'my experience' in some abstract way. The reason courts want experienced expert witnesses is so that they can point to specific experiences that help them interpret evidence in a manner that is superior to an average civilian from outside a specialized field of knowledge. For example, Urquhart's expertise and experience meant that he knew various different methods for determining the speed of a vehicle. Being experienced should also mean that you know the limits of your knowledge, the limits of the evidence, and the uncertainty of what you are presenting. Did Urquhart learn from his experience of giving an opinion on the camber of the road before it was measured, which showed that his opinion was wrong? Isn't that the type of experience we hope our experts draw upon? That they will say something like, 'I had an experience where I offered an opinion before taking the measurements, and later discovered that my opinion was wrong. I am therefore reluctant to give opinions that are not supported by evidence.'

Finally regarding the rightward veer, there is the matter of the different tyre sizes, with the left tyre higher than the right. Police mechanic Senior Sergeant Robert Leguier testified that this 'wouldn't make any difference whatsoever'[36] in terms of the tendency of the car to veer leftward or rightward. No tests were performed to verify this assertion.

The Straight Section

The defence put forward a scenario whereby the car followed a constant arc through the long grass, an arc with radius of 112.5 metres. They argued that this was a possible path that would not require inputs from a driver, because the car was veering rightward down the slope of bank. They argued that such a path was consistent with the physical evidence. When asked about this possibility, Sergeant Urquhart stated that 'in order to calculate any sort of radius accurately you need clearly defined edges. In this case when you look at the plan you have lines and you can say there's a clearly defined edge, but when you look at the photographs it is not simply the case that you can look at the photographs and say there's a clearly defined edge and it's safe to use that as an edge from which you can take those measurements.'[37] This is consistent with his comments that 'the tyres were rolling across grass so the grass was being displaced. It's more difficult under that condition to actually define clearly an edge of a tire mark'.[38]

Firstly, this does not rule out the defence theory, it merely means there is uncertainty in where the edge of the tyres went, so the evidence is also consistent with a range of other possibilities. Urquhart has not fulfilled his obligation which was to rule out a possible path that an unsteered car would take. Secondly, despite outlining this uncertainty, Urquhart nevertheless insisted that 'those tyre marks certainly appeared to be straight.' Again, he is giving an opinion that is contrary to his own assessment of what can be garnered from the available evidence. He first says that there is uncertainty in the edges, but then professes an opinion that the path has a section that is straight. This opinion is the basis of the second steering input in the second trial. Regarding the defence theory of an arc, Urquhart had looked hard for reasons to oppose it, and found that the edges are difficult to define so the theory is not reliable. For his own theory of a straight line, he had not even looked hard enough to find the exact same objection.

Finally, if the car followed an arc through the long grass, it will continue on this rightward arc, causing it to miss the tree trunk. Meaning that the 3rd alleged steering input is predicated on Urquhart's opinion that the car travelled straight through the long grass. The slope of the terrain was to the right in this region: the fact that the car continued to veer right is not evidence that there was a steering input by a conscious driver.

On the subject of the 3rd steering input, Urquhart also gave an opinion that crashing through the fence, which caused the fence wire to cut through the front right hand panel of the car, did not alter the direction of the car 'my view is that there was certainly not enough force that it caused the vehicle

---

36. Trial 1 1761
37. Trial 1 2022
38. Trial 2 3438

to change direction... So yes there was an impact with the wire fence, yes it cut through the metal but it did not change the direction or the path of the vehicle at all.'[39] Again, no testing or experiments were done, no studies of this type of collision were cited, no experience directly related to this type of collision was recounted. An opinion was simply asserted, with certainty. Again, an opinion that happened to go against the interests of Farquharson.

Figure A.1.4. Arial photo which shows the path of the car leaving the road at a gentle angle. The mark highlighted, used by the prosecution reconstruction expert, are not where the car left the road.

The misplaced photos

The day after Farquharson drove into the dam, September 6, 2005, Sergeant Peters took a series of aerial photographs of the scene. These somehow got misplaced, and were not seen by Urquhart when he did his analysis. They were finally provided to the defence some eight days into trial one[40]. Urquhardt had not taken them into account when drawing his conclusions regarding three steering inputs. One of those photos is shown in **Figure A.1.4**. It shows pretty clearly some tracks that seem to show the path that the car took. A path showing a car smoothly veering rightwards, down the slope.

---

39. Trial 1 2034
40. Trial 2

APPENDIX B: OTHER 'CHANGING STORIES'

As with the Lindy Chamberlain case, every time Farquharson added a small detail to his version of what happened, it was alleged by the prosecutor that he had again changed his story. For example, Farquharson told paramedic David Watson that Jai had slightly opened his door and water had started rushing in,[1] and so he had closed it. He told the same thing to Dr. Bartley[2] at the Geelong hospital and again during the police interview. Yet, because he had not included this detail in earlier tellings, it was somehow significant, according to the prosecutor, as it was a 'detail given for the first time. It was for the first time that the accused claimed that his son had opened the door of the car causing the car to fill up with water and sink. That hadn't been said to anyone before…'[3]

During another police interview, Farquharson was trying to describe what happened and, according to the prosecutor, 'he then introduced the new claim, an entirely new claim that perhaps they were rocking on a ledge'.[4] Again, the basis of this supposedly 'new claim' is just that Farquharson had not repeated the story verbatim. Previously he had said that when he 'had come to', that he was 'confused where the car was', that he 'thought I was in a ditch',[5] that he 'thought I was in a drain, in a ditch',[6] and that when Jai opened the door 'we nose-dived a bit'.[7]

1. Trial 2 p4944
2. Trial 2 p4943
3. Trial 2 p4943
4. Trial 2 p4950
5. Trial 2 p3746
6. Trial 2 p3764

When asked to explain what he meant, Farquharson said that 'I thought I might have been on the side of the road'[8], indicating with his hands how the car was angled over a ditch or drain or some other drop off. Is his description of the car as seemingly rocking 'on a ledge or something like that'[9] inconsistent with what he had about being on the side of the road and then nose diving a bit? Isn't it just a different way of explaining it? Of trying to express what had happened? Why couldn't he think he was in a ditch, but when the car moved after Jai opened the door, he started to wonder if they were on a ledge? He was asked the same questions many times, so maybe he was trying to clarify things, to find a better way to describe what happened.

Isn't that what the police wanted when they asked him the same questions over and over? A better description as to what had happened? Aren't they asking again because they did not quite understand what he meant in his previous descriptions, so a different analogy may help? Or would a verbatim recount have satisfied them? You can be sure that if he repeated the story verbatim every time, the prosecutor would have jumped on this as being a rehearsed story, and therefore evidence of guilt. Damned if he did, damned if he did not. That is the nature of confirmation bias, that is the nature of tunnel vision. Of course, a cynic may say that the police asked him the same questions over and over because they know that skilled prosecutors will be able to highlight inconsequential changes in the responses, painting them as evidence of guilt. This is just another reason that innocent people should ask a lawyer to accompany them to interviews. A simple answer interruption 'my client has answered that question' can go a long way to blunting this prosecution tactic.

It is also very normal that Farquharson's re-telling of the story would incorporate ideas suggested by his friends or family, and hence evolve just like the memory of all witnesses. For example, the morning after the tragedy, grief counsellor Leona Daniel

---

7. Trial 2 p1093
8. Trial 2 p 3699 See also similar words used in a phone call to Cindy (Trial 2 p4950)
9. Trial 2 p1093

suggested to Farquharson that 'he couldn't have opened the doors because the water pressure would have been so great'.[10] So when, in a subsequent interview, Farquharson said that 'I got out and I, and just the pressure and then I tried to get around the other side and I couldn't...'[11] the prosecutor again attacked on this point, 'why did he ever mention the concept of pressure?', cross examining him extensively on his use of this word, implying that adding this detail somehow counted against Farquharson's credibility.

---

10. Trial 2 p4306
11. Trial 2 p3866

APPENDIX C: PROFESSOR NAUGHTON'S REPORT

STATEMENT

Name: Matthew NAUGHTON

STATES:

My name is Matthew NAUGHTON and I am an Associate Professor of Medicine at Monash University and the head of the General Respiratory and Sleep Medicine Service at The Alfred Hospital, Prahran. My qualifications are MBBS, MD (both Melbourne University) and a Fellow of the Royal Australian College of Physicians. I have been practicing in the field of respiratory and sleep disorders for 20 years. I am on the editorial board of 8 medical journals and I also review manuscripts for an additional 17 medical journals.

I have been asked to express my opinion as to the likelihood that Robert FARQUHARSON suffered from an episode of "cough syncope" in the moments prior to his vehicle leaving the highway or whether, assuming that he did lose consciousness at that time, in my opinion there is any other likely cause for such a loss of consciousness. I have been supplied with the following documents by the Office of Public Prosecutions:

1. Police summary;
2. Statement of Dr Ian McDonald together with his evidence at committal;
3. Statement of Greg KING together with his evidence at committal;
4. Statement of Darren BUSHELL;
5. Statement of Gary HUNTINGTON together with his evidence at committal;
6. Statement of Shane ATKINSON together with his evidence at committal;
7. Statement of Tony McCLELLAND together with his evidence at committal;
8. Statement of Stephen MOULES;
9. Statement of Kiri FAUSETT;
10. Statement of Carolyn FAUSETT together with her evidence at committal;

11. Statement of David WATSON together with his evidence at committal;
12. Statement of Lindsay ROBINSON together with his evidence at committal and notes;
13. Statement of Dr Bruce BARTLEY together with his evidence at committal;
14. Statement of Dr Paul MESTITZ;
15. Statement of Dr Thomas YIP;
16. Statement of Dr Chris GORE together with his evidence at committal and notes;
17. Statement of Dr John KING together with his evidence at committal;
18. Statement of Edward HARMAN together with his evidence at committal;
19. Statement of Geoffrey EXTON together with his evidence at committal;
20. Statement of Rohan COURTIS;
21. Statement of Susan BATESON together with her evidence at committal;
22. Statement of Glenn URQUHART together with his evidence at committal;
23. Statement of Joanne GERSTNER-STEVENS;
24. Transcript of tape-recorded conversation with Robert FARQUHARSON en route to the Homicide Squad Offices; and
25. Transcript of the Record of Interview with Robert FARQUHARSON.

In formulating my opinion I have had regard to my own experience and training in the field of respiratory illnesses and diseases and the textbook Respiratory Medicine, 2nd Edition, eds Murray & Nadel. I have also made inquiries of my medical colleagues and physiotherapy and nursing staff who practice in my field.

Cough syncope is a very unusual and rare condition. In my opinion it is extremely unlikely that Robert FARQUHARSON suffered from cough syncope.

I have come to this opinion for the following reasons:

a/ No one had witnessed him to collapse previously. His employer witnessed a coughing fit where he went red in the face but he did not collapse or lose consciousness.

b/ Cough Syncope when it does occur usually occurs in patients with advanced lung disease eg. emphysema, pulmonary fibrosis, cystic fibrosis or if the patients has a combination of disabling heart and lung disease. Even in these situations, cough syncope is extremely rare. The accused seemed otherwise to be in good health, had a physical employment and led a normal life. There is no evidence from what I read that he had advanced lung disease.

c/ Patients who suffer from cough syncope may be thirsty or dehydrated before suffering from an episode. Being dehydrated exacerbates the condition cough syncope. In this instance, Robert FARQUHARSON went to a fast food outlet with his children just prior to the event and consumed food and drink.

d/ Cough Syncope is an incredibly rare condition. None of my colleagues, who are eminent respiratory specialists, have ever personally witnessed it. I have never witnessed it, yet I have treated very ill patients suffering from severe respiratory and cardiac conditions for 20 years. I have also consulted with nursing and physiotherapy staff, experienced in treating respiratory and cardiac patients, and none of whom have witnessed it either.

It is also significant that after the vehicle entered the water and the driver exited he dove down into the cold water, swam to the shore, ran to the road but did not suffer any fits of coughing afterwards, nor from any fever.

Other causes for loss of consciousness, but which would be extremely unlikely to have occurred include:

1. Epileptic seizure, but this would be highly unusual and there is no recorded history of epilepsy.

2. Cardiac arrhythmia, again he has no known heart disease and the monitoring done after the event was normal and there have been no subsequent attacks.

3. Falling Asleep – again unlikely because there is no history of sleep deprivation in this case. Further, the terrain over which the car travelled after it left the highway is such that I would have expected the accompanying jolts to awaken a sleeping driver.

(signature)
(Matthew NAUGHTON)

Statement taken and signature witnessed by me at 2:43 AM/~~PM~~ on 7/5/07 at Prahran.

(signature)
Gerard CLANCHY
Detective Sergeant 26157

I hereby acknowledge that this statement is true and correct and I make it in the belief that a person making a false statement in the circumstances is liable to the penalties of perjury.

(signature)
(Matthew NAUGHTON)

Acknowledgment made and signature witnessed by me at 2:43 ~~AM~~/PM on 7/5/07 at Prahran.

(signature)
Gerard CLANCHY
Detective Sergeant 26157

APPENDIX D: DAWN WAITE TESTIMONIES

AT VOIR DIRE (9 March 2010)

Morrisey (Defence) Asking Questions: **Waite Responding**

At the time when you were looking, when you drove up behind that vehicle did you have high beams on or not?—

Actually I did flick my lights at first because you know I just wanted to make sure that the driver in front of me knew that I was behind and you know that I wanted to pass so I did flick, that's when I noticed that there was no adult head in the front seat of the passenger side, there was no, there was only one head in the front seat.

I see. And how were you able to see that there was one head, is that because there were no head rests on the vehicle?—**I don't recall.**

Do you know whether what you were seeing was a head or whether it was a head rest?—**No, I don't.**

So what you saw could have been a head?—**Yes.**

But it could have been a head rest?—**It could have been, yeah, correct, but..**

Could you demonstrate how you do the flick, what was your car, what was the mechanism for doing the high beam, was it turn or a push?—**No, it was just a flick forward.**

...it's a split second flick, is that correct?—**Yes, it's a, yes, yes.**

And apart from the flick that you did?—**Yes.**

You had your lights on normal?—**Just normal, yes.**

Did you notice whether that vehicle had darkened windows or not?—**No, I didn't notice that.**

You didn't notice that?—**No.**

I take it you were unable to see the dashboard of that vehicle?—**No.**

To the best of your recollection there is no street lighting on that stretch?—**No, no.**

Of highway No.1?—**No.**

And to the best of your recollection, you had your lights on, correct?—**Yes, that's correct.**

So, how slow did your vehicle get to, perhaps I should ask you this, how close did you get to that vehicle, were you- - -?—**I kept a fair distance so it would have been a couple of car lengths back enough, enough time to give me, if the car had braked, it gave me enough time to stop myself.**

So you weren't tailgating this car?—**Oh, no no, no way.**

That's okay. And I asked you before whether you could tell that it was darkened glass or not and you said you couldn't tell?—**No, but I knew I had my lights on. That's all. I definitely had my lights on.**

No, no of course. Because it was effectively dark, wasn't it?—**Yes.**

****

AT TRIAL (13 & 17 May 2010)

Tinney (Prosecution)Asking Questions: **Waite Responding**

This might sound a silly question, but was there any other street lighting around or any other source of lighting other than say your headlights?—**My headlights were on high beam but that was the only lighting around.**

Did you leave your lights on full beam?—**Now, I may have, I remember flicking my lights to - - -**

Sorry, go on?—**I remember flicking my lights after a minute or two I had been behind the car, and I flicked my lights to let the driver know that I wanted to pass. But I, I didn't, and then I – I remained, my lights were on full, but I don't remember actually having, when I actually took my lights off full behind the vehicle, when I was behind the vehicle. I just know I had them on high beam when I passed and as I was approaching... I sat behind the vehicle, but I had taken my cruise control off quite a long way before that because, as I said, the vehicle was going very slow, so I'd taken my cruise control off and from the time I took my cruise control off and I sat behind the vehicle, that would have been about a minute or two.**

So how much of that time do you think was when you were actually behind it, about a car length back?—**I would say half of that time.**

Now, in that period of time when you were still behind the vehicle, were you able to notice anything about the driver or any other occupant of that vehicle?—**Yes, I noticed when the car had veered to the left, and I had had my lights on full beam then, I noticed that the driver of the car had kept on looking out to his right.**

And that situation of the driver looking out, apparently looking out to his right, is that something that you were able to observe only at the point when he, a point when the vehicle came over to the left or- - - ?—**Yes, because I couldn't, I couldn't see the driver when he was at, on, you know, on the right-hand side, it was only when he moved over to the left-hand side that I could see that the driver's head kept on turning to the right.**

You told the members of the jury that he, that the vehicle went from the lane in which it was to the right and then over to the left of the left lane at least three times?—**Yes, that's correct.**

So on all of those occasions were you able to see that the driver appeared to be looking to the right?—**I remember that the last time he was moving, looking to the right, I, I don't recall seeing that observation the last – the previous two times**

****

Morrisey (Defence) Asking Questions: **Waite Responding**

Now, what I want to put to you is this. You had literally a split second of vision in which to see that; is that correct?—**Yes, I believe it was a little bit longer than a split second but no, I did observe that.**

It was a little bit longer than a split second. Would you like to put some - - - ?—**Well, the car, at the time the car was over the left-hand side and my lights were on full beam.**

How long were they on full beam for?—**I believe I left the**

lights on full beam to see the way clear for me to pass the vehicle. As I said before, I, I wasn't very happy about passing him until I knew it was safe.

While you were sitting behind the vehicle are you saying you left the lights on full beam?—**Yes, I – yes, I believe I did.**

... Morrisey then reminds her of her answers from Voir Dire before he continues

That was your position about the view that you had at that time; is that correct?—**Yes, it was but you never asked me did I, did I, when I put my lights on full.**

Just a moment. You talked about a flick?—**Yes, I did.**

You didn't talk about turning it on and leaving it on, didn't you?—**No, I didn't but you didn't ask me when I put my lights on full.**

You have thought about that quite a lot, haven't you, what you were asked and what you didn't, is that correct?—**I read my transcript.**

Who gave you the transcript?—**The police.**

Sorry?—**Mr Clanchy.**

Mr Clanchy gave you the transcript. I see. All right. So you went through your transcript very carefully; is that correct?—**No, I just - - -**

Is that right?—**Browsed through it, but I was very nervous that day, I was unwell, as you know, and I was - - -**

Hang on a second?—**Very nervous.**

Hang on, Ms Waite, just stop there please. You are going a long way from the question there please. All right, now, this issue about the head rests, you don't recall seeing a head rest, do you?—**No, I don't.**

So that when you are looking at what the driver does is the fact is you are looking through a back windshield, is that correct?—**Yes, that's correct.**

And it's got, well, you say it's got no shutters in it, is that correct?—**I didn't recall shutters but I didn't - the car was to** the left of the road when I was observing – that's – my lights, I could see into the car.

So you're – – – ?—**I could see into the side of the car.**

Just a moment. Are you saying that you made the observation not through the shutters, not through the back window, but through a side window?—**Because it was over to the left.**

Okay. So, there was a head rest right in the way of the driver's head, wasn't there, when you were making these observations, is that correct or not?—**Well, I saw it so it must – he must have been on the side, he – it must have been to the left when I saw him looking to the right, because, I was still behind the vehicle, and I could see the driver turning right. His face turning right, his movements.**

So which window do you say you were looking through when you made that observation?—**I was behind the car, so, he was pulled over to the left at that time, so, it would have been, would have still been behind.**

Which window?—**It was – it still would have been behind I would say.**

I will give you a third chance, which window? Or are you just figuring it out?—**No, no, no, no, no, I am just, I am re-thinking it in my mind. I would say it was the back window.**

And you, I suggest to you, had your high beams up, it was not a question of turning it on and leaving it on, it was a flick as you described like you used to do in New Zealand, is that correct?—**Yes, that's correct yes.**

And in New Zealand when you do a flick you don't leave your high beams blazing, do you?—**You do put your high beam when you pass.**

Now, anyway, just to come back to that, you were asked

questions by me on the voir dire at page 30, Your Honour, question, "I asked you before whether you could tell it was darkened glass and you said you couldn't tell?"

Answer by you, "No, but I knew I had my lights on, I definitely had my lights on"?—**But when you were saying that I didn't say full beam and that's what I meant, when I kept on saying I had my lights on I didn't actually say the full beam.**

You are jumping ahead of me there?—**I am sorry.**

But we will get to that. You said you had your lights on, you did not say you had the full beams on?—**That's right but that's what I meant, by saying I had my lights on, I had my lights on.**

That's what you meant, you meant that you had your high beams on?—**Yes.**

But until you came to court here on Thursday you had never said that?—**That's correct.**

Not to the police and not in this court, is that true?—**That is correct but they were on, I failed to put that.**

All right, so it was, it was a- - - ?—**Well, you don't drive on a country - - -**

It was a world premiere, wasn't it?—**No, you don't drive on a country road without your lights on full, I just naturally presumed that you realised I had my lights on full, I didn't think I had to explain that.**

At page 27 were you asked this question, "Apart from the flick that you did, you had your lights on normal?" Answer, "Just normal, yes." Were you asked that question and did you give that answer?—**I was but they were on full. As I said - - -**

Well can I suggest to you rather than being confused and nervous, what happens is, you are now trying to defend a position when you say you could see into a car which you just couldn't see into at all?—**No, that's not, that's not true, I saw into that car and my lights were on full.**

Well, and you went on at that time to say, "I could see into both the back window and the front window if that makes sense", correct?—**Yes.**

All right. And anyway I think you have confirmed that until last Thursday you had never mentioned having your lights on full(?)?—**No, that's, that's right.**

Thanks. Do you think it's a safe thing to do to put your lights on high beam when you are passing a car?—**Well, yeah, I do.**

Is that your claim, that you do that all the time or- - -?—**When, when I pull out into the lane, I flick my light on full, but I, to pass, yes.**

What, before you have got past the driver?—**Yes.**

You don't think it might dazzle them in their mirror?—**No, well, that's what I do.**

Yeah, but just answer the question, you don't think it might dazzle them in their mirror?—**Yeah, probably does.**

Well can I suggest to you rather than being confused and nervous, what happens is, you are now trying to defend a position when you say you could see into a car which you just couldn't see into at all?—**No, that's not, that's not true, I saw into that car and my lights were on full.**

Well, and you went on at that time to say, "I could see into both the back window and the front window if that makes sense", correct?—**Yes.**

ABOUT THE AUTHOR

Dr. Chris Brook is an astrophysicist with a legal background, who is concerned about the way that science is mis-understood and mis-used in our criminal justice system, and the lack of science in so-called forensic "science".

Chris works at the Universidad de La Laguna and at the Instituto de Astrofisica de Canarias in Tenerife in the Canary Islands, which houses some of the world's largest and most important telescopes. The Instituto de Astrofisica de Canarias is one of Spain's premier science institutes.

"I am interested in how the legal system could learn from science in terms of how to analyse evidence. I believe that scientific methods and knowledge should be used for analysis of all evidence in all criminal cases.".

Chris lives in the Canary Islands with his wife Arianna and daughter Miranda.

You can follow Chris and his blog on the problems of forensic science at sci-cri.com

www.ingramcontent.com/pod-product-compliance
Lightning Source LLC
Chambersburg PA
CBHW020317010526
44107CB00054B/1881